# CHRISTIAN PATIENCE

THE STRENGTH & DISCIPLINE OF THE SOUL

BISHOP ULLATHORNE

SENSUS FIDELIUM PRESS

*Christian Patience: The Strength & Discipline of the Soul* was originally published by Burns and Oates, Ld. in 1886, and is in the public domain.

Sensus Fidelium Press edition © 2023.

All rights reserved. The typesetting of this edition is copyright of Sensus Fidelium Press. No part of this work may be reproduced in print or ebook formats without the express permission of the publisher, except for quotations for review in journals, blogs, or classroom use.

Print ISBN: 978-1-962639-31-6

SensusFideliumPress.com

# DEDICATION

To His Eminence,

The Most Illustrious and Most Reverend<br>CARDINAL NEWMAN.

My Dear Lord Cardinal,

    I do not forget that your first public appearance in the Catholic Church was at my consecration to the Episcopate, and that since that time forty years of our lives have passed, during which you have honored me with a friendship and a confidence that have much enriched my life. Deeply sensible of the incalculable services which you have rendered to the Church at large by your writings, and to this Diocese of your residence in particular by the high and complete character of your virtues, by your zeal for souls, and by the influence of your presence in the midst of us, I wish to convey to you the expression of my affection, veneration, and gratitude, by the dedication of this book to your name. It is the last work of any importance that I shall ever write, and I can only wish that it were more worthy of your patronage.

I am ever, my dear Lord Cardinal,

Your devoted and affectionate Servant in Christ,

✠ WILLIAM BERNARD ULLATHORNE,<br>Bishop of Birmingham.

Birmingham, 18th July, 1886.

# CONTENTS

| | |
|---|---:|
| *Preface* | vii |
| 1. The Work Of Patience In The Soul | 1 |
| 2. On The Nature And Object Of Christian Patience | 19 |
| 3. On Patience As A Universal Virtue | 43 |
| 4. On Christian Fortitude | 63 |
| 5. On The Patience Of The Son Of God | 84 |
| 6. On Patience As The Discipline Of The Soul | 104 |
| 7. On Patience As The Perfecter Of Our Daily Duties | 126 |
| 8. Encouragements To Patience | 147 |
| 9. On The Gifts Of The Holy Ghost | 168 |
| 10. On Prayer | 194 |
| 11. On Patience In Prayer | 218 |
| 12. On The Cheerfulness Of Patience | 243 |
| *Notes* | 269 |

# PREFACE

This volume completes the series originally contemplated. The Author's object has been to explain and inculcate those fundamental principles of the Christian virtues which, from their profundity, are least understood, but which most contribute to the perfecting of the human soul. The first volume, under the title of the Endowments of Man, establishes the doctrinal foundations of the Christian Virtues. The second, under the title of the Groundwork of the Christian Virtues, treats chiefly of Christian Humility as being the receptive foundation of the other virtues. This third volume treats of Christian Patience as being the positive strength and disciplinary power of the soul. The sovereign virtue of charity is explained throughout the three volumes. In the production of the last volume, the Author has found much less assistance from the Fathers of the Church and the great spiritual writers than in the two previous ones. As a rule, they have limited their instructions to that side of the virtue which is exercised under sufferings; and only a limited number of them, among whom I may mention St. Zeno, Tertullian, St. Gregory the Great, St. Bonaventure, and St. Catherine of Siena, have treated of that most important side of the virtue by which it gives strength and discipline to all the mental and moral powers, and perfection to all the virtues.

One remark is due to the reader. The only solid way of explaining the virtues is by their principles and their mutual connections. But to do this effectually requires that the same principles be often repeated, as well to fix them in the mind as to show their connection with the practical details, and to give to those details greater light. In the preface to his translation of the famous treatise of Albert the Great, On adhering to God, Sir Kenelm Digby observes: "He often repeateth the same thing, but still with some addition and further explication of the matter, to inculcate it the deeper."

# 1

# THE WORK OF PATIENCE IN THE SOUL

*"The trial of your faith worketh patience. And patience hath a perfect work; that you may be perfect and entire, failing in nothing."—St. James i. 3-4*

The perfection of the Christian soul consists in that complete and exquisite charity whereby we love God above all things, and our neighbor as ourselves, for the love of God. This love, this charity that perfects the soul, is the sublimest gift that we can receive from God in this our exile, because God Himself is charity, and the life of God is charity. In partaking of His charity, according to our condition and capacity, as St. Peter says, "We are made partakers of the divine nature,"[1] that is, by a created participation, and are made the children of God. For by charity God lives in us and we in Him. The divine gift of charity is the richest fruit of the sacrifice of our Lord Jesus Christ, who in most humble and patient charity gave His life to His Father, not only to deliver us from sin, but to obtain for us the supernatural life of charity. This life is the work of the Holy Spirit of God, dwelling in us, abiding in us, operating in us, uniting our life with the life of God, and raising our will into a holy co-operation with the unspeakable movements of His divinely given love. "If anyone loveth Me," saith our Lord, "he will keep My commandments, and My Father will love him, and We will come to him, and will make Our abode with him."[2]

The love of charity is the greatest thing that we can give to God, because it originates with Him, and is moved by the action of His Holy Spirit; with it we freely give ourselves to God, and through its means we return all to Him that He has given to us.

The love of God is our spiritual life; it makes the will good, the affections good, the soul good, and the work of the soul good. St. Paul calls charity the bond of perfection; it unites us with God, unites us within ourselves, unites us with all spirits that love God, and with all things whatever that God loves. It is the old commandment, the new commandment, the greatest commandment, the comprehension of all the commandments, the life of all the virtues, the fulfilment of the whole law of God.

Hence all the other commandments, and all the other virtues by which the will of God is fulfilled, look to the love of God, are perfected by the love of God, and have their end in the love of God, for charity brings them all to God. Faith is the steadfast and unfailing light that guides the soul to the love of God; its divine truths are the reasons of that love, and they shine into the believing soul from the light of the Eternal Word Incarnate, and flow from the teaching of His Church. Hope wings our aspirations towards the Eternal Good which is promised to our love. Humility subjects our nature in the consciousness of its great needs to God, that we may be the subjects of His love. Charity makes us like to God by the flame of living, life-giving love, upon which we ascend in will and desire to Him whose nature is love, and whose love is His unspeakable goodness.

Whatever affection is sinful or dishonouring to God and to the soul is unworthy of the sacred name of love, because it is the enemy of charity. Its true name is cupidity, which is vile, or self-loving pride, which is a base perversion of our nature. These are affections that move against the light of faith and the very reason of things, and are hostile to the sovereign laws of love. But the charity of God makes the soul chaste, beautiful, and wise, whilst she reaches towards God with the arms of love through the very heart of grace. Countless considerations of God's goodness, mercy, and compassion may join with the emanations of His charity to move our hearts to love Him; but when we have once entered into His goodness and mercy, have felt His love, and tasted His sweetness, we love Him for His own most pure and perfect excellence, and pass from sense to spirit, from self to God, and from thinking of Him to adoring Him, who lives for ever and ever. This is the infancy of beatitude; the first dawn of the principle of the glory to come; the beginning of heaven amidst the dreary obscurations and desolate confusion of this blind world.

In the Most Holy Trinity charity is the principle of the Divine Unity, and the substantial energy of the Divine Life. Yet who can form any true conception of that uncreated charity? In this life we can only know it by the sense we have in our spirit of the resemblance of the gift of charity to the Divine Giver. In the Holy Scriptures it is compared to a fire, but to a fire that is living, life-giving, and unconsuming. In Daniel's vision of the Ancient of Days, the throne on which He sat is "like flames of fire, and the wheels of it like a burning fire". In Ezechiel's vision He is seated upon glowing cherubs moving on fiery wheels, to represent the unceasing action of His charity towards His intelligent creatures. The Prophet Daniel beheld "a swift stream of fire that issued forth before Him; thousands of thousands ministered to Him, and ten thousand times a hundred thousand stood before Him"[3]. When St. John beheld the glorious vision of the Son of God, "His eyes were as a flame of fire"[4]. The Seraphs, those spirits nearest the throne of God, are, as their name signifies, spirits of fire, that is, of love. Our Divine Lord declared that He came to cast fire on earth, and promised that His disciples should be baptized with fire, that is, with the burning ardor of charity. Accordingly the Holy Spirit came down upon the Apostles from heaven in tongues of fire, thus outwardly expressing the interior ardor of charity that enkindled their hearts with the unconquerable love of God and of souls. That fire consumed the infirmities of their nature, and gave them strength to conquer in the power of God. Hence the prayer of the loving soul: "Send forth the fire of Thy charity".

From charity God created all things, and for the sake of charity He moves all that He has created. He made the material world for the probation of souls, that in preferring their Creator to the things created they might prove themselves worthy of His love, and of receiving the rewards of love. For souls are made for the high and noble prerogative of receiving and returning the love of God. The saving providence of God moves through His creatures from the bosom of His charity. His mercies, which are above all His works, are the tender yearnings of His charity. He endures the evils of sin and ingratitude with the patience of His charity, waiting as a merciful Father the return of His children from evil to the good that He holds in readiness for their repentance.

Woe, then, to that false science which puts matter before spirit, sense before conscience, darkness before light, and the creature before God, and professes to find the cause of light and love, those sublimest gifts of the eternal charity of God, in the lowest and least spiritual elements of His creation. It is an awful proof of the extent to which cultivated intellects, lost to charity, can be gained to pride, and of the utter perversion of that light of intelligence which their minds have received from God. "The fool said in his heart: There is no God."[5] The wise man exclaims: Without the charity of God we are nothing.

Not only is the charity of God all-embracing, but it is most abundantly communicative. The bosom of our Heavenly Father is open to all His children made in His divine image; to hear their sighs, to receive their desires, to accept their prayers, to relieve their wants, to deliver them from evil, to rescue them from misery. Then does He cheer them with light and enkindle their souls with love. He asks but their goodwill, and to their goodwill He gives all that they are capable of receiving. To the souls that love Him and seek His presence He sends down from His high heavens perpetual streams of light and grace, to draw them who are sanctified in the Blood of His Son more closely to His love, to perfect their charity.

In your love you must also of necessity love that charity by which you love God, because it is the most beautiful and inspiring of the gifts of God. What can be so beautiful, what so enlarging, what so delightful as that all-embracing charity which descends like fire from God, unites us in life with God, and also with all His good angels and saints, and with all pious souls on earth, in one sacred and living bond of union and communion of good? Every one who is brought out of the dark region of sin into the divine circle of universal charity is not only made beautiful in his soul by the love of God, but that soul partakes in her degree in all the charity with which she is in communion by her charity, be the possessors of that charity in heaven, on earth, or in the region of purification. For we share in the charity of all whom we love and who love us in God; and true charity loves all that God loves. What a sublime view does charity open into the communion of saints!

Nor does charity rest contented within this immense circle of spiritual life; but as the God of all charity is merciful, patient, and bountiful even to those who love Him not, and is always ready to pardon their sins, and to give them His unspeakable love, even so works the charity of God imparted to Christian souls. That charity imitates His goodness, His patience, His benignity, His bounty, and is patient, kind, and beneficent to all. "Love your enemies, do good to them that hate you, and pray for them that persecute and calumniate you: that you may be the children of your Father who is in heaven, who maketh His sun to rise upon the good and the bad, and raineth upon the just and the unjust."[6]

But it is one thing to receive the divine gift of charity, another to have the virtue of charity, and another to have that virtue in perfection. For although the gift is the principle of the virtue, it is not the actual virtue, not that which makes charity our own. It can only become the actual virtue when the will enters into the gift, acts with the gift, and performs the interior and exterior works of charity. For the will is the seat and power of love; so that what the will desires the will loves, and what the will seeks above all things, the will loves above all things. When, therefore, the will enters into the grace of charity, and is clothed with it, it receives a divine power, exalting it above the order of nature, and giving to it the supernatural flame of divine love. The heart is the seat of our sensible affections, but these sensible affections are purified and made spiritual, when moved by the will, and clothed with charity towards God, the supreme object of our actions and desires. And it is by the pure and perfect exercise of the will, free from all mixture of what is contrary to the love of God, and exercised in the perfect gift of charity, that this holiest of virtues is made perfect.

We must also bear in mind this solemn truth, that the supreme and final object of all charitable service to our neighbour is God Himself. For all charity moves towards God, as its divine origin and final end. It moves as it were in a circle, from God to us, and from us to God, then to our neighbour, and through our neighbour to God, in virtue of the intention of charity. We thus imitate our Heavenly Father's love to us, and join ourselves to that love, and are the ministers of His love, kind, patient, and forbearing to all from His gift; and especially when, for His sake, we give our help and service to those who are in affliction, in poverty, in ignorance, or in distress. This is a holy communion in which we partake in the good that we impart, and receive increase of love from the love we put forth, growing in the good that we communicate, and gaining strength from the resistance we make against the reluctance of our nature, and from the evil that we overcome in others.

"All the glory of the King's daughter is within."[7] This daughter of the King is the soul born of charity. The glory of that soul is in the abiding presence of the Holy Spirit, and in the principle and the promise of eternal glory. Charity is the living beauty of the soul that seeks God through all the virtues; it is the sweet odour of God, the living flame that breaks out of His truth, establishing order, purity, justice, goodness, and wisdom in the soul. It is the sacred fire placed by the Holy Spirit upon the altar of the heart. What is all philosophy compared to charity? Charity is the most practical philosophy, which from the heart illuminates the understanding, because it is the noblest action of truth, and reaches lovingly to the Divine Cause of all things.

But if the perfection of the soul consists in complete and exquisite charity, what room is there for other perfections? Why does St. James teach that "patience hath a perfect work"[8] Why does he insist that by patience we are made "perfect and entire, failing in nothing"? St. Paul enforces the same doctrine, where he says: "Patience is necessary for you: that doing the will of God, you may obtain the promise"[9] And our Blessed Lord gives us this solemn instruction: "In your patience you shall possess your souls"[10] What, then, is the work of patience in the soul?

In the first place, it must be observed that charity takes hold of the other virtues, animates them with her fire, inspires them with her motive, draws them into her service, and employs them, whether faith, hope, humility, patience, or whatever other virtue, for her own completion and perfection. In the second place, such is the irritability, restlessness, weakness, and inconstancy of the powers of our nature, considered in themselves, that they require the firm control of patience to conquer them, and to bring them into subjection to the sovereign virtue of charity. Hence, St. Paul teaches that "charity is patient";[11] and that it is patient charity which enables us to "bear all things," and to "endure all things". Hence, the Fathers and great spiritual divines have concluded that the grace of patience is given with the grace of charity, as well to protect it as to bring it to perfection. True patience for the love of God is therefore the highest test and most evident proof of the presence of a noble degree of charity; because patience is its perfecting quality, making it whole and entire, failing in nothing. It is the surest test, because it cannot be easily mistaken, as it can only be obtained, even with the help of grace, by dint of labour, self-combat, and effort; but we have the sensible result in the possession of one's self and in peace of soul.

What do we find so difficult as to keep ourselves in our own possession, so that no part of our nature shall slip away from the command of the will, or from the empire of charity? Our Divine Lord seldom gives His reasons for His precepts, because they carry in themselves their own light; but He has given us the whole reason why we need the virtue of patience, when He tells us that it is by this virtue we hold the possession of our souls.

This vigorous virtue of patience is the spiritual remedy which God has provided against the weakness, perturbation, and inconstancy of our nature, exposed as it is to irritations, fears, temptations, cupidities, vanities, pride, and sadness. Every creature, by reason of its origin from nothingness, when left to itself, is exposed to division, dissolution, and failure; unless it receive a divine support, and a bracing strength of patience to hold it together, that it may endure and persevere. But in our fallen nature, and especially in that part of it which is material and animal, there is a darkness, a baleful fire of cupidity, a root of selfishness, and a restlessness, that war against the light and law of God in the soul, darken her light, dissipate and trouble her powers, and draw her away from the possession of herself. But the less she is in the possession of herself, the less capable is the soul of ascending to God, and therefore the less capable of knowing God and loving Him.

The soul cannot possess herself when she is held in the possession of her mortal senses, appetites, or passions, or when held in bondage to creatures that are less than herself, and that trouble, degrade, and divide the soul, and take off her mind and will from what is greater and better than herself. Nor can the soul possess herself within herself, because she is made for God, and without God for the chief object of her mind and affections she is poor, disturbed, and discontented. She can only possess herself in God through charity and patience, in love adhering to God, in patience persevering in that adherence despite of all the perturbations and fears of her inferior nature. Then will the soul find her powers united and in possession of her will by reason of her union with God; but this will only be in proportion to her patience.

Hence, St. John Climachus observed that "to the spiritual man patience is more essential than food,"[12] and justly so; for food strengthens the body, and preserves it from weakness, but patience fortifies the soul, and without it no virtue can be firm and solid. But as we are bound to take more care of the soul than of the body, it is evident that we ought to be more solicitous for patience than for food. For, in the words of St. Peter Damian, "the man whose patience breaks down may have other virtues, but he will never have their strength and solidity"[13]. Patience is concerned in all that we have to resist, in all that we have to deny ourselves, in all that we have to endure, in all that we have to adhere to, and in all that we have to do. This includes all human acts that bear the character of duty or devotedness, whether those acts be purely interior, or come forth into the exterior life and conduct. For wherever patience fails, the act is weak and the work imperfect.

This comprehensive view of the work of patience in man is enlarged upon by that profound thinker Tertullian in the following terms: "Patience protects the whole will of God in man and enters into all His commandments. It fortifies faith, governs peace, helps charity, prepares humility, conducts to penance, leads to confession, rules the flesh, preserves the spirit, bridles the tongue, controls the hand, breaks down temptations, expels scandals, and consummates martyrdom; it consoles the poor man, moderates the wealthy man, suffers not the infirm man to sink under his weakness, and allows not the strong man to consume his strength; it delights the believer, attracts the unbeliever, adorns the woman, and makes the man approved; it is loved in the youth, praised in the maturer man, and is looked up to in the aged man. Patience is beautiful in both sexes and at every age. The features of the patient one are calm and pleasant; the brow is pure, because free from the signs of sadness and of irritation; the eyes are peaceful; the mouth is sealed with discretion.[14]

Yet, next to the virtue of humility, there is no Christian virtue that stands more in need of careful exposition than the virtue of patience. Although well known in a popular way, and on the surface, as it is opposed to anger, or as our sustainer under sufferings, it is but little understood as a fundamental virtue of the soul, and that only by those truly spiritual persons who are well exercised in interior self-discipline, of which this virtue is the basis. It is therefore of great importance that we should be instructed in its ways and in the methods by which it is obtained.

So intimate is the connection between patience and humility, that neither of these virtues can make much progress without the other;

nor can charity advance towards its perfection without their aid. The seraphic St. Francis, so deeply founded in these two virtues, was wont to exclaim: "Hail humility with thy sister patience!" What humility begins patience consolidates. Humility purifies the soul, patience fortifies the will; humility subjects the soul to God, patience rests the soul on God; humility makes the soul simple and sincere, patience makes her firm and constant; humility keeps the soul in her just and true position, patience protects her in the peaceful possession of that position. It is not, therefore, humility alone, or patience alone, but humility and patience in their happy combination with charity, that establish the groundwork of the Christian virtues; and on this secure basis we are able to work out our perfection. Hence St. Catherine of Siena calls patience "the pith and marrow of charity"

If we examine the Eight Beatitudes, we shall find that patience is an essential constituent in every one of them; if we hear the spouse of Christ, the loving soul, declare in the Canticles, "He hath set charity in order within me,"[15] the order of charity is secured by patience. By patience was the Church of God built up; by patience every holy soul is built up. In his great vision of the combat throughout the ages of the Church with the world, St. John sums up the final triumph of God's servants in these words: "Here is the patience of the saints, who keep the commandments of God and the faith of Jesus".[16] Not only does St.

Paul teach in various places that patience is the virtue that completes and perfects charity, but in a special prayer for his disciples he asks for them the combination of these two virtues: "May the Lord direct your hearts in the charity of God and the patience of Christ".[17]

If we contemplate the provident action of God as it moves through His creation, we everywhere see the signs of His divine patience, sustaining what is by nature feeble, upholding what left to itself must fall, enduring evil and disorder for the sake of final good, providing for all things according to their needs, and conducting all things to their destinies according to His eternal designs. If we contemplate the ways of God in souls, with what a sovereign patience

He endures their wayward follies and ungrateful crimes, to bring them from their evil to His good! If we contemplate those souls themselves, or look carefully into our own, our experience of the weakness and inconstancy of our nature will teach us how greatly we stand in need of the gift and virtue of patience. This truth has been so admirably expressed by a holy Bishop and Martyr of the third century that we here give his words.

St. Zeno says: "Whilst we seek the blessed life with the earnest sighs of our nature, and look for it through the various virtues, they are all brought to their rest through patience. Without patience nothing can be conceived by the mind, nothing can be understood, nothing can be taught. For all things look to patience. Neither faith nor hope; neither justice nor humility; neither chastity nor honesty; nor concord; nor charity; nor any act of virtue; nor even the elements of nature; are able to hold together, or keep their consistency, without the nerve, restraint, and discipline of patience. Patience is always mature: it is humble, prudent, cautious, provident, and contented under every necessity that arises. Tranquil in the day of clouds and amidst the tempests of provocation, it allows nothing to disturb the serenity of the soul. The patient man knows of neither alteration nor regret. Who can say that he ever suffers loss? Whatever he has to endure, you will find him as complete at the end of his sufferings as though he had suffered nothing. How can we calculate the results of his patience? When he seems to have undergone defeat, we find he has got the victory.

"No force, no violence, can drive patience from its position. Neither labor, nor hunger, nor nakedness, nor persecution, nor fear, nor danger, can move patience from its resolution. No power, no torments, no death, come it in whatever shape, no ambition, no enjoyment of felicity, can shake the constancy of patience. Robustly balanced in a certain elevated and divine temperance that calms the soul into peaceful moderation, patience abides immovable; and to enable it to master all difficulties, its first conquest is over the soul herself. The virtues cannot be virtues; nor can the state of the elements be lasting; nor can they flow in their well-known connection through their solemn circles, unless patience like a solicitous mother be the keeper of things and the regulator of their changes."[18]

It is an obvious truth that what is weak by nature or constitution, and liable to fail, can only be made strong by the infusion of strength, or by adhering to what is strong and unchangeable. But moral strength, that which makes the soul strong, whether in action or endurance, is patience. Let us examine these principles by the light of the inspired Psalmist. When surrounded with trials, oppressed, and almost smothered with temptations, he feels all the weakness of his nature, and is troubled with disturbing fears. But he breaks away from them in this fervid cry: "Shall not my soul be subject to God? For from Him is my salvation. For He is my God and my Savior: my protector, I shall be moved no more." The Hebrew text, as the commentators observe, is more forcible. It indicates a silent subjection to God that neither doubts, murmurs, complains, nor listens to temptation, and a resting on God as the rock of his strength. After describing his enemies rushing upon him, as though he were "a leaning wall and a tottering fence," he thus addresses his own soul: "Be thou, O my soul, subject to God, for from Him is my patience. For He is my God, and my Savior: He is my helper, I shall not be moved."[19]

In other Psalms the Royal Prophet invokes the Almighty as his "firmament and his refuge," and as the fortress of his strength; and calls God his patience, because from Him he derives the strength of patience, rests on Him as the foundation of His strength, and finds in Him his protection. In the seventieth Psalm he says: "Be Thou to me a God, a protector, and a place of strength, that Thou mayest make me safe. For Thou art my firmament and refuge. . . . Thou art my patience, O Lord; my hope, O Lord, from my youth."[20] He thus teaches, from his own interior experience as well as from his light, that our patience is derived from adhering to the unchangeable strength of God, and from receiving the gift of strength from His bounty. Rising in another Psalm to that more fundamental and steadfast patience which takes the name of fortitude, of which he has received the gift, the Sacred Singer says: "I will sing Thy fortitude, and will extol Thy mercy"[21]. And in the consciousness that this noble gift is mainly given that by its force he may adhere to God, he says again: "I will keep my fortitude to Thee"[22].

We are here taught by the Holy Spirit, through the soul of David, that God is our patience, our fortitude, and our strength, provided we rest our souls on Him, adhere to Him, are subject to His strengthening influences, and work with them in loyal co-operation. "Patience is so great a gift of God," observes St. Augustine, "that it is even ascribed to Him who waits so long for the conversion of the sinner. God cannot suffer, yet though incapable of suffering He takes the name of patience. But as He neither suffers nor is subject to impatience, who can say what the patience of God is? It is as incomprehensible as His zeal, His anger, or anything of like kind."[23]

But if we consider patience as it is the enduring strength of charity, that admits not the entrance of evil within the divine circle of good, whilst it endures the existence of external evil for the sake of greater good, then we shall approach nearer to understanding the patience of God; because God is charity, and charity is patient. As what is weak of itself obtains strength by adhering to what is strong, the weak human will obtains strength to keep the whole man in discipline by adhering to God and receiving power to repel the movements of temptation and the risings of irritation, and to quiet the perturbations of the spirit, come from whatever cause they may. "We are directed," says the profound Tertullian, "to exercise the authority of patience, not from any cynical affectation of equanimity (like the pagans), but from the divine disposition of a celestial and life-giving discipline, of which God is the example.[24]

We shall better understand the divine power of patience if we consider how all moral evil has sprung in the first instance, and still springs in its beginning, from impatience. St. Zeno, Tertullian, St. Cyprian, St. Augustine, and several other early Fathers have treated on this subject. Every kind of spiritual creature was first created by God in a good state, and received grace to love Him and to adhere to Him as the supreme good of their nature. This implied the grace of charity and patience—charity to love, patience to persevere and to endure their probation; but being weak by nature, owing to their origin from nothingness, and having free will to choose their own acts, they were exposed to the danger of neglecting their grace, and of giving themselves to self-love, self-will, and cupidity. So long as they remained with patient perseverance in the love and will of God, they were sinless; but so soon as they yielded their will to temptation, they lost the patience by which they adhered to God, to His love and to His will, becoming impatient of the good they possessed through the curiosity and desire of trying what was evil; and thus, with the loss of patience, they became weak, irritable, sinful, separated from God, and divided within themselves. It must also be remembered, according to the Scriptures and the traditions both of the Rabbins and the Christian Fathers, Satan and his angels fell through jealousy of the high dignity conferred on man at his creation.

After this explanation, let us hear the words of Tertullian, which are repeated in substance by St. Cyprian and St. Augustine. He says: "As patience is in God, we must expect to find the first adversary of patience in the first enemy of God. We detect the birth of impatience in Satan, when he could not patiently endure that God should subject all that He had created to His image in man. Then it was that his impatience conspired with his malice. Adam, again, would never have fallen had he stood with patience within the divine commandment. He was innocent; he was the friend of God; he was in possession of paradise. But in losing his patience he fell from the wisdom of God and ceased to be capable of divine things. Cast out of paradise, he became a man of the earth, and was easily taken hold of by impatience in things offensive to God. Look upon the catalogue of sins, and you will find that they all begin with the loss of patience; for evil is impatience of good. No one is impure who is not impatient of purity, or unjust who is not impatient of justice, or unquiet who is not impatient of tranquility. Whoever is evil is impatient of good."[25]

The seat of patience, as of all the virtues, is in the will. Its office is to hold the will with firm steadfastness to what is reasonable, just, orderly, and true, and to withhold the will by refusing it to what is unreasonable, unjust, disorderly, or false. For example, the patience of faith holds the will with firmness and constancy to the truths revealed by God, and keeps to the divine motives of faith, whatever sufferings the soul may have to endure for the sake of her faith; whilst this same patience of faith refuses the will to error and to whatever may tempt the soul to relax her hold of faith. The patience of hope holds fast by the will, with unswerving confidence, to the goodness, mercy, and promises of God, and refuses to let the will be moved into despondency or sadness, or to whatever may tempt the soul to lessen her confidence in God. The patience of charity adheres by the will habitually to God with love and gratitude, and that notwithstanding every kind of obscuration, trial, or loss of sensible devotion, and refuses to yield up the will to whatever might weaken, diminish, or contradict the love of God.

So it is in every other virtue. Patience holds the will with constancy to the good upon which it is engaged, and withholds the same will from those provocations or temptations that would weaken or destroy the virtue in its act by putting evil or falsehood in its place. Hence you will find that the first movement towards evil is always a disturbing movement of impatience.

It is therefore laid down as a principle, as well by the pagan philosophers as by the Christian moralists, each taking their own view of it, that patience is the virtue of the virtues, that is to say, it is the force that gives them their vigour, endurance, and solidity. St. Gregory calls it "the root and guardian of the virtues".[26] It is the root, as supplying them with strength and consistency; it is the guardian, as protecting them from perturbation and evil. As the tree obtains its strength from being rooted in the ground, the soul, which is the tree of virtue, obtains her strength from patiently adhering to God. As a fortress girds round its inhabitants and defends them from the assaults and alarms of their enemies, so patience defends the virtues from the temptations and alarms that assail them. Hence St. Zeno observes that "the worth of patience is not so much in the multiplying as in the perfecting of the virtues"[27]. When St. Paul speaks of the faithful who are "rooted and grounded in charity,"[28] he evidently refers to that charity which is firm and constant by reason of its patience.

Taking this profound view of Christian patience, St. Augustine defines it in these terms:—"Patience is the enduring of evils with an equable mind, lest through an evil disposition we should give up that good which brings us to our greatest good"[29]. The good we have already as devout Christians is the sense of God, the light of faith, the grace of Christ, the friendship of God through communication of His Holy Spirit, and peace of heart through the absence of grievous sin. This good, already in the soul, brings us through the exercise of charity to our supreme good. But through impatience, vexation of spirit, and sadness, patience glides away, and the good we have is disturbed, scattered abroad, and diminished; and what is worse, if we enter into an evil disposition, patience is relaxed more and more, and as impatience and sadness take its place, the habits of grace and virtue are weakened and lowered, the light of the soul becomes obscured; and if we altogether lose the patience of charity, that divine gift itself becomes extinguished together with our supernatural life.

In St. Paul's magnificent description of charity, the object of the Apostle is to show, that whilst it is inseparable from faith, it is perfected by unselfishness and patience. Weigh the qualities one by one which the Apostle ascribes to this most excellent of virtues, and you will find that this is the sum of their sense: "Charity," he says, "is patient, is kind; charity envieth not, dealeth not perversely; is not puffed up. Is not ambitious, seeketh not her own, is not provoked to anger, thinketh no evil. Rejoiceth not in iniquity, but rejoiceth with the truth; beareth all things, believeth all things, hopeth all things, endureth all things."[30] From the nature of charity it must have these qualities. Without faith it could not be grounded in supernatural truth, without unselfishness it could not be generous, without patience it could not endure, nor could it repulse its enemies. In the words of St. Cyprian: "If you take patience away from charity, it languishes in desolation and cannot endure."[31]

If you consider the human soul as a spiritual coin that bears the image and superscription of God, faith is the mold that gives it a divine figure, and charity is its golden quality. Humility gives it gravity, discretion flexibility, and patience durability. When that soul is tried in the fire of tribulation, and its charity put to the test by reproaches and calumny, then will the degree of her patience show how far the virtue of that soul bears the character of durability. For, as it is said in the Proverb: "He that is impatient suffers damage"[32]. And again: "The learning of a man is known by patience, and his glory is to pass over wrongs"[33]. But as the vice of obstinacy makes pretensions to the virtue of patience, although it is but the stupidity of pride, true patience must also stand the test of humility. For there may be a proud endurance of contumely that is nothing better than folly; just as the worm of pride may be concealed in the apparent humility of sackcloth.[34]

After this general exposition of the work of patience in the soul, what shall we say in conclusion? As a divine attribute of God patience is infinite and eternal. In His divine benignity He exhibits that patience towards us in bearing with our offences and ingratitude, and in waiting for our repentance and return to His love. As He has made us to His image that we may be formed to His likeness, He sends to us the grace of patience through the gift of charity, that through its faithful exercise we may imitate His patience. This virtue is the tonic medicine of our enfeebled nature; it fortifies the will, soothes down the irritabilities that derange the soul, braces the powers into unity, and gives stability to all the virtues. It secures the mind from dissipation, the will from perturbation, and enables us to preserve our self-possession.

It is the pith and marrow of charity, strengthening the love of God in the children of light, that it may persevere under every cloud of tribulation and adversity.

As the rock resists the surging waves, patience resists the surges of temptation, and scatters them into empty foam. In the day of weakness and suffering it upholds the spirit above them in the serene atmosphere of cheerfulness, and will not suffer her to sink into the wasting disease of sadness. In a word, and that word shall be St. Cyprian's, "Patience is not only the keeper of good but the preventer of evil, repelling whatever is adverse to good. Obedient to the Holy Spirit, it adheres to celestial and divine things; and standing in opposition to those solicitations of the body that assault and capture the soul, it contends for the virtues as from a fortress of strength."[35]

"Oh, patience," exclaims St. Zeno, "thou art the queen of all things, and I know that thou restest more safely on thy own foundations, on thy own counsels, and on thy own good ways than in the words of those who are strangers to thee. Thy praise is not in multiplying, but in strengthening the virtues. Thou givest to virginity the flower that never fades. Thou art the safe harbour of widowhood from the storms of life. Thou art the strength of the yoke of married life, enabling its burden to be borne with the forbearance of an equal love. Thou teachest friendship how to will and to forbear the same things. Thou givest freedom to the rugged labourer, and art the consoler of his toils. To poverty thou givest the privilege of bearing all things, that so it may possess all things. The Prophets were raised to their sublime office by patience. The Apostles adhered to Christ through patience. Thou art the nursing mother of the Martyrs, and their crown. As the knot binds the flowing tresses on the head of the modest maiden, thou bindest up the virtues into unity with beauty and honour. Happy, eternally happy, is he who hath thee always in his company."[36]

## 2

# ON THE NATURE AND OBJECT OF CHRISTIAN PATIENCE

"Patience is necessary for you: that doing the will of God, you may receive the promise."—HEBREWS x, 36.

When we have obtained a clear insight into the precise nature of any virtue, of how it works in the soul, and to what purpose it is directed, we have gained the knowledge both of what it is and of what it is not; and we are able to distinguish its action from every other movement of the will. This knowledge is of great importance for the cultivation of virtue; for, as an engineer cannot work his engine satisfactorily unless he knows what belongs to every part of its construction, a soul cannot manage herself with intelligence unless she knows what belongs to her several powers in the exercise of the virtues. When one thing in the soul is confused by the mind with another, the will cannot work in clear light, and may even confound what is opposed to a virtue with the virtue itself, causing error, perplexity, and uneasiness.

There are many people who read expositions of the virtues in books, and have a real desire to profit by them; yet the knowledge they gain is but little compared with what they might obtain, because they look more into the book than into themselves. They do not reflect upon their own interior state, or upon their own interior operations, in doing which the book is intended to assist them, nor do they carefully observe what passes within their souls. Their knowledge is book-knowledge, not self-knowledge, and is consequently shallow, without roots within them, and quickly fades and passes away. Such unreflecting readers are like the man who beholds his face in a glass, goes his way, and presently forgets what manner of man he is; but if we look upon a book as no more than a help to self-knowledge and the perfecting of the virtues, and if we second the book by interior reflection and observation, then it will enable us to read and understand the interior book of the soul, which has the immense advantage of being illuminated with spiritual light; and we shall thus obtain a knowledge all our own, a true and lasting possession always ready to do us service. But this demands for its accomplishment that very virtue of patience which it is the object of this book to inculcate.

The first thing required to be understood is that patience is an immediate exercise of the will, which is the spring of all free and moral action. It must not, therefore, be confounded with the sentiments, sensibilities, or feelings, because it is a pure act of the will. But although, like all real virtue, it springs from the resolution and action of the will, as enlightened by the mind and conscience, patience, like every other virtue, uses the other faculties of the soul, and even the members of the body, as its instruments, the will making them obedient to execute its commands, and to act in submission to its force and direction. But the will of the good Christian is elevated by divine motives and sentiments, and is energized by divine grace, so that the strength of virtue depends upon the supernatural gifts of God. But what has to be mainly looked to is the will, because when the will is good and resolute, and goes in the right direction, the whole man follows as a matter of course.

The second thing to be understood where patience is concerned is the double action of the will, the action by which the will advances, and the action by which it recedes and refuses its co-operation. It advances to what it loves; it recedes and refuses to be united to what it dislikes or hates. The virtuous will desires and wills what is good, but refuses to give itself up to what is vicious or disorderly; and although this refusal is often said to be passive, it is in fact a strong act of the will, and often requires more strength and resolution than it does to desire and will what is good. Hence this kind of action is the greatest practical proof of the freedom of the will. For, when the will is attracted by some strong inferior appetite, or urged by some strong passion, to move in the direction of evil or disorder, and yet, adhering to higher and better motives, that will draws back upon itself and refuses to be drawn away by that appetite, or to be driven by that passion; this is not only the greatest proof of the freedom of the will, but it is the greatest act of virtue. But what we have here described is the interior action of patience.

But left to its own nature, the will is so weak, movable, and restless, it is so readily attracted by curiosity, its attention is so quickly turned to whatever is felt within us or that moves around us, that it cannot be truly firm and patient unless it have a firmament upon which to rest far stronger than nature can provide, and a strength incomparably beyond its own, as well as a motive more exalted than mere nature can supply. This firmament is the God in whom we live, and on whom the soul must rest by adherence to Him. This strength is the supernatural grace of God given to the will. This motive, greater and stronger than all others, on which to place both the attention and intention of the will, is the light and love of God. When the will thus rests on God, looks to God, and draws strength from God, that patience is generated which resists all evils and disorders, gives us the possession of ourselves, and keeps the soul in peace. "Be thou, O my soul, subject to God, for from Him is my patience."[1]

If we take the common definition of Christian patience, it is the virtue that strengthens the soul to resist provocations and temptations, and to endure afflictions, so as neither to give up the good of virtue nor to commit sin. This definition is sufficiently comprehensive to include the different ways in which patience is exercised, as well as the different adversaries to which it is opposed; and it shows that the chief object of the virtue is to keep the soul in the peaceful possession of herself. But it should be clearly understood by every one who values the perfection of his actions that this virtue of patience depends a great deal more upon the interior management of the soul than upon our exterior conduct; not only because it must necessarily begin there, and make progress there, and there in the interior establish order and peace; but also because if the interior man is patient the exterior man will be preserved in patience. For impatience begins within the soul, and from thence proceeds to the exterior man.

Patience is both a special and a universal virtue. As a special virtue it is opposed to two special vices. As a general or universal virtue it gives strength, stability, and protection to all the virtues, and is opposed to every vice. We have here to consider it as it is a special virtue; and as such it is opposed to vexation and anger on the one hand, and to sadness on the other. For these are the chief destroyers of patience.

Vexation and anger are both opposed to the good of reason and to the good of virtue. They darken the light of justice, take us from our self-possession, bring us into disorder, disturb our peace, and diminish or destroy charity. They set fire to the other passions and appetites, and lead us into evil. But they are also mixed with sadness, and when anger subsides sadness remains, and is increased by the reaction from the excitement and folly of anger. Hence St. Thomas defines the special virtue of patience to be the virtue that preserves the good of reason against sadness, so that reason may not sink under its influence. For the moral virtues have good for their object, and protect the good which the light of reason dictates against the disturbance of the passions. But amongst those passions sadness is one that greatly hinders the good of reason from guiding the soul aright, and in accordance with the light of justice.[2]

Sadness is a very subtle vice, working often in its beginning without being perceived. But grief and sadness are at the beginning of vexation and anger, and act as stimulants to these passions; and when the excitement of passion subsides the dregs that remain are a more bitter grief and more desolating sadness. St. Paul says: "The sadness of the world worketh death",³ And according to Ecclesiasticus: "Sadness hath killed many, and there is no profit in it",⁴ Hence the soul has great need of patience to keep her from sadness.

Vexation is the beginning of anger, which has many degrees from mild resentment to outrageous fury. Anger is a sensitive, irascible, vindictive passion, a complication of many passions with one prevailing appetite, the appetite of revenge. It springs out of grief and sadness, owing to some real or imaginary disparagement, offense, contempt, or injury, threatened or inflicted upon us, or upon some one dear to us, and it awakens in us the appetite of retorting wrong or avenging injury. As anger rises to the height of passion the blood starts up, the nerves are shook, the heart becomes timid, the brain is suffused, the mouth trembles, the tongue is impeded in its utterance, the face glows with baleful fire, the whole man is a painful and unsightly spectacle. The excitement of the animal man overwhelms the spiritual man, and reason sinks under the masterful dominion of passion. It is an intoxication and a madness for the time it lasts.

If we look into the interior of the angry man, he can be no longer recognized for what he was. Imagination has usurped the place of reason, and crowds the mind with hateful images and vindictive motives. "Lashed with anger, the soul is all in disorder, her peace has fled, and, rent and torn with sharp and bitter trouble, that soul is herself no longer. She has lost the power derived from her resemblance to God."⁵ The mind has lost its guiding light, the will its rational power, pride takes the place of good sense, hatred the place of charity, and vindictiveness the place of justice; and yet anger affects to be nothing less nor more than justice. To quote the experience of one who had long to contend with great anger under great and ignominious sufferings: "An excited mind ceases to reason; carried away by a resistless torrent of wild ideas, it forms for itself a sort of mad logic, full of anger and malignity; it is a state of soul as unphilosophical as it is absolutely unchristian".⁶

Anger opens the door to all the vices and passions; and as that guardian virtue of patience is thrust aside, there is nothing left that can prevent their entrance. Hence timidity, grief, rashness, audacity, clamour, contention, strife, hatred, insult, contumely, indignation, and violence, all follow after anger, and feed its desolating flames. It smothers reason, confounds wrong with right, extinguishes prudence, breaks up friendship, treads down the wisdom of counsel, befools the wise, lacerates gravity, destroys peace, and shuts out the Holy Spirit from the Christian soul. It has been well observed by Hugo of St. Victor that "as pride takes man from God, and envy takes the man from his neighbour, anger takes the man from himself".[7]

We have described the vice of anger in its full-blown pride and disorder, and in its deadly degree, because when a vice is seen in all its magnitude we are better able to see what vicious and hateful elements it contains; and so can more easily understand that even in its less and lower degrees the germs of those same vices are not wanting, although they escape the observation of those who are unaccustomed to much self-examination. But sensitiveness, touchiness, annoyance, and such smaller degrees of impatience are not without irritation and interior disturbance; but when it comes to displeasure, discontent, murmuring, resentment, vexation, retort, indignation, or disdain, there is a degree of anger in the soul, not without at least an equal degree of sadness.

But it is precisely these degrees of irritation and vexation, when first rising from our inferior nature, and making themselves sensible to our superior nature, to our light, and to our conscience, that present the most numerous occasions for self-discipline, by the exercise of which our patience may be armed and fortified against more serious attacks of anger. The first movements of impatience, the first uneasiness of dissatisfaction, are warnings to patience to be upon its guard, lest trouble arise to disturb the soul and take hold of the will. If we calmly look down from the superior soul upon the first movements of irritation or impatience, nothing can appear more contemptible; and under the rebuke of the gaze of our interior eye they vanish in shame. One has seen from Alpine heights a little white cloud down in the valley below, which, unless some wind blows it away, will rapidly swell and grow until the whole region is enveloped in mist, fog, and rain. So is it with the first little cloud of trouble and discontent that moves in our lower nature: the breath of patience will disperse it, but if left to itself it will quickly grow on what it feeds upon, and will envelop and fill the soul with anger and vexation. For anger is a brooding vice that feeds on sensitive self-love and imaginary wrong far beyond the original offence, if indeed offence has been given.

It is a good point of prudence to realize to ourselves the good qualities of those with whom we have to act, and which are almost always more and better in the heart than appears on the surface, and yet not to forget their obvious limitations and infirmities; that we may not only not misjudge their intentions, but may also know what we can justly expect from them, and what we cannot reasonably look for. This will save an enormous amount of misconception, rash judgment, irritation, and vexation. We have all very different characters, and the difference arises from our personal limitations, which are owing partly to nature, partly to the circumstances that have attended upon our several lives, and much to the habits in which we have been formed. But it is absurd to expect the same habits, sentiments, qualities, and powers in all persons, to judge all persons by the same standard, to exact what does not exist, and then give way to annoyance and discontent because we have not found what we desired. As the old proverb says, we must take people for what they are, and make just and due allowances, remembering that others have to allow for our limitations.

If a man chooses a partner in life for certain good qualities, and finds with time that some others are deficient, the whole happiness of that family depends upon his forbearance with respect to those limitations, and upon his doing his best to supply them. The same may be said of those who elect their superiors; one is chosen by preference for certain leading qualities, but there may be limitations as well; yet how preposterous would it be for subjects to fix their minds upon those minor deficiencies, and to make them the occasion of murmuring, complaint, and discontent, forgetting all the good qualities for which that person was chosen. A little society comes together, under certain regulations, for one common purpose; but unless the members of that society make mutual allowance for the diversity of characters and limitations of which it is composed, unless they bear and forbear, give and take, with equal goodwill, contention and anger will enter that society and rend its happiness asunder. The Apostolic rule: "Bear ye one another's burdens, and so you shall fulfill the law of Christ,"[8] is the law of patient charity.

Applying this law to religious societies, the venerable Gerard, commenting on the Rule that formed the author of the Imitation of Christ, breaks forth in this exclamation: "Never, no, eternally never, can charity and concord reign in a community where holy patience does not absolutely rule"[9].

Such is the difference of natures, temperaments, and inclinations, that it is impossible for a number of persons to live and act together in peace with each one, and in concord with all, unless each one holds his sensitive self-love under the control of patience, and merges his private interests in the common good.

St. Paul had this great law of Christian society in view when he wrote these words to the Galatians: "You have been called unto liberty: only make not your liberty an occasion to the flesh, but by charity of the spirit serve one another. But if you bite and devour one another; take heed you be not consumed by one another. ... If we live in the Spirit, let us walk in the Spirit. Let us not be made desirous of vainglory, provoking one another, envying one another."[10]

Almost every one has some defect in body, manners, conduct, or way of thinking and speaking; and we have not unfrequently to come in contact with those who are rude or even vicious; but if we lose sight of what is due to the immortal soul, and give way to annoyance, disgust, or loathing, we lose our patience, become deformed ourselves by that loss, and inflict wounds on our own charity and on that which is due to our neighbour. Now, if we trace this conduct to its root, we shall find that it originates in the impatience of fastidious self-love; yet if we profess to follow Christ, and to imitate His ways, we should remember that He chose for Himself a society of simple, uncultivated persons, and conversed affectionately with publicans and sinners. We forget how others have to bear with our defects, and that we are a cause of trial to our neighbours. Blinded by self-love, we see the mote in our brother's eye, and forget the beam in our own.

There is nothing that drives us to impatience so vehemently, or throws us into greater interior disorder, than an injury, or the imagination of an injury, which is far more frequent than real injury. For sensitive persons, who have but little interior self-discipline, are prompt to imagine themselves injured in word or deed; and what is greatly to be noted, they are much more inclined to imagine themselves injured by their friends and by their superiors than by other persons. The reason is because they attach more importance to their affection, claim more of their indulgence, and suffer more intensely if they think that they are undervalued or disparaged by them. Should they become dissatisfied with themselves, and therefore conscious of blame, they readily suspect that others disesteem them, and are quick to interpret their words and acts in that sense. Then a little spark sets their soul in flames. Such persons ought to set a law on their imagination, and keep their inflammable suspicions of wrong under the control of patience; they ought to suspect their own suspicions, which experience tells them are often unjust, or their sensitive self-love will never leave them in peace. For many things are said and done without the least intention of injury; some from quickness of tongue, some from inadvertence or thoughtlessness, some in good-natured jest, some from good intentions, some from mere imprudence; and no one has any right to take any of them in bad part, and so commit himself to anger, grief, and sadness.

Few there are who have not observed that even the just correction of those whose duty it is to correct, instead of being taken in good part, is too often converted into anger, grief, and sadness by weak souls, who exhibit thereby a spirit at once mean and ungrateful. Where such is the case, rebuke has justified itself, and has revealed to that soul an interior state of disorder that calls for the most vigorous redress. It is high time for that soul to become offended with her own conduct.

But if any one should falsely or maliciously assail our good name and reputation—a mode of detraction not limited, alas! to the children of the world—let us, in that case, keep our magnanimity, that our virtue may be stronger than another's vice, and that our patience may suffer no loss by reason of another's improbity. Rather should we rejoice in the Lord that He has called us by these means to greater justice, which is commonly born, receives its growth, and obtains perfection among injuries and insults. In the nature of things, justice is hated by injustice; and therefore our Lord was hated by Judas, by the Sadducees, and by the Pharisees. But He has promised a great beatitude to those who suffer injuries with patience.

There are also abundant occasions given us for the discipline of patience in those material things and events, which are opposed to our inclinations and desires by necessity, and independently of our choice. Such are corporal infirmities and maladies, intense heat or cold, severity of weather, the uncomplying nature of materials in which we work, and other like things. However unreasonable it may be to give way to vexation or anger with things insensible, yet many have so little wisdom as to lose their peace and patience over them. Nay, some have so little patience as to lose temper over the bite of a fly, the dulness of a pen, the bluntness of a knife, or the tightness of a shoe. Like little children devoid of reason, they will ascribe guiltiness to things incapable of intention, and have their little revenge upon them at the expense of their sense, patience, and serenity.

We come at last to those great calamities in which individuals, families, and whole communities are involved or overwhelmed, whether by the injuries of men or the visitation of God. Such misfortunes try the constancy of the brave, and expose feebler souls to the danger of desponding sadness. Now, if reason should prove unavailing to set a measure to grief, let faith prevail; and when all seems lost on earth, let us look up to Heaven for better things. For when things are at their worst according to the world, if the calamity is rightly used, they begin to be at their best according to God. All things are in God's hands, to give or take as He chooses; and an immortal soul is more precious in His sight than all that the world can give. When He strips a soul of earthly things, He calls upon that soul to look to Him and to trust in His care and providence. His dispositions are wonderful; He plays in the world with the children of men, stripping but to clothe more generously; striking but to heal; casting down but to raise up; bringing to the gates of death, and restoring to life. When holy Job was stripped of his earthly goods and all his dear ones, the God who holds all things in His hands remained to Him; and therefore he kept his patience, and held to God with unswerving trust; whilst the voice of his resignation arose in these memorable words: "The Lord gave, and the Lord hath taken away: as it hath pleased the Lord, so is it done: blessed be the name of the Lord. In all these things Job sinned not with his lips, nor spoke any foolish thing against God."[11] "And the Lord blessed the latter days of Job more than the beginning."[12]

There is nothing really lost so long as God is with us, nothing therefore to be despaired of. As long as we are simple, upright, fearing God and departing from evil, placing our hope in God and not in the prudence of the world, He has care of His servants, will turn their calamities into blessings, and will not leave their patience unrequited. Divine is that patience of hope which in the heaviest as in the lightest trials looks to God, trusts to God alone, and fills the soul with the conviction that whilst God is with us nothing can be against us.

It would seem needless to advance more reasons on the duty of bearing adversities with patient resignation, because on this subject every one can be his own teacher. Who is not ready to raise up the mind of his friend or neighbor from the depth of grief? Who is not able to direct the mind of one saddened with affliction to the divine help, to the unreasonableness of too much sorrow, and to the inestimable value of patience? He will even minister gentle rebukes on the folly of being overwhelmed with too much sadness. Yet when his own turn comes, he forgets the excellent teaching that he gave to others, and will let no one soften down his grief. Thus the words that Eliphaz babbled so unjustly to the patient Job come home in all their truth and justice to many a consoler: "Behold thou hast taught many, and thou hast strengthened the weary hands: thy words have confirmed them that were staggering, and thou hast strengthened the trembling knees: but now the scourge has come upon thee, and thou faintest: it hath touched thee, and thou art troubled. Where is thy fear, thy fortitude, thy patience, and the perfection of thy ways?"[13]

How shall we explain this apparent inconsistency? The fault is not in the light of the understanding but in the resolution of the will. Our faith, our instructions, our meditations, and our prayer leave us in no ignorance of what we ought to do. We know well that in every grief and trial we ought to direct our mind and acts to God; but when we have neglected to form our interior to habits of patience, and our will has been too much devoted to the service of self-love, many things become difficult to endure. So when the hour of trial comes, the will loses sight of the truth, refuses to be patient, and casts off the law of light. The disorder therefore is in the will; but the cure is also in the will. Holy Job was not patient by nature, but by the force of virtuous habits in his will. The remedy is to waken up the will to the generous resolution of enduring with a magnanimous spirit whatever God ordains that we should endure with resignation and hope; looking to no secondary causes, but accepting the will of God as the first and ruling cause, until it be His good pleasure to take away the burden.

Returning for a moment to the vice of anger, it should be thoroughly understood that all inordinate anger includes in it a disposition to revenge, greater or less according to the degree of anger, even though it be but a retort in word or feeling, and that word or feeling be concealed in the breast. In fact, the anger that is kept within is more wasting and consuming than the anger that finds relief in expression. St. James has this element of vindictiveness in view where he says: "Let every man be slow to anger, for the anger of man worketh not the justice of God"[14]. And St. Paul is more explicit. He says: "If it be possible, as much as is in you, have peace with all men. Not revenging yourselves, my dearly beloved, but give place to wrath; for it is written: *Revenge to me; I will repay*, saith the Lord."[15]

Anger is not a movement of power, but a weak affection of nature destructive of power, although the angry man mistakes it for power, and at the time revels in it with a sense of satisfaction, as if it were a triumph of strength. But that satisfaction is already mixed with the misgivings of sadness; unless resisted on its first approach, nothing grows so rapidly. Hence the apostolic rule: "Give place to wrath". Yield before it, retreat from it; if needful, and occasion offers, retreat from the occasion of it. If anger comes upon you, says St. Ambrose, if it begins to take hold of you, give place to it, and take your own place. Your place is in patience; your place is in reasonableness; your place is in calming down your indignation. It is no small thing to calm down anger; it is an act as great as if you had remained unmoved. This is nature, that is virtue.[16]

But the question arises: Is there a just anger? Unquestionably there is a just anger, or rather a just indignation, which belongs properly to parents, to those who are placed in authority, and to those whose duty it is to correct and amend disorder or vice, and especially the disorder of insubordination. And sometimes this just indignation becomes a duty that cannot be omitted without sharing the evil that is fostered by the absence of it. But we must carefully distinguish between vicious anger and just indignation. Vicious anger springs from passion, virtuous indignation moves from reason; vicious anger blinds the reason, virtuous indignation acts in the light of justice; vicious anger has an evil purpose, virtuous indignation has good for its object; vicious anger multiplies evil, virtuous indignation corrects evil; vicious anger is moved by the malicious appetite of revenge, virtuous indignation is moved by the zeal of vindicating the law and order established by God. Hence the Psalmist admonishes us: "Be angry and sin not"[17]. And our Divine Lord arose in the spirit of indignation against the Pharisees on account of the pride and hypocrisy with which they misled the people of God from the truth, and against the buyers and sellers who profaned the temple of God.

But where correction requires the emotions of indignation to give it due effect, this ought not to be allowed to go beyond just reason and measure; and, therefore, reflection should go before correction. For whoever corrects another from the impulse of inordinate anger will himself be inflamed by the vice of anger; he will exceed the measure of justice, and do more harm than good. Explaining the text,

"Be angry and sin not," St. Bernard justly observes: "You may sin as much by excess of anger as by omitting anger altogether. Not to be angry when you ought to be angry, not to correct the disorder, is sinful; but to be more angry than you ought to be is to add sin to sin."[18] It is with a view to keeping the just measure of anger that St. Gregory gives us this most valuable advice: "Take great care that when you use anger as an instrument of virtue you do not let it become your master. Make it the obedient servant of your reason; let it never depart from the support of reason. It will rise with vigor against vice when made the minister of reason."[19]

Reflecting in after life upon the grief and bitter anger against which he had to struggle under harsh and inhuman treatment during the ten years of his imprisonment, Silvio Pellico makes the following reflections, which, as coming from experience, are not unworthy of being here entertained:

"If I were a divine I should often insist upon the necessity of correcting irritability and inquietude of character; none can be truly good without that being effected. How nobly pacific, both with regard to Himself and others, was He whom we are all bound to imitate! There is no elevation of mind, no justice without moderation in our principles and thoughts, without a pervading spirit which inclines us to smile at the events of this little life, rather than fall into a passion with them. Anger is never productive of any good, except in the extremely rare case of being employed to humble the wicked, even as the usurers were driven by our angry Saviour from defiling His holy temple. Excitement and violence, perhaps different altogether from what I felt, are no less blameable. Mine was the mania of affliction and despair; I felt a disposition, while suffering under its horrors, to hate mankind. Several individuals in particular appeared to my imagination in the most revolting colours. It is a sort of moral epidemic, I believe, springing from vanity and selfishness; for when a man despises and detests his fellow creatures, he necessarily assumes that he is much better than the rest of the world. ... It is a curious fact that living in a state of hostility and rage actually affords a pleasure; it seems as if people thought there was a kind of heroism in it. ... Such is the world, and without uttering a libel, it is not what it ought to be."[20]

To complete this part of our subject, St. John Chrysostom has an admirable discourse in which he demonstrates that no one can be spiritually injured except by himself.[21] The only good we have that is excellent and imperishable is our soul, and the good which God gives to the soul. But by nothing except our own will can the soul or its good suffer injury. So long as one possesses one's soul in patience, no one can take any part of that good away from us. We can only lose the good of the soul by not holding to it with constancy, and we thus sin by losing patience. If we yield up the will to provocation or to temptation, it slips from our control, and suffers its force to be scattered and blown away at the word or stroke of another; and it is thus at the mercy of our lower nature, becoming weakened, impassioned, and unreasonable. Yet the injury and loss to the soul comes not from the provoker, not from the temptation, but from our own want of patience, in not holding the will to a better object, that we may endure with constancy until the trial pass away. Vexation, anger, and such like weaknesses, that give the will up to disorder for the time, are like mental derangement, in that they are attended with excitement, delusion, and the clouding of reason, to such an extent, that when calm and sober sense returns, we are surprised and grieved to find that we have not only lost our self-command but have committed ourselves to a great deal of folly.

But when the soul is truly patient, neither what afflicts the body nor what assails the soul can really do us injury. On the contrary, the soul becomes enriched with stronger virtue, and that fortitude is confirmed whereby we hold to God. "For which cause," says St. Paul, "we faint not; but though the outward man is corrupted: yet the inward man is renewed day by day. For our present tribulation, which is momentary and light, worketh for us exceedingly above measure an eternal weight of glory, while we look not at the things which are seen, but at the things which are not seen. For the things which are seen are temporal, but the things which are not seen are eternal. For we know, if our earthly house of this habitation is dissolved, that we have a building of God, a house not made with hands, eternal in heaven."²²

Every inordinate outbreak of impatience, vexation, or anger is accompanied with sadness, and terminates in greater sadness. Self-love is wounded, pride humiliated, vanity disappointed and put to shame, and sadness follows, depressing the soul, enfeebling the spirit, clouding the mind, warping the judgment, and paralyzing all generous virtue. The tendency of sadness is to brood over one's self, and to consider one's self as an ill-used and disappointed creature, deserving of better things. Then the fumes of melancholy take possession of the heart, which becomes sullen, heavy, and bitter, and finds a miserable satisfaction in nursing the wounds of self-love in loneliness of soul, as though God and our friends were our adversaries. In the virulent accesses of this morbid disorder, the sad one even imagines that this lonely isolation is a sort of revenge upon others, as if they were the inflictors of this bitterness, although it is only inflicted by one's own self-love and pride.

Hence sadness is the most selfish of all selfish things, and the very essence of self, eating and consuming the very heart of virtue. The serpent coiled round its slimy self, with no other feeling but of self, is the image of sadness. In itself, so long as it lasts, it has neither reason, hope, charity, nor generosity. We have described this vice in its darker degrees; but there are many other kinds of it, which, if not so gross or offensive, are more subtle and less observed, but which, nevertheless, become great impediments to the freedom and generosity of the soul, especially in the performance of duty and in the exercise of prayer.

In his comment on the definition of patience given by St. Thomas, Cardinal Cajetan gives us these pertinent remarks: "'In your patience you shall possess your soul'. This possession consists in having the undisturbed and peaceful dominion of the soul. But it is patience that keeps away whatever disturbs this quiet possession of one's self; and it is in this sense that St. James tells us that 'patience hath a perfect work'. But whilst cheerfulness looks to what we love and desire, sadness looks to what we do not like and would not have; and what we do not like we hold in fear, and fear is much less in our power than those delightful thoughts that inspire cheerfulness. If, then, we take a morbid pleasure in sadness, it becomes far more injurious to the soul than the fear of evil. We must not forget that the virtues are connected with each other, and that charity is patient. But as charity prefers God to all things, it must prefer God to all those things that sadden the soul; and as Christian patience is caused by charity, and cannot exist without charity, whatever we have to suffer should be endured with patience for the sake of the greatest good, that is, for the love of God, and the doing of His will."[23]

From this exposition the conclusion is obvious. Charity looks with the cheerful eye of generous love to God as the greatest and most desirable good. Sadness looks with the troubled eye of self-love to the things we dislike and would not have. Thus sadness takes us from the greatest good, the good of charity, and places us in the evil condition of cheerless and discontented self-love, in which the soul feeds on the bitterness of self in a state of privation and disappointment. But that this may not happen, patience is given to charity, that by its power of endurance charity may be protected, and the evil of sadness may be kept away from invading the soul.

There is "a sorrow according to God," which, says St. Paul, "worketh penance steadfast unto salvation"[24]. But this steadfastness implies its patience. This is a sorrow that does not depress or sadden, but it elevates the mind and brings consolation to the soul. It causes no loathing for prayer as the sadness of the world does, but attracts the soul to God, and only laments those things that separate the soul from Him. It is the fulfillment of the beatitude: "Blessed are they that mourn, for they shall be comforted". But that morbid sorrow or "sadness according to the world," which, as the Apostle says, "worketh death," and to which patience is opposed, is an animal passion that dwells in the sensual appetite. It springs out of irascibility and from repugnance to the evils which it fears, and is seated in the flame of anger. For the object of sadness is always some temporary evil, real or imaginary, which is thought to be injurious, although offensive to nothing but self-love.

When sadness is much indulged in, there follows a contraction of mind, a weakening of the soul's power, a dissolving of the heart's strength, and an embittering of the spirit, which causes restless discomfort, and brings forth indignation and melancholy. These unhappy feelings generate impatience, discontent, despitefulness, sloth, and weariness of heart. A certain darkness closes over the mind immersed in the turbid unction of self-love, so that the soul sees not her own folly; and although the will commonly shrinks in its morbid entanglement from expressing the condition of the soul, yet whenever speech is given to it, it comes out in some way like this: "I am not at comfort with myself"; or, "I am annoyed with myself"; or, "I am vexed with myself"; or, "I have no peace with myself"; or, "I am thoroughly miserable". Observe how all this language of sadness begins and ends in self. Observe also how it points to the drowning of patience in the flood of sadness. Remark again how it breathes of nothing but wounded self-love mortifying in its own bitterness.

Very much of this sadness comes from fixing the mind on the secondary causes of what tries or afflicts our nature, instead of looking to the first and most beneficent cause in the will of God. The winds of heaven, the plunderers from the desert, and the malignity of Satan were the secondary causes of Job's afflictions; but he in his patient resignation went straight to the first cause: "The Lord gave, and the Lord hath taken away. Blessed be the name of the Lord." The privations, trials, or sufferings that befall us are either directed or permitted by the ordinance of God, and that with a view to our final good. And the virtue of patience is given us that we may be able to meet them and profit by them.

God knows what we stand in need of far better than we know ourselves. Our trials are the fatherly dispositions of His providence; and it is idle to fix our mind on human causes, when they are ruled in the results that affect us by the one Divine Cause. They are brought upon us for our probation, our correction, or the expiation of our sins. They are designed to wake up in us the nobler and more vigorous and enduring virtues. They establish the soul in discipline by the force of that patience and magnanimity which they demand of us. They prove our love of God and our neighbor, by the forbearance and the endurance which they call upon us to exert. They refine away those noxious humors, the products of self-love and sloth, that obstruct and impede the generous flow of spiritual life. They plant in us the ground seed of merit, and prepare the rewards of endurance. They make us generous in conforming our will to the will of God. Hence the cheerful endurance of trials and sufferings is a virtue truly sublime, reaching its heroic degrees in the martyrs and confessors of God. It places us in spirit with Christ upon the cross, upon that cross which He commands us to carry after Him all the days of this mortal life. It gives us a likeness and a lot with Him in the great work of our salvation, which is all included in the mystery of His cross. With the exceeding patience of His love for us, He suffered exceedingly; and our patient endurance of labour and suffering is the greatest proof we can give of our love of God in Christ Jesus.

But when we come to those interior trials that touch the very marrow of our life, we must apply these reflections in a yet more exalted sense. We are made to enjoy God, and the soul delights in the first fruits of the Holy Spirit. But we must be purified before we can be sanctified; and we must deserve God, as far as we are able, by becoming more like to His Incarnate Son, crucified in spirit as well as in body. Those interior aridities and desolations of spirit, those anxieties arising from unpremeditated scruples, those unsought distractions and temptations that try the patience of the soul, are the crucifixions of the spirit, and call upon us for fortitude and endurance. They reveal our native weakness, correct our self-love, sweep out pride and levity, teach us humility, purify the soul of her vain conceits, put our fidelity to the proof, and compel us to have recourse to the remedy of patience. For unless we are very patient and enduring under these interior trials, sadness will invade the soul, will greatly endanger her light, her freedom, and her charity, and bring her under the dominion of the worst form of self-love, of that self-love which murmurs and complains in its bitterness, and makes prayer a painful and reluctant exercise.

Be it then understood and remembered that the darkness of trial is not evil, that dryness of spirit is not sin, that confusion of mind is not malice. They are invitations to patience, calls to resignation, beckonings to the healing cross, admonitions to be humble and obedient to the will of God. Faith is asked to adhere with patience to God in the dark; but this is the perfection of faith. Hope is called upon to cleave with trust to the good which, though present, is neither sensibly felt nor seen; but this is the sublimity of hope. Charity asks in those hours of desolation for the substance rather than the accidents of the love of God; for the pure will and desire of love without its sensibilities; for patient conformity with Christ crucified and desolate; for the courageous desire of God without the reward of present delight. But this is that strong, pure, unselfish God-seeking love, which is the more meritorious from the absence of present delight. The test of this brave and vigorous love is in the earnestness of its desire, and in the patience of its resignation. Yet God is secretly present with the soul, and whilst that suffering soul is humbled in the consciousness of her infirmity, in reward for her patience she receives a secret strength and peace, infused into the depths of her spirit, of which she is not altogether unconscious.

We have said that desire and patience are the proofs that the soul still adheres to God in the hour of interior trial. For she will then enter into the spirit of the Psalmist: "Be thou, O my soul, subject to God; for from Him is my patience. For He is my God, and my Saviour: He is my helper, I shall not be moved."[25] But when the dark cloud breaks, and the sun of justice shines forth anew to the thirsting soul with brighter beams than before, she emerges from her trial more pure, luminous, and firm in virtue by reason of her faith and patience in the day of distress. "Son," says the wise Ecclesiasticus, "when thou comest to the service of God, stand in justice and fear, and prepare thy soul for temptation. Humble thy heart, and endure; incline thy ear, and receive the words of understanding; and make not haste in the day of clouds. Wait on God with patience; join thyself to God, and endure, that thy life may be increased in the latter end. Take all that shall be brought upon thee; and in thy sorrow endure, and in thy humiliation keep patience. For gold and silver are tried in the fire, but acceptable men in the furnace of humiliation. Believe God, and He will recover thee; and do thou direct thy way, and trust Him." Then, to lift us out of fear and disheartenment, the Wise Man sets before us these high motives for our encouragement: "My children, behold the generations of men; and know ye that no one hath hoped in the Lord, and hath been confounded. For who hath continued in His commandment, and hath been forsaken? Or who hath called upon Him, and He hath despised him? For God is compassionate and merciful, and will forgive sins in the day of tribulation, and He is a protector to all who seek Him in truth."[26]

But if in our interior trials we lose our patience, then we fall into sadness, and so become weak, troubled, and discouraged. For as by patience we adhere to God, and receive his strengthening influence, by the same patience we endure the privation of consolation, and resist discouraging fears. But if, in the darkness and dryness of the soul, we give way to disheartening fears, and lose our confidence because we are deprived of comfort, then patience gives way to impatience and discouragement, which open the door to sadness, that greatest enemy of hope, which loosens the bonds of charity, and leaves us in a weak and helpless condition, a prey to mortified self-love; for sadness brings with it a disrelish of devotion.

Yet the remedy for sadness is prayer. "If any one of you is sad," says St. James, "let him pray."[27] But as sadness broods in selfishness, and is inclined to rest rather in our own unhappy thoughts than on God, the soul turns to prayer with reluctance, and therefore in the first instance by an effort. Hence the saddened one must first turn to God by vocal prayer, persevering in which, that reluctance will be overcome, and so the disposition will be recovered for the recollection of mental prayer; and, as the sadness subsides, the spirit will enter anew into the heart of prayer.

The second remedy against sadness is to break out of it by some external act of kindness or generosity. For the malady consists in a morbid concentration upon one's self, and a brooding within one's self, that repels sympathy and kindness, as being adverse to this melancholy mood, a mood that can only be cherished in isolation of spirit. But let the will make a little effort to be kind and considerate towards another, and it is amazing how soon that malignant charm is broken that held the soul spell-bound to her saddened thoughts and imaginary grievances. A smile, a kind look, a few gentle words, a considerate action, though begun with effort, will suffice to open the soul, and set the spirit free from its delusion. Action, again, in the line of duty, and from the sense of duty, will enable the soul to throw off the morbidity with which she is encumbered; and by the return to more cheerful thoughts she will recover her patience.

As every virtue holds on its way between two vices that bear some resemblance to it, the one in excess, the other in defect; patience holds on its way between the vice of obstinacy, as an excess, and the vice of impatience, as a defect. Obstinacy arises either from stupidity or pride. It looks like patience, because it seems to hold its own, and to resist what is not its own. But patience is reasonable, and obstinacy is unreasonable; patience resists what is evil, and obstinacy resists what is good; patience is tranquil, and obstinacy is turbulent. Impatience is the vice in defect of patience. When it rises into irritation and anger it is often mistaken for strength, but the strength of the soul is in her patience. When a man is filled with the impatience of anger from head to foot, he will tell you that he was never more calm or self-possessed in his life; he mistakes the equable balance of excitement and disturbance throughout his system for calmness and self-possession. He is possessed indeed, but possessed by an impatience and a weakness that hurry him away from the light of reason and the judgment of prudence into acts of folly, the retrospect of which produces sadness.

Charity and patience form the Christian character. To love God, and in that divine charity to love all that God loves, is to expand the flame of life in the soul, whereby the spirit is enlarged with the communion of eternal good, and with every kind of good. But patience is the strength and solidity of charity, that makes this golden virtue firm and steadfast; that keeps back the impetuosity of nature and its temptations from injuring the flame of love; and, by its discipline, preserves the soul in serenity and peace. The union of these two virtues into one ardour and strength, brings the sweetness of meekness, and completes the lucid image of Christ in the soul, making her beautiful in the sight of our Heavenly Father.

When it is considered what a power is given by Christian patience to creatures by nature so feeble and inconstant, we cannot but see that its origin is divine. What a motive for striving to bring its grace into the virtue that gives us the possession of ourselves! There is only one evil in the sight of God, and that evil is sin. Sin arises from the impatience that will not adhere to God, and keep the will steadfast to His law and commandments. But it is the nature of Christian patience to rest on God, and to hold with firm tenacity to whatever He enjoins. Whatever else are called evils, such as temporal privations, trials and sufferings, are so far from being evils to the patient soul, that in this present providence they are in the order of good. They are evils to those impatient souls that make them the occasions of sin; but those patient ones derive their power from God to transform the sense of these evils into virtues that enrich the soul, and bring her to her Eternal Good.

The restoration of man to God should therefore bring him back to that patience, through the loss of which he ceased to abide in God and in His will. But that restoration is accomplished through Jesus Christ, the Son of God, who exhibited, both to His Father and to men, the perfection of humility and patience from the beginning to the ending of His mortal life. The Father gave His patience to the Son, and with that divine patience the Son overcame all His enemies and ours; and gave that patience to us, that by its help we may master our weakness, and overcome in every hostile encounter. For, in the words of St. Leo: "The Passion of the Lord continues still, and even to the end of the world. As He is loved in His Saints, and is fed and clothed in His poor; so He endures in those who suffer patiently for justice' sake."[28]

Wherefore the great Apostle sets patience before us as the power that resists the entrance of sin, and exhorts us in the vehemence of the Holy Spirit, to keep the patience of Christ before us in all its exercise. He says to the Hebrews: "Laying aside every weight and sin that surrounds us, let us run by patience to the fight proposed to us:

looking upon Jesus, the author and finisher of faith, who, having joy set before Him, endured the Cross, despising the shame, and now sitteth at the right hand of the throne of God. For think diligently on Him that endured such contradiction from sinners against Himself: that you be not weary, fainting in your minds. For you have not yet resisted unto blood, striving against sin."[29] And, to show the great value of trials for perfecting patience, and how intimately patience is bound up with charity, the Apostle says again: "We glory also in tribulations, knowing that tribulation worketh patience: and patience probation; and probation hope. And hope confoundeth not; because the charity of God is poured forth in our hearts, through the Holy Ghost, who is given to us."[30]

# 3

# ON PATIENCE AS A UNIVERSAL VIRTUE

"In all things let us exhibit ourselves in much patience."—2 Corinthians vi. 4

Owing to the habit of thinking of the virtues individually and separately, and to the method of thus treating of them in books, we are too much disposed to lose sight of their close connection with each other, and of the way in which they act, not only with each other, but within each other. The distinctions between them have their foundations in their objects, and to understand these distinctions is a valuable and useful instruction. But that knowledge is equally valuable and instructive which enables us to understand how they act in union and mutual co-operation, giving animation, support, vigour, or protection to one another. One color cannot make a picture, nor one virtue a saint; many colors unite and blend their shades to form a beautiful work of art, and many virtues unite and blend together in happy mixtures to make a beautiful soul.

As all the virtues have their seat in the will, and there unite, they flow into each other, help each other mutually, and are most perfect when most united. But this connection and co-operation is much more intimate in the Christian than in the natural virtues, because they have their origin in the divine principle of grace, converge proportionately to their perfection to one final end, and are all animated by one and the same life of charity. All the Christian virtues live in the light of faith, all look to hope, all obtain their life from the love of God. They are founded in humility, ruled by justice, guided by prudence, sustained by fortitude, preserved by temperance, strengthened and protected by patience. Christian fortitude is a profounder degree of Christian patience. It is a gift of the Holy Ghost, and patience is included in it as the less in the greater.

Whilst each virtue has its own object, certain virtues are called universal, because, besides their own special object, they enter into every other virtue, and assist every other virtue in obtaining its object. Of these, next to charity, patience is the most important; for, to recall the words of St. Zeno, "all things look to patience". Neither faith, hope, charity, nor justice—neither humility nor charity nor any other virtue can hold together, or keep on its way, without the nerve, restraint, and discipline of patience. Hence it has been called the virtue of the virtues, as giving to them all their strength, stability, and perseverance. It has also been called the chief part of virtue, as being the abiding force that carries them through their difficulties. If you ask the reason, you will find it in the weakness, irritability, and inconstancy of our nature, rendered so much more infirm through its fall and sin. But this requires a large explanation, which will help us to know ourselves and to understand what help we require to make us constant and peaceful.

If we examine the whole of the virtues, we shall find them divisible into two kinds according to the work that they do for the soul. One of these kinds seeks to reach good, the other removes the obstacles that prevent us from seeking good. Of the kind that directly seeks good are faith, hope, charity, justice, and religion; of the kind that removes the obstacles to good are humility, temperance, self-denial, and repentance. But patience, which, as St. Zeno remarks, "is less in multiplying than in perfecting the virtues," belongs to both kinds of virtue. It comes with charity, derives the fire of its energy from the charity of the Holy Ghost, and gives it perfection. On that part it causes the will to adhere to God with constancy, and sustains the other virtues that directly seek God; for they work perfectly in proportion as they work patiently. But it has another work, a work of which we are more conscious, in strengthening those virtues that resist evil and all that disturbs the peace and self-possession of the soul. Whilst, therefore, patience is conservative of the virtues that seek good, it is the strength and stay of those virtues that remove the obstacles to good. It is for this reason that St. Gregory calls it the root and guardian of the virtues, and that St. Cyprian teaches that it is both the expeller of evil and the keeper of good. This brings us back to St. Augustine's definition of the virtue, that by patience we cheerfully endure evils with an equable mind, that we may not, through an evil disposition, desert that good which brings us to our greatest good.

A soul given to impatience loses strength from every virtue and weakens her hold of all that is good; she has not the spiritual nerve to hold herself together; for in the impatient soul there is a restlessness, a wavering, a want of spiritual fibre, a swerving from good intention, and a want of steadfastness in action that disturbs the soul and undermines the most virtuous resolutions.

Any change that passes in the sense and feeling of such a person —a little restlessness in the nerves, a little weariness of mind, a little trouble in the affections—will disturb her slender patience, lower the tone of her virtue, and even change her intentions. Almost any change in outward circumstances—an alteration in the weather, a piece of bad news, a sharp word, or some little interference with what one is doing, however well intended—will be sufficient to alter the dispositions of the heart and change the current and color of one's thoughts, as the impatient soul vibrates from one thing to another, and rushes in desire from the present duty to something that the imagination represents as more congenial. With the growth of impatience comes the disinclination to dwell on those divine and unchangeable truths which agree not with the spirit of restless change, and a yet greater disinclination to hold to those divine motives that invite us to constancy and lead us to act with a view to our spiritual good; for our impatience engages us with the sense of our own discomfort, dissipates the spirit of recollection, and scatters the power of attention, to the great damage of all stability of purpose.

Think of the unregenerated condition of the mortal body, with its flame of concupiscence lusting against the spirit, its restless sensibilities, its petulant appetites, its disorderly movements, its reluctance to be brought under subjection to the law of the spirit, its ever-changing irritabilities, and those crooked instincts of evil that through the imagination move upon the soul, all tending to trouble her peace, and to overthrow the virtues. Unless patience be there to resist and withstand the inflowings of irritation, curiosity, and cupidity, it is impossible for the soul to preserve her own proper good, or to secure its augmentation; for every virtue and the good of every virtue is open to temptation and loss through yielding to the restless irritability of our mortal frame. Even those who have obtained a calm external demeanor for social purposes by artificial training are not thereby delivered in any degree from their internal disturbances.

Then in the soul herself there is that terrible disorder of self-love, giving birth to pride and vanity, those fearful irritators, weakeners, and dividers of the soul, that interfere so much with the advancing movements of all the virtues, and give rise to such an amount of impatience and disturbance, and, being in close league with the animal senses, leave nothing in its right place, nothing in its just union with its proper good and strength, nothing in enduring peace.

The good of the soul is spiritual like herself, but immeasurably greater than herself. It is the littleness of self-love that makes her impatient of a good so much greater than self-love can aim at, or anything short of charity can aspire to. To reach that good requires a most patient cooperation with the grace of charity. But the disinclination that makes the soul slow and reluctant to seek that spiritual good, reveals the feverish impatience of her greater good with which she is afflicted.

In a perfect spirit thought and will must act in perfect unison, the thought one with the truth, and the will one with the justice contained in that truth. The will must at once reject the evil which truth reveals to the thought. And all the powers of the soul, with the virtues that belong to them, must act in perfect accord with the light in the mind and the justice in the will. This implies a perfect union of the soul with God, to the complete annihilation of inordinate self-love; and a state of stability in that union, which neither moves from the light of God, nor wavers from the love of God. This stability is the perfect patience of charity. Change that patience into impatience, and the unity of that soul with God, and through God with herself, will be shaken and impaired, if not altogether lost.

In the degree in which the soul loses her union with God she glides off from the divine basis of her strength, and there arises division within herself. In consequence of that division her spiritual acts become feeble, wavering, and impatient. The will is often at discord with the mind, and the mind with the truth. Good intentions fail for want of resolution, and feeble acts falter after wavering intentions, and these are soon lost sight of for want of the patience that gives them perseverance. Conscience and conduct are often at disagreement from want of that strength and stability of will which faithfully follows the inspirations of conscience. Such is the fallen man, weakened in all his spiritual joints and sinews through the wasting disease of impatience.

"Man alone is headstrong," says St. Zeno, "alone impatient, taking his daily pleasure in his disorderly emotions. He is given to change. He thinks it a misery to be himself. He is unwilling to see that when he keeps not himself in his just and proper state, he subjects himself to a derangement that is not unlike to lunacy. What is this impatience but a slippery condition of mind, in which the soul acts with hasty and frequent perturbations against her own well-being? Her actions are unstable, incautious, blind, and improvident; and she excites herself to her own undoing. Impatience is a thing without substance, a busy failure divested of personal dignity, putting everything in a state of trouble, disturbing all things in an instant. Impatience is the mother of sin, the nurse of curiosity, the goad to rashness, the author of detestable evils. The death that strangled human salvation burst forth from impatience in the beginning of the world."[1]

If there is truth in this description of mankind when living in quiet times, how much more applicable is that truth to the unquiet times in which we are living. All the present conditions of life seem to combine in making men restless and unstable. It looks as if we had fallen upon those latter times predicted by the Prophet Daniel, when "many shall pass to and fro, and knowledge shall be manifold"[2]. Whatever have been the benefits resulting from the investigations, speculations, and inventions of our times, they have had the effect of producing a moral intoxication on the minds of men, that has turned them away from the pursuit of divine and eternal things, and has changed the tranquil habits of our fathers into habits of restlessness and the love of perpetual movement. Most men have become eager for novelty and change, and they live so much outside themselves as to neglect or even abandon the interior good of their souls. The tree of the knowledge of good and evil has been shaken for its fruits, and if the knowledge of good has fallen to those who are inclined to good, the knowledge of evil has fallen in great abundance to those who are inclined to evil. We live in the midst of a restless, impatient, and fevered life, that more than ever demands for our security patience of will and stability of mind.

We have not yet completed the account of the fever of impatience. A great number even of persons desiring the better things are habitual sufferers from a low, malingering, and silent form of the malady; because, ignorant of themselves, they are unable to perceive how their want of interior patience deprives their virtues of their vigor, and undermines their spiritual health. They feel that something keeps them back from advancing to more solid virtue, but they see not that it is their want of patience with themselves, and with what they are engaged upon, that distracts the mind, dissipates the heart, and makes the soul inconstant in her purposes. They have never disciplined their will, that central power of the soul, in that fundamental patience which gives a firm and assured basis to all the acts of our life. They have not realized to themselves the sense of the Psalmist, when, conscious of his natural weakness, he exhorts himself: "Be thou, O my soul, subject to God, for from Him is my patience". "There is something so singular in this virtue," observes the learned and contemplative Harphius, "that even those who seem to have the other virtues are often devoid of patience."[3] They are not only devoid of interior and spiritual patience, but they have no idea what an immense defect it is, or how much their interior impatience is the cause of their inward troubles, and the obstacle to their interior advancement.

"Patience is of God," says St. Cyprian, "and whoever is gentle, mild, and patient, is an imitator of God. If the patience of God the Father abide in us, who are repaired by the Divine Nativity, if we have that likeness of God in us that was lost in Adam, it ought to shine from our interior outwards, and become manifest in our actions."[4]

What we have thus far endeavored to say on this virtue as the groundwork of the other virtues has been most happily expressed by the reigning Pontiff Leo XIII. In his Encyclical Letter on the Third Order of St. Francis, the Successor of Peter teaches us in these words: "The perfection of Christian virtue is a disposition of soul that is patient of all that is arduous and difficult. Its symbol is the Cross, which those who follow Christ bear on their shoulders. What belongs to this disposition is a soul detached from mortal things, a vigorous self-control, and a gentle and resigned endurance of adversity. Finally, the love of God and of our neighbor is the mistress and sovereign of the soul; such is its power, that it wipes away all the hardships that accompany the fulfilment of duty, and makes the hardest labors not only endurable but actually pleasant.

Whenever the will separates from the foundation of its strength by departing from God, the instruments of the will, be it the mind, the hand, or the tongue, lose their patience, and in losing their patience lose their wisdom and skill. The thoughts wander from their purpose, the imagination seduces and carries away attention, the hands relax in their work, the tongue becomes imprudent, the sense of duty is enfeebled, and duty itself lingers on its way, or is imperfectly done. The workman suffers as well as the work, because impatience is trouble, and has an element of sadness in it. As it is obvious that all the virtues and the whole condition of the soul are enfeebled by the fever of impatience, it must be equally obvious that the whole soul is strengthened and made healthy by the discipline of patience. Hence the old French proverb, that patience surpasses science. But this is the last virtue obtained in its perfection, because human nature is so weak and inconstant, and the acquiring of this virtue is laborious. But when it has reached a certain perfection, it secures to the soul a cheerful serenity and sweetness, and a constant peace.

Viewed as a universal virtue, St. Cyprian describes it in the following terms: "Patience commends us to God, and keeps us united with God. By its force we keep down anger, control the tongue, govern the mind, and guard the peace of the soul. By the same virtue we govern ourselves with discipline, break down the assaults of concupiscence, repress the swellings of pride, and extinguish the heat of malice. It restrains the wealthy from abusing their power, and supports the poor in their wants and distress. It protects the blessed integrity of virgins, the laborious chastity of widows, and the mutual charity of married life. It makes the soul humble in prosperity, strong in adversity, and meek under injuries and calumnies. It teaches us to be quick in pardoning offences; and when we have offended, to ask much and long for pardon. It repels temptations, endures persecutions, and brings to sufferings and martyrdom a happy consummation. Patience gives strong and firm foundations to our faith: patience exalts our hope to a sublime degree of confidence: patience enables us to follow in the steps of Christ, and walk after Him in the way of endurance: it gives us the perseverance of the children of God whilst we imitate the patience of our Heavenly Father."[5]

To put the subject in its widest point of view, all the appetites and passions of our nature are good when in their just order, their right measure, their due direction, and in true accord with the light of reason and of faith. But they become disorderly, incline us to evil, and become evil themselves, when through inordinate irritability, which is the result of weakness, they spring up in a disorderly way, and lead us into disorder. As St. Thomas teaches from St. Paul, what is irritable or irascible in our nature has its root in concupiscence, or in the passionate desires of our animal appetites, and ends in them.

Whence it follows that patience grounded in fortitude is the proper remedy for all inordinate passions and appetites. And this reminds us of the teaching of so many of the early Fathers, that if Adam had kept his patience he would not have lost his innocence. You see impatience in the sensitive feebleness of childhood, in the restlessness of youth, in the instability of manhood, and in the returning feebleness of age. But you never see it in the saints, because they have laboriously disciplined themselves in patience, and have obtained the cheerful possession of themselves.

Some persons are by nature and the temperament of their constitution more choleric and irascible than others. This temperament is compounded of two elements, sanguine ardour and irascibility. But when this irascibility has been brought by laborious self-discipline under the rule of patience, the ardour of it is most valuable when in its right direction, both for the overcoming of difficulties, and for the undertaking of good works. And thus it is with every force of human nature: deliver it from the disturbing influence of impatience, place it under the discipline of patience, and it will work in good order and to the best effect of which it is capable.

Not only does the invigorating and steadying virtue of patience proceed from charity, but it perfects charity. "Charity is patient." In the words ascribed to St. Dionysius the Areopagite: "That love of God which first moves the soul towards divine things is a most sacred and unspeakable operation, whereby a divine state is established in us".[6] This divine state is the work of the Holy Spirit dwelling in the soul, and, as St. Paul shows, the grace of charity brings with it the grace of patience. But charity is the life-giving form of all the virtues. First, it is the divine principle of their supernatural life. Secondly, it gives to them their supernatural value, and the condign merit of eternal life. Thirdly, charity communicates to them that high moral good from which they obtain their perfection.[7]

But let the reader specially take note, that grace is one thing and virtue another. Grace is the divine gift; virtue results from the co-operation of the will with the divine gift. But as there is so much more to overcome, and consequently so much more labour of the will in the exercise of patience than in the exercise of any other virtue, that is the reason why there are so few who reach the more perfect degrees of patience. Having never experienced the wonderful strength and peace which the fundamental virtue of patience gives to the soul, or the clearness and vigour which it gives to her interior acts, they have never realized the extreme importance of striving to obtain it at whatever cost. Yet it is by patience that charity is perfected; and this was manifested in our Lord Jesus Christ, whose divine charity was so wonderfully patient, and who consummated His love of His Father and of mankind by His most patient sufferings. St. Bonaventure justly remarks that to suffer and endure with patience for the love of God is a much greater thing than to do great works for the love of God. But in this pious souls are often at fault: they will attach this principle to external sufferings, and will not see that it applies with even greater truth to internal and spiritual sufferings. Yet our Divine Lord suffered much greater things in His soul than in His body.

There is a sentence of St. Maximus which every good Christian should carry in his mind: "The sum of Christianity is to give love for love, and patience for suffering; whoever is most patient under suffering will be the greatest in the kingdom of heaven".[8] But it should be equally remembered that spiritual sufferings are far greater than corporal sufferings. And here a remark of the learned and pious Cajetan will not be out of place. Commenting on the first of the Beatitudes: "Blessed are the poor in spirit, for theirs is the kingdom of heaven"; and also on the last: "Blessed are they that suffer persecution for justice' sake, for theirs is the kingdom of heaven"; after pointing out that the poor in spirit are the humble, he says: "By the word persecution you must understand every kind of pain and suffering. You see then that one and the same reward is given to those who act patiently (the poor in spirit), and to those who suffer patiently, provided they persevere to the end. They both obtain the kingdom of heaven, and it is theirs already, although they have not yet come into their possession." In short, the reward of heaven, so magnificently described in the Book of Revelations, is there repeatedly promised by our Lord to those who by patience conquer their adversaries by overcoming themselves.

The intimate relations of patience with charity have never been expressed with greater force and beauty than in the parable dictated by St. Catherine of Siena whilst in a state of ecstasy. It occurs in her dialogue on discretion, and we shall here give it in a free translation. Be it first however observed that St. Catherine uses the word discretion in the sense of spiritual recollection, in which we obtain perception of the relative value of divine and human things. In this sense of the word she follows that illustrious Doctor of her Order, Albert the Great, who thus describes it: "True discretion is to judge prudently between the Creator and the creature, between what the Creator is and what the creature is, and in how much the Creator differs from the creature. It likewise judges between what is good, what is better, and what is best; and also between what is evil, what is more evil, and what is most evil; whilst it decides how much the good is to be loved, and the evil to be detested."[9]

The just man is compared in the Psalm to a tree planted by the waters, whose fruits do not fail. If you plant a tree within a circle of fertile earth, the earth will nourish the tree and make it fruitful. But if you take it up from the circle in which it is planted, it will die and produce nothing. The soul is a tree made to be fruitful in love: it can only live in charity. The roots of that tree are the affections of the soul, which should be planted within the circle of self-knowledge, of that self-knowledge which is united to God by humility. But God is likened to the circle in this, that He has neither beginning nor ending. And the soul that is planted in the earth of humility, and is united with God, finds herself within that divine circle, within which she obtains the knowledge of God and of herself. If the soul be thus united with God, she will find that her knowledge, like that circle, has neither beginning nor ending. But if the soul is not united with God, though she may have a beginning of knowledge, it will end in confusion.

In the measure in which the tree of charity is nourished by humility, it will put forth the branches of discretion; but the pith and marrow of the tree is patience; and this patience is the demonstrative proof that God is in the soul, and that the soul is united with God. Thus sweetly planted, the tree will put forth the virtues as its flowers, and will produce such fruits as will be profitable to our neighbours, such at least as are willing to accept them from the servants of God. The soul herself will praise God, who is the Creator of the tree and its fruits, and will come to her final end in the everlasting God, from whom, without her consent, she never can be removed. But the fruits hang on the boughs of discretion by the force of patience, from which they derive their excellence.[10]

Food is not more essential to strength of body than patience is to strength of soul; and God in His goodness makes us conscious of our weakness, that we may be induced to seek the means of strength. What God loves and approves in us is the cheerful and loving patience that we put into our duties, because that is the spirit of charity, and expresses the amount of charity with which we serve Him. Every new restraint that we put upon the hurry and impetuosity of our excitable nature is a reduction to order, a power gained, a weakness removed, a further subjection of nature to grace, a step in the way of peace, that makes us less unlike to God.

We read much of the self-denial and self-mortification of the Saints; we know how effective this is in purifying nature, and in subjecting the body to the spirit and the spirit to God, so long as it is under the safeguard of obedience. We know that self-denial is enjoined by our Divine Lord upon all His followers, and that without self-denial there can be no solid virtue, because it directly attacks self-love, which is the source of all evil. "And He said to all: If any man will come after Me, let him deny himself and take up his cross daily, and follow Me."[11] Whoever, again, is acquainted with those schools of sanctity, the Religious Orders, will not have failed to observe, that where the spirit of the founder is duly observed, cheerfulness and spiritual joy are always in proportion with the amount of self-abnegation and austerity enjoined by the Rule. This fact opens a great light to us, and shows that the secret of cheerfulness and content is in the freedom of spirit obtained by the conquest of the body. It must be so, because the sacrifice of self to God invigorates the will, makes the soul patient and healthy, and quells that sensual self-love which is the source of impatience and sadness, changing it into the generous love of God.

But when we come to that interior and spiritual mortification to which exterior self-denial is subservient, we shall find, upon careful examination, that it is all reducible to patience. Take the mortification of inordinate curiosity for an example. This is a vice that is very injurious both to self-control and to recollection, and opens the door to many temptations. It leads the mind away in search of distracting and dissipating novelties. It peeps into other people's conduct and affairs, with which the soul has no concern. It will even pry into error and vice, and long to taste the evil that is in them. This evil not only dissipates the mind, but breeds many rash judgments, and lays open the heart to many temptations. But it is patience that withholds the mind from curiosity, and mortifies this inordinate vice to death.

Take the mortification of the interior sensibilities for another example. These sensibilities produce the affections, which when directed to their right objects influence the will to good, but when directed to wrong objects influence the will towards evil or disorder. Their lawful use is to attach the soul with love and pleasure to what is good for us, and to withdraw the soul with dislike and abhorrence from what is evil or injurious to our well-being. But it is by patience that the will withholds the sensible affections of the soul from mingling with the disorderly movements of the body, or the inordinate movements of self-love; and so the soul is kept back from entering into the disorders of the irascible passions on the one hand, and from entering into the inordinate movements of the sensual appetites on the other. Thus the true mortification of the interior affections of the soul is reducible to that patience which, whilst adhering to God, refuses to surrender the will to the sensibilities, passions, and sensualities of the animal man, that, when followed, lead to confusion and spiritual death. St. Paul points to this internal discipline where he says: "If you live according to the flesh, you shall die. But if by the spirit you mortify the deeds of the flesh, you shall live."[12] But "the deeds of the flesh" are not merely its external acts, but much more those internal sensibilities, irritabilities, and sensualities that spring from the body, and which St. Paul calls "the spirit of the flesh". When any part of the body mortifies, the arteries no longer bring to it the life-giving blood, the veins no longer take from it what is injurious to life. But spiritual mortification acts on the side of life; it is an act of the patient will refusing entrance into the soul to whatever obstructs the freedom and flow of spiritual life.

Having put the interior process by which the soul is disciplined into patience in various points of view to assist the reader in understanding it, we will now resume what has been stated in one comprehensive view.

If you are placed within a fortress founded upon a rock, within that stronghold you will feel secure from the enemies who seek to injure or destroy your life. The walls and the rock hold together, and resist all efforts to break through or undermine them. What is the secret of the strength and security which they give you? It consists in that invisible and mysterious power which is called the attraction of cohesion, whereby all the parts hold together, and the whole is made firm and inaccessible. But if your adversaries have an accomplice within the fortress, it is still in danger of being betrayed and surrendered. The soul is a living, free, and most sensitive spirit, having the will for its central power. The fortress which protects the soul from her enemies is patience. It rests upon God as the rock of its strength, and is fenced round as by a wall from the invasion of its enemies. The secret of the strength of this fortress is in the spiritual cohesion by which all the powers of the soul hold together, through the patience of the will, and are thus enabled to resist the efforts of the enemies of the soul from entering within its defenses, and there spreading disorder, confusion, and desolation.

But if the will becomes relaxed and careless, all the powers that depend on the will become loose and negligent, and the adversaries of the soul find their accomplice, whose name is impatience, within the stronghold, the fortress is betrayed, and all sorts of trouble and disorder make their way within the soul, the will and its powers are driven from one disorder to another, and the soul herself becomes a pitiable spectacle to God and His angels. But, to use the figure of the Psalmist, God is the firm rock and fortress of the soul, and when the will adheres to God, His truth surrounds her as a shield; and His grace pours in its strength, enabling the will to hold her powers together, and to resist by their cohesion all the efforts of temptation, and every disorder that would trouble the peace of the soul or do injury to her life.

What we have here endeavored to put in figure is to illustrate the truth, that we become strong to resist temptation, to endure trials, and to keep ourselves above the wasting influence of sadness, in proportion to the firmness with which the soul adheres by her center to God, as the supreme and central foundation of her life; by which adherence her powers are kept in unity, and in obedience to the will obedient to God. The will, or central power of the soul, should never be thrown off from its own true centre, but should be patiently held to its divine support, so that the soul may never go off from her foundation or lose her balance: "The Lord is my firmament, my refuge, and my deliverer".[13]

This is what St. Catherine of Siena means, when, in her inspired wisdom, and from her own example, she advises us to form a little cell by recollection in the centre of the soul, protected by patience as by walls, into which the spirit of God, His light and grace alone shall enter; a little sanctuary into which the world and its cares shall never enter; a centre of peace into which no trouble shall be allowed to come. 'So that when troubles come, that come to all, they may be kept by the intervention of patience outside of that secret sanctuary of the soul, and never be allowed to come between the soul and God. If they are allowed entrance into the soul they will confuse the vision, and disturb the will, which will not know how to deal with them. But if kept outside the soul, they will have no power to disturb either her judgment or her peace. She will see through them after a time, and will know how to deal with them. This is one of the most important rules for the patient management of the will.

Whilst the soul is able by her fundamental patience to keep a calm and recollected center, she will be able to use her faculties and put them forth with tranquil energy from that calm and recollected and immovable center, in their due order, towards their work, as duty, obedience, and the will of God require. An immense amount of fatigue and trouble will be saved, for nothing fatigues so much as the interior disturbance resulting from disorder and the want of central calmness. We are now in a position to better understand the words of our Divine Lord: "In your patience you shall possess your souls". But if we throw out the very center of the soul upon the creature, and thus part with our interior union with God, we shall become nothing but weakness and disorder.

Extreme cases best illustrate intermediate ones. Observe two persons in a high state of quarreling. Both have lost their self-control. Whatever is within them is thrown out in a flame of passion. Their judgment is gone with their self-command; and you see all round and through them, a pitiable spectacle of human weakness, driven by animal instincts, ungoverned by the light of reason. The whole center of the man is thrown out, and there is nothing reserved within him by which he can control himself. Observe another example, in which one is the victim of uncontrollable passion, and the other in full possession of himself, derived from patience and endurance. You have here the whole contrast between moral strength and moral weakness; strength prevails and weakness is put to shame.

Take the case of one, who, devoid of that central patience and strength, finds himself suddenly involved in some complicated trouble, in which both persons and affairs are concerned. The trouble gets inside of him, takes hold of his feelings, confuses his faculties, and clouds his judgment, which is too much embarrassed to help him through his difficulty. If he is at all wise he will seek the counsel of a prudent and experienced friend. Take another who possesses his soul in patience. He will keep his trouble outside his soul, hold it at due distance, which will give him a calm, objective view of it, and after a time he will see his way through it, and know what to do with it.

Whilst, then, the primary object of patience is to keep the centre of the soul recollected and protected in its recollection, the second is to govern the exterior life from that recollected centre, whether in action, speech, or demeanor, so that the strength, calmness, and moderation of the soul may shine out in our exterior conduct, in a way that may commit us to nothing but what is peaceful and edifying. The remoter objects of patience are the evils, trials, temptations, and disturbing influences that come against us without our will or choice. Upon these we can impress no image of virtue, because they are not within us, they form no part of us, but are altogether independent of us. But if we suffer these outward causes of trial to enter into us and take possession of us, they break down the strength of patience, throw us into disorder, and defile us with their vices. But if these evils are kept outside of the soul, when they cannot be removed, they must be endured, with the consoling reflection that the endurance of them will strengthen and increase our virtue, and prepare us for the rewards of endurance.

But, as we have already observed, the effect of patient endurance is not to make us hard and insensible to trials and sufferings. This would defeat the beneficent designs of God in allowing them for our probation and greater virtue. "Some think," observes St. Gregory, "that it is a sign of great constancy not to feel the scourges and sufferings that come upon us from the correcting hand of God; others feel those trials to such an excess as to indulge in grief and sadness beyond all right and reason, and give a murmuring tongue to their pains. But the true virtue of patience holds the midway between these extremes; for insensibility of heart gives no weight to virtue. And when a man feels no sense of pain from the trials that God sends him, it only proves his incorrigible stupidity and numbness of heart. When, on the contrary, under the rod of trial and rebuke he gives himself to excessive grief and sadness, he throws away that patience which guards the virtues; and whilst his heart suffers to excess, he breaks into impatience, and perhaps into injuries, and instead of being amended by his troubles, he gives himself to worse evils on account of them."[14] There is also an impatience with one's self; and who is not acquainted with that infirmity? It may have its beginning in some venial fault or error into which we have slipped or glided with no great deliberation. But the failure has wounded our self-love, and produced an interior annoyance and vexation, which is far worse than the original fault. Like throwing away the medicine when the disease appears, patience is given up at the very moment when wanted to cure the infirmity. Had we taken to that steadying virtue at once, the mischief would have been stayed; but the shame and humiliation of failure is allowed to disturb the heart, to discomfort the soul, and to bring on a certain sadness that goes from one act of interior impatience to another, doing more harm than a hundred of those faults from which this disorder is allowed to rise. Yet, as St. Bonaventure tells you, "patience would have purged the sin, and would have saved you from it in future". "Charity is patient" and patient charity covers a multitude of sins. The Church proclaims this in the tribunal of penance, that not only the works of charity but the endurances of patience are satisfactory for sin. The priest says to the penitent: "May whatsoever good thou dost, and whatsoever evil thou endurest, be to the remission of thy sins and the reward of eternal life". We may well say with St. Gregory, that "patience is the cure of every grief". Delay not the cure, or the grief will turn to sadness. Take hold of patience, or the one fault will bring you others that are greater in its train.

It remains to show how this strenuous virtue is the fundamental principle that gives power to the Beatitudes. The poor in spirit are the humble. They know they have nothing of their own but their weakness and sins, and that they are dependent on God for all things. They therefore hold themselves in subjection to God, and keep themselves with patience in their lowly position. The meek are those whose patience has made them gentle and forbearing in the sweetness of charity, and who possess the land of their soul in peace. The holy mourners whom God comforts are they who in patience lament before God, and do penance for the evils whereby He is offended, and who patiently persevere in their supplications for the removal of evil.

They who hunger and thirst after justice must patiently mortify their sensual appetites and selfish desires, that their spiritual appetite may be filled with good things. The merciful cannot be merciful unless their patience restrain them from anger and selfishness, that their charity may flow forth in pardon and generosity. The blessed peacemakers are they who possess their own souls in peace. And they who suffer persecution for justice' sake are they who bear and endure whatever is inflicted upon them for the love of God, for whose holy cause they stand. Then, to crown the exposition of the Beatitudes, our Divine Lord calls upon His followers to rejoice in suffering for His sake because of its exceeding reward. "Blessed are ye when they shall revile you, and persecute you, and speak all that is evil against you, untruly for my sake: Be glad and rejoice, for your reward is very great in heaven."[15] Truly patience is golden, and patient suffering in devoted charity is a pure diamond.

One good example is worth a thousand when taken to heart, and we will therefore conclude with an example of the power of patience in illustration of what has been said from the life of St. Francis Xavier, as given in the nervous language of Dryden.

"When St. Francis brought the Gospel into Japan, on the first occasion on which it was heard in the city of Amanguchi, the Saint and his companion, John Fernandez, met with great opposition, especially among the Bonzas; when an action of Xavier's companion did not a little contribute to the gaining over of the most stubborn. Fernandez preached in one of the most frequented places of the town; and amongst the crowd of auditors were some persons of great wit, strongly opinioned of their sect, who could not conceive the maxims of the Gospel, and who heard the preacher with no other intention than to make sport of him. In the midst of the sermon, a man, who was of the scum of the rabble, drew near to Fernandez, as if he were to whisper something to him, and hawking up a mass of nastiness, spit it full in his face. Fernandez, without a word speaking, or making the least sign that he was concerned, took his handkerchief, wiped his face, and continued his discourse.

"Everyone was surprised at the moderation of the preacher: the more debauched, who had set up a laugh at this affront, turned all their scorn into admiration, and sincerely acknowledged that a man who was so much master of his passions as to command them on such an occasion, must needs be endued with greatness of courage and heroic fortitude. One of the chief of the assembly discovered somewhat else in this unshaken patience: he was the most learned of the doctors of Amanguchi, and the most violent against the Gospel. He considered that a law which taught such patience and such insensibility to affronts, could only come from Heaven, and argued thus with himself: 'These preachers, who with so much constancy endure the vilest injuries, cannot pretend to cozen us. It would cost them too dear a price; and no man will deceive another at his own expense. He only who made the heart of man can place it in so great a tranquility. The force of nature cannot reach so far; and this Christian patience must proceed from some divine principle. These people cannot but have some infallible assurance of the doctrine they believe and the recompense which they expect; for, in fine, they are ready to suffer all things for their God, and have no human expectations. After all, what inconvenience or danger can it be to embrace their law? If what they tell us of eternity be true, I shall be eternally miserable in not believing it; and suppose there be no life but this, is it not better to follow a religion which elevates a man above himself, and which gives him an unalterable peace, than to profess sects which continue us in all our weakness, and which want power to appease the disorders of the heart?'

"He made his inward reflections on all these things, as he afterwards declared; and these considerations being accompanied with the motions of grace, as soon as the sermon was ended, he confessed that the virtue of the preacher had convinced him; he desired baptism, and received it with great solemnity. This illustrious conversion was followed with answerable success. Many who had a glimmering of the truth, and feared to know more plainly, now opened their eyes to the light of the Gospel." [16]

# 4

## ON CHRISTIAN FORTITUDE

"Thou, O God, art my strength."—Psalm xlii, 2.

When King Solomon had completed the Temple of God in Jerusalem, he erected two majestic columns of bronze in the great porch by which the people entered to perform their worship. These columns were crowned with beautiful capitals of the same enduring metal, in which rows of pomegranates were placed one above another, and the whole was enclosed with a network of chains, which again was crowned with lilies. To the column on the right he gave the name of Jachin, and to the column on the left the name of Booz.[1] In the Hebrew language Jachin signifies rectitude, and Booz fortitude. These noble monuments stood before the temple to express to all who entered that the law of God is rectitude, and that the will of God which His law reveals is accomplished by fortitude. The first column taught the people of God that all things proceed from the wisdom of God, and are guided to their ends by His justice; the second taught that all things are upheld and strengthened by the fortitude of the divine will. They also taught that to obey the light of justice we need from God the gift of fortitude, that we may have a strenuous will to obey His divine behests.

The pomegranate is the symbol of fruitfulness, and the clusters of them that crown these columns may be taken to express the fruits that grow from the union of fortitude with justice. The network of chains is the bracing patience that protects and preserves them: and the lilies express the purity with which the soul is graced in virtue of these fundamental gifts.

St. Paul is supposed to refer to these prophetic columns, where he calls the Church "the pillar and firm foundation of truth".[2] Speaking in figure, every Christian has need of the support of these two columns, that he may be a holy temple of God : of Jachin, the light of truth and justice in his mind; of Booz, the firmness of fortitude in his will; that in the face of all trials he may be able to accomplish the will of God. Finally, it is through the two virtues of justice and fortitude that he enters the glorious Temple of God, the "house not made with hands, eternal in Heaven".[3]

The greatest moral strength of which the soul is capable comes from the Christian grace and gift of fortitude, of which patience is a potential part, that is to say, it agrees with patience in some respects and differs from it in others. Patience is mostly concerned in overcoming the restlessness of nature, in enduring adversities, in resisting temptations, and in subduing or keeping away impatience, anger, or sadness. Fortitude is a braver and a stronger virtue, is more deeply woven into the constitution of the soul, and is concerned with difficult action as well as with difficult endurance.

Fortitude is required to face great dangers bravely, to undertake great works beset with difficulties, or to undergo martyrdom, or the equivalent of martyrdom.

It must, however, be remembered that difficult action, that is, the action that surmounts great difficulties, includes endurance as well, on account of the obstacles opposed by, the greatness or stubbornness of the work to be done, or of the opposition which other persons raise up against it, or of the misgivings or reluctances that arise within ourselves, and which have to be overcome with courage. Patience, then, is included in fortitude. But fortitude is a virtue more deeply seated in the soul, is more calm in its operations, and less the subject of consciousness than patience. We are less conscious of fortitude because it is a force that works with greater ease : we are more conscious of patience because it is exercised with greater effort, and is felt by the greater resistance which it encounters from irritability, impatience, or sadness. The whole man moves together in fortitude, but in patience only a portion of the faculties are brought into exercise at one time.

Whoever has great fortitude ought also to have great patience; but this is not always the case. For a person who can call up great fortitude on great occasions will often be found irritable and impatient, nay even angry, on smaller occasions. This is owing to the want of a good habit of self-discipline over the imagination and the temper in the daily and hourly conduct of life. But this defect belongs more to natural than to Christian fortitude, which last is a gift of the Holy Ghost, and, where perfection of life is diligently cultivated, it includes the gift of patience. But as fortitude chiefly concerns the greater and patience the lesser labours and trials of life, both branches of the virtue require to be well and carefully cultivated; and whoever is well exercised in patience will not be wanting in fortitude.

The word fortitude is derived from the Latin word *fortis*, which means a morally strong and brave man, whilst the word *fortitudo* signifies the state or habit of moral strength and bravery. The Greek word *andreia* bears the same signification of masculine bravery. The pagans looked upon it as their chief, most honourable, and almost only virtue, considering that the other virtues belonged to manners more than to manhood. It is still honoured and rewarded by the world as the greatest of human virtues, and the most valuable to the republic. Nor does it hold a less position among the Christian virtues, where it is guided by faith, exalted by hope, animated by charity, and regulated by humility. Christian fortitude is the highest gift of spiritual strength, and the source of Christian magnanimity. It is not limited to man alone, as the pagans limited this virtue, but, according to their respective conditions and duties, is equally given to both sexes. Hence the Church has had many great and glorious martyrs, confessors, and spiritual workers among her virgins, wives, and widows, who have exhibited the greatest fortitude and magnanimity. This has been especially the case among her devoted virgins, whose vocation and consecration to their holy state imply the gift of fortitude, implanted by the Holy Spirit in their weakness.

The fortitude of the natural man neither goes beyond his native powers, nor ascends above natural motives, although it is not without a providential assistance from God. Aristotle treats of it under the head of bravery, and says that "the brave man endures and performs those things that belong to courage for the sake of what is honourable". And he thus explains himself: "He who bears himself bravely, and fears what he ought, from the right motive, in the right manner, and at the right time, and feels confidence in like manner, is brave".[4] Cicero gives a wider scope to the virtue, and defines it to be "the undergoing of labours with considerateness, and the enduring of sufferings with constancy".[5] Elsewhere he describes it as "a condition of soul that is patient in encountering perils as well as labours and sufferings, apart from fear".[6] The Greek assigns honour for its motive, and the Roman the benefits which it brings to man.

But Christian fortitude has its foundation in the supernatural strength of divine grace, and its motive in the honour and love of God, and in the good we are able to accomplish. St. Augustine defines it in general terms as "the firmness of the soul amidst the troublesome things of time",[7] and more especially as "the love of enduring all things in peace for God's sake".[8] And elsewhere he calls it "an affection of the soul whereby we despise whatever inconveniences or injuries we may suffer, that are placed beyond our power to remedy".[9] If we put St. Augustine's descriptions together, we shall find them to correspond with St. Paul's exposition of Christian fortitude. "Who is he that shall separate us from the love of Christ? Shall tribulation? or distress? or famine? or nakedness? or persecution? or the sword? As it is written: For Thy sake we are put to death all the day long. We are accounted as sheep to the slaughter. But in all things we overcome for the sake of Him that loved us. For I am certain that neither death, nor life, nor angels, nor principalities, nor powers, nor things present, nor things to come, nor might, nor height, nor depth, nor any other creature shall be able to separate us from the love of God, which is in Christ Jesus our Lord."[10]

In this inspired description of the brave and magnanimous Christian we are taught that fortitude is the strength of charity; that it derives its ardent force from adhering to God through Christ; that it is mighty above all created powers to repel the adversaries of the soul, be they earthly or unearthly, come they with fear or enticement; and that this fortitude of charity overcomes every temptation, trial, and suffering by still adhering with constancy to God.

The world admires its own heroes, who, for honour, interest, or the excitement which it gives them, undergo great labours, do works that look large in the eyes of men, encounter great perils with risk of life, or endure extreme sufferings with constancy for some public cause. And though these men are not unfrequently known to have their moral deficiencies and failings, yet the world exalts them, rewards them with honours and benefits, and erects monuments to their memory. The hope of these things is often their leading motive, next to the pride that moves within them. But the heroes and heroines of God, although the world takes little note of them, are far more wonderful. Armed with Christian fortitude their hearts are set on God, in whose strength they do great things, and suffer great things, and, whilst wholly indifferent to the world's opinion, are a spectacle to God and His angels.

Their audience is in the invisible, infinite, and most glorious world of spirits. They know that the power of God is perfected in their infirmity. They have no confidence in themselves; all their trust is in the divine help. In their valiant combats they first conquer themselves, that they may be in a position to surmount all outward dangers and difficulties. They have no fears but the fear of God, and no will but His will. Let but the will of God be known, and, however difficult the task may be to human nature, no fear, no obstacle will daunt their ardour in accomplishing His will. They may hear many discouraging voices, they may meet with many obstacles, they may often find the way dark before them, and have to wait for the light that shines from providential conditions; but the light and strength from God within them will carry them bravely on, and even though visible success should fail them, invisible success will be surely gained. For God often ordains that one shall sow in tears and another reap in joy. The Martyrs seemed to fail in the world's eyes, when amidst their sufferings they gave up their lives with their blood; but whilst they were crowned in Heaven, the faith they loved to spread sprang up to numbers from their blood. Nay, Christ Himself, when to the eyes of the world He seemed to have utterly failed, at that awful moment redeemed the world and saved mankind. The way of God in His servants is the way of fortitude in humility; and it is the sublimity of heroic faith to seem to fail when all is gained.

Keeping in mind St. Augustine's definition of fortitude, that it is the love of doing and enduring all things peacefully for God's sake, let us hear his exposition of the virtue: "That love," he says, "of which we speak, and which should animate us with the flame of sanctity towards God, is temperate in withholding the will from all the things of concupiscence, and strong in rejecting them. Of all the burdens laid upon us in this life the heaviest is our own body, and this is owing to the just law which God passed upon that old sin, which is so widely known but so little understood. The soul trembles and quakes with fear, lest the body be vexed or tormented with pain or labour, or be taken from us by death. Through the mere custom of always carrying the body, we love the burden of it, and find it hard to realize that, if through the help of the law of divine love we govern the body wisely and well, it will obtain its resurrection and salvation, and its rights will suffer no injury. But when the soul is turned to God with the fortitude of love, these things become known, and death is not only endured but welcomed with desire.

"There remains the great conflict with pain and suffering: yet nothing of this kind is of such iron hardness and obstinacy but the fire of love will master it. When this fire bears up the soul towards God, she soars up freely and wonderfully on strong and beautiful wings over every torment inflicted on the body, until her chaste desire brings her to rest in the embrace of God. Can we ever allow that God would permit the lovers of money, or of praise, or of sensual pleasure, to become stronger than His own lovers? Their affections are not love, they deserve no other name than that of concupiscence or lust; yet they show what a force the soul can put forth, even in the heated and noxious pursuit of those poor objects. But this is an argument for us, for if the lovers of these things can endure so much whilst deserting God for the sake of them, how much ought we to be ready to endure to save us from the unhappiness of deserting God."[11]

Elsewhere the great Doctor concludes: "As we have such great need of the gift of fortitude, we must implore it of Him who commands us to be strong; for unless He makes us strong, we cannot be what He commands us to be. We must, therefore, ask it of Him who says: He who perseveres to the end shall be saved; lest we claim a fortitude of our own, and so become weakened of all strength.[12]

We may consider the virtue of fortitude either as it is a special virtue, having its own immediate object, or as a universal virtue, giving its strength and firmness to all the other virtues. In this last sense it is one of the four cardinal virtues. As a special virtue its office is to restrain and overcome the fears and the audacities that spring up in the sight of dangers, and particularly the danger of death. Yet even here it stands not alone, but is accompanied with other virtues, and especially with prudence, temperance, and moderation. "Although fortitude is a high virtue," observes St. Ambrose, "it is never without the co-operation of other virtues; without justice it would promote iniquity." And in calling it "the temperance of the heart," the Saint expresses its whole character.[13]

The theologians therefore maintain, that those who encounter perils and death from unjust or evil motives have not the virtue of fortitude, but only a habit that has some external resemblance to it; because the virtue of fortitude has always some good for its object. The pagan world exalted the fortitude of Cato and men of his character, because they put themselves to death to escape the humiliation of defeat; but the Christian can see nothing in this conduct beyond the ignominious cowardice that springs from pride and shame.

The special virtue of fortitude is exercised amidst the perils of war, on occasions of great danger, under the infliction of severe sufferings, or wherever there are great fears or difficulties to be overcome. In warfare this virtue contends with fearless bravery and firm constancy. But there is another kind of warfare that cannot be waged effectually without the gift of Christian fortitude, both in action and endurance, and that is the war of the spirit against the world, the devil, and the flesh. This is the most vital and protracted of combats, a combat for life against the bringers of death, in which fortitude is both the inward strength and the defensive armour of salvation, having patience and magnanimity for its supporters.

Not only abroad amongst enemies, but at home in social life, fortitude must uphold the mind and heart with firmness amidst the temptations, contradictions, and adversities that are wont to raise unreasonable fears, or to break down courage. Such are loss of fortune, of friends, of honour, or of deserved respect. Such, again, are detractions, unjust dealings, insinuations of evil, and seductive flatteries, which, unless the soul be firm in fortitude, are wont to afflict the heart with sadness, or to weaken the soul's sincerity.

The heroes of the Old Testament, who stood for God's cause, were endowed by Him with this admirable gift of fortitude. Such were Abraham, Moses, Caleb, Josue, Jepthe, Samson, David, and the Machabees, "who by faith conquered kingdoms, wrought justice . . . recovered strength from infirmity, became valiant in battle, put to flight the armies of foreigners". Nor were there wanting valiant women, like Judith and the Mother of the Machabees. Such also in the spiritual warfare were the prophets and holy men of God. "They had trials of mockery and stripes, moreover of bonds and prisons. They were stoned, they were cut asunder, they were tempted, they were put to death by the sword, they wandered about in sheep-skins, in goat-skins, being in want, distressed, afflicted: of whom the world was not worthy: wandering in deserts, in mountains, in caves of the earth."[14] All these were divinely fortified to be the witnesses of God and the soul against the errors and sins of the world.

Such heroes of God were the Apostles of Christ, strong and brave in their fortitude, subduing the world to His truth at the cost of everything that nature holds dear, until they gave up their lives to the tormentors. Such were the holy Martyrs of both sexes, who for the love of God endured every ignominy and suffering, and sealed their faith with their blood. Such the noble Confessors, those holy men and women who sacrificed the world, gave up all things to God for the love of souls, and welcomed sufferings as others welcome treasures, that they might prove their love of God by their endurance. We are certainly not less weak by nature than they were, and our souls are encompassed with enemies, if less violent, more subtle and numerous; and we have therefore as great a need of the virtue of fortitude, as well to contend against our adversaries as to keep our souls in peace and safety. We have not less reason, then, to take to heart the admonition of St. Paul: "Be ye strengthened in the Lord, and in the might of His power. Put ye on the armour of God, that you may be able to stand against the deceits of the devil."[15]

We have now to consider what vices are opposed to fortitude. On the side of defect they are timidity or cowardice, and also intimidation, which causes a false instead of a just fear; whilst on the side of excess is to be found that audacity or foolish daring which amounts to rashness. Yet neither fear nor daring are to be taken for vices when rightly used and properly regulated, but only when they become inordinate passions that run into excess beyond what is just and reasonable.

The vice of timidity or cowardice arises from fearing without just reason what we ought not to fear, when we ought not to fear, or more than we ought to fear. All fear springs from the love of something that we dread to lose, or that we dread lest it should suffer. Thus the fear of God springs from the just dread of being separated from Him who is the Supreme Good, and our supreme good, and whom we ought to love above all things. The fear of reverence is altogether different; it is an inspiration of awe and wonder that comes upon us through contemplation of the Divine Majesty. The fear of losing one's life comes of inordinate love for this mortal and transitory state of existence, which the love of the Supreme Good is not strong enough to conquer. Self-love has many fears, all of a more or less foolish and inordinate kind. Every kind of love has its own fears, and every kind of sin, having a love of its own, has also its fears and its angers. The avaricious man loves his wealth, fears to lose it, and is angry with every person and thing that imperils it. The sensual man loves his sensual pleasures, but is disturbed with fear and anger against those who would deprive him of them. The ambitious man loves honours, fears dishonour, and is angered by those who would lessen his position.

But it is the fear of great dangers, and especially of death, that is opposed to fortitude as a special virtue; whilst all the fears that drive men into sin and injustice, or into the danger of them, are opposed to fortitude as a universal virtue. For example, when a man from fear of losing his property, or his reputation, commits perjury; when a woman from fear of evil treatment, or of starvation, gives up her virtue; or when a person gives up the exercise of his religion from that fear of the world's opinion which is called human respect.

Intimidation is that fear which is struck by other persons into the soul so as to overcome the fear of God, and make a man fear what he ought not to fear, where he ought not to fear, or to fear more than he ought to fear, to the danger or evil of his soul.

Audacity or rash daring is an excess that attempts to imitate fortitude, and that is without the prudence and modesty of mind which belongs to that virtue. It mostly springs from vanity and the love of vain glory, for the audacious are boasters of what they are not, and wish to seem strong and brave when they are only weak and timid.

It may be noted that the fear caused by intimidation and the rashness of audacity both proceed from one or more of these three causes: first, from not setting a sufficient value on the good or the life to be protected, and especially the good and life of the soul; secondly, from pride in trusting too much to one's self whilst despising others, as though they had no power to injure or overmaster us; thirdly, from stupidity, which is too dull to see the danger to which one is exposed.

To complete the anatomy of fortitude, we must examine the parts of which the virtue is composed, and which combine to give elevation, steadfastness, and splendour to its exercise. These are confidence, patience, magnanimity, magnificence, constancy, and perseverance. Confidence is the assured hope of bringing what we undertake to a successful end. Patience, as we have seen, resists perturbation, grief, and sadness, and victoriously endures molestation. Magnanimity is that greatness of soul which rises above difficulties and dangers. Magnificence is that largeness of soul which projects and carries out great works from high and noble motives. Constancy stands with unchangeable firmness to its resolutions, and shuns the levity that flits in restless moods from one thing to another. Perseverance is the resolute continuance in good once begun, despite of all obstacles and discouragements.

It is obvious that perseverance must greatly depend on patience and constancy. And here St. Bernard will instruct us. "Perseverance," he says, "and that alone, brings the glory that crowns the virtues. Without perseverance the warrior wins no victory, the victor wins no palm. It comes of the vigour of the powers, and gives completeness to the virtues. Perseverance is the offspring of constancy, the sister of patience, the friend of peace, the bond of friendship. Take perseverance away, and fidelity will fail of its reward, well-doing of its grace, and fortitude of its praise. For not he who begins but he who perseveres to the end will be saved. When Saul was made king of Israel he was little in his own eyes, but he did not persevere in his humility, and so lost his kingdom and his life. Had Samson persevered in prudence and Solomon in devotion, the first would not have lost his strength, nor the second his wisdom. I entreat you, then, that you keep with firmness to this sure sign of justice to this one and only faithful guardian of integrity."[16]

The vices opposed to perseverance, as St. Thomas observes, are softness and pertinacity or stubbornness. Softness comes of ease and pleasure. A soft and easy life melts away those energies whereby we endure labours and hardships, and dissolves the force that encounters and conquers the difficulties that are met with in doing good works, and especially in doing them in the best and most patient way. The proper cure for the contemptible vice of softness is labour and self-denial.

Pertinacity is that blind and stubborn vice which sticks to one's own sense and clings to one's own way, despite of what is right and reasonable. Careless of being in the wrong path so long as he has his own will and way, the pertinacious man disregards the wisdom that would show him the right way, and will probably look upon advice as an insult to his consistency. "We have heard," says Isaias, "of the pride of Moab: his pride, and his arrogancy, and his indignation, are more than his strength."[17]

Martyrdom is the crown of fortitude. It exceeds every other human act in its perfection, and this because it gives the most positive proof of the greatest charity. Yet it is not the sufferings but the cause that makes the martyr. God delights not in sufferings, but He delights in the brave and patient love with which the martyr suffers. He delights in the calm, resigned, and cheerful trust with which the martyr looks up to Him amidst his torments. The blood of the martyrs consecrates the earth beneath, from which their souls look up to Heaven above—that Heaven which awaits them on their deliverance from the body. Their faith falls in light on the spectators of their combat, and reaches the hearts of men of good will. In the words of St. Cyprian, himself a martyr, and the witness of many martyrdoms: "Christ rejoices in them, the Divine Protector of their faith fights in them, and conquers through them, giving them all the gifts that they are capable of receiving. Christ is there, the conflict is His own; He upholds them, He strengthens them, He loves the assertors of His Name. After conquering death in Himself, He conquers death in us."[18]

Happy are they who share the honour and glory of the martyrs! But this is refused to no one by Him who commands us to take up our cross daily, and to follow Him. For a life of self-denial is a martyrdom, and calls for the martyr's fortitude. St. Gregory tells us that, "when persecution ceases, there is left for us still the martyrdom of peace. The neck is not brought under the weapon of steel, but the desires of the body have still to be slain with the sword of the spirit."[19]

St. Bernard distinguishes three kinds of martyrdom: martyrdom in will alone, martyrdom in act alone, and martyrdom in act as well as will. Martyrdom in will alone is found in those who are ready to give their blood and life for the virtues, although the occasion does not present itself. Martyrdom in act alone is found in the Holy Innocents, slain in the place of Christ before they reached the use of reason, and crowned by Christ with the martyr's palm. Martyrdom in will and act is the prerogative of the glorious army of martyrs, who cheerfully sealed their faith with their blood for the love of Christ.

Three things must unite to make the true martyr: first, the state of grace and charity; secondly, the actual surrender of life in public testimony of the choice of things invisible in preference to things visible; thirdly, the cause of death, which must be in defence of the faith or of some virtue. Wherefore, whoever would imitate the martyrs must be clothed with charity, must endure their sufferings with fortitude, and must die to the passions of their nature for the sake of God and the virtues.

St. John Chrysostom often insists on this spiritual kind of martyrdom. Speaking to the people of Antioch on the actual martyrdom of their former Archbishop Eustathius, he puts to them this question: "Who, then, can be a martyr?" And he answers in these words: "I have frequently told you that it is not death that makes the martyr, but that resolute will can do the same. Not I, but St. Paul gives this definition. He says: 'I die daily, I protest'. How can one die daily? How can one take six hundred deaths into one and the same body? By that resolution of will that makes us ready to die. Abraham stained not his sword with blood, he did not redden the altar with the gore of his son, he did not slay Isaac. Yet he perfected his sacrifice. Who says this? He who accepted his sacrifice. God said to Abraham: 'Thou hast not spared thy beloved son for My sake'. Yet Abraham received him back alive, and took him home. How was it, then, that he did not spare him? He spared him not in the resolution of his will; and of such sacrifices I am accustomed to judge. His hand did not immolate, his will made the sacrifice. It was a sacrifice without the shedding of blood. Those who are initiated in the divine mysteries know what I say: even the unbloody sacrifice is perfect, and Abraham's was the figure of it."[20]

Let us hear the great St. Gregory again. "If," he says, "we strive in earnest to have the virtue of patience, although we live during the peace of the Church, we may still have the palm of martyrdom. For there are two kinds of martyrdom, one of mind, another in act as well as in mind. We may be martyrs without the violence of the sword. To die by the hand of the persecutor is martyrdom in open act; to endure contumelies and still pardon our enemies is martyrdom in the hidden soul."[21] Standing at the tomb of a martyr the great Pontiff speaks yet more impressively: "We are standing," he says, "at a martyr's tomb, and we know by what death he reached the Kingdom of Heaven. We may not be called upon to give up our bodies in the manner he did; but we conquer the world in the spirit. God accepts this sacrifice; in the judgment of His fatherly spirit He accepts this kind of victory. Our Lord Jesus Christ beholds this combat within the heart, helps us to wage the war, and rewards the conqueror."[22]

We may dwell on the sufferings of the martyrs until we almost fancy ourselves in their place, but unless we imitate their fortitude by dying to ourselves, this is an idle delusion. Even to honour the martyrs without imitating them, as St. Augustine says, is but a false adulation. Our kind of martyrdom is marked out for us by St. Paul, and demands that we ourselves be the executioners. "If," he says, "by the spirit we put to death the deeds of the flesh, we shall live."[23]

The life of man on earth is a warfare, says holy Job. The life of the true Christian is a daily cross and martyrdom. To deny one's self, to combat the corrupt propensities of our nature, to keep the desire of Eternity well advanced before the things of time, and to endure whatever may come upon us, demands a patience, a fortitude, and a perseverance like the force that carried the martyrs through their sufferings. Yet let no one think that this daily fortitude is hard, stern, and pitiless like the boasted virtue of the Stoics. There are critical moments when fortitude demands that we become stern and severe with ourselves, but never with others, unless to check some great evil. But where this virtue is habitual, and in good exercise, it is gentle, free, and cheerful. As it is the gift of the Holy Ghost, and works with the sweet flame of charity, it sweetens the soul, and by its resistance to the vices that produce fear, hardness, and disconsolation, true Christian fortitude makes the soul peaceful, pleasant, and cheerful.

This view of the subject has been well expressed by the learned and devout Gerson. "The gift of fortitude," he observes, "is different from the virtue, although both regard what is arduous and difficult. As a virtue fortitude withstands or endures perils, such as we must suffer if we would not part with good; with the good, for example, of holding to the faith, of pursuing justice, or of doing good to others. But as a gift of the Holy Ghost fortitude is a gratuitous and abounding grace, given to those who seek perfection of life through the divine counsels. It may be defined as an affection of the soul that restrains concupiscence and the fears arising from adversity. Those who are in the charity of God have it in habit, but those who are perfect have it in action. But those who have this gift more in habit than in action, and are therefore imperfect, have the power of becoming perfect, if they will only bring out the habit into actual work and complete exercise.[24]

Some persons are stronger by nature than others, and some have larger and freer powers. Some, again, are by constitution more temperate, and by the soundness of their frame have their irascible and sensual passions under greater control. This firmer constitution of nature may be of great advantage to the Christian virtues; but if pride takes the place of humility, and sensuality that of temperance, this very strength of constitution will contribute its energy to the ruin of soul and body. But as Christian fortitude is a gift of God, and not a quality of nature, when brought from habit into exercise, it will do the bravest and most valiant deeds even in the weakest natures. Witness those virgin martyrs of tender years and delicate bringing up, who for the love of God did the noblest acts and underwent the greatest sufferings devoid of all disturbing fear. Witness again those heroic servants of God, who amidst corporal infirmities that would lay common mortals on their beds as permanent invalids, have expended the energies of a dozen ordinary mortals in laborious and unceasing acts of charity to their neighbours. It is the contrast between conscious weakness and the divine power working through that weakness that gives to Christian fortitude its splendour and sublimity.

St. Paul has expressed this conscious power in conscious weakness with magnificent generosity. "And He said to me: My grace is sufficient for thee, for power is made perfect in infirmity. Gladly therefore will I glory in my infirmities, that the power of Christ may dwell in me. For which cause I please myself in my infirmities, in reproaches, in necessities, in persecutions, in distresses for Christ. For when I am weak, then am I powerful."[25] Of his daily necessities and trials the great Apostle speaks in the same language of fortitude. "I speak not for want. For I have learnt in whatever state I am to be contented therewith. I know both how to be brought low, and I know how to abound: everywhere, and in all things I am instructed, both to be full, and to be hungry; both to abound, and to suffer need. I can do all things in Him that strengtheneth me."[26]

In his Book on the Duties of the Ministers of the Church St. Ambrose treats professedly on the virtue of fortitude. He calls it the firm and energetic force of virtue, which is higher than the other virtues, because it commands and invigorates them. With justice is this virtue called fortitude, because it is through its help that man governs himself, keeps down anger, and refuses to let himself be relaxed or softened by the allurements of the world around him. What can be higher, what more magnificent, than for a man to rule his body from the elevation of his mind, and to bring it under servitude; to insist that it shall obey his will, and work with diligence in the way that his resolute will shall determine?

Of the two kinds of fortitude, the first looks upon the things of the body as the least, and as if they were superfluous, and as rather deserving to be despised than thought much of. The second kind follows the Supreme Good of the soul, and whatever makes the soul herself good and beautiful; all this it follows with affectionate attention. What can be so exalting as to form the soul to an elevating energy, that looks on the things of this world as neither great in themselves nor deserving to be constantly pursued. If you have this much judgment in your soul, you will of necessity prefer what makes the soul herself good and beautiful, and will give your mind and affections to that good.

But whatever befalls you, let it not upset or disturb your mind. Be not like those who let any loss of this world's goods, any lowering of their honour or respect, any gainsaying of their adversaries, bring them down from their superiority over such things. Finally, let no peril to health or life that ought to be encountered for justice' sake ever move you. This fortitude belongs to those whom Christ sets in the field, and who after lawful striving shall be crowned. What think you of this law? Does it seem weak for your guidance in the combat? "Tribulation worketh patience; and patience trial; and trial hope; and hope confoundeth not, because the charity of God is poured forth in our hearts, by the Holy Ghost who is given to us."[27]

The most eminent spiritual writers lay it down as a principle that fortitude is the moral foundation of contemplation. A little consideration will make this evident. What is contemplation but the resting of the mind and heart upon God as their supreme object, and as the highest object of all desire? For in contemplation the mind passes not from object to object, nor from reason to reason, by an ascent from inferior to superior things, as in meditation, but rests with fixed attention and wonder upon God Himself, and devotes the affections to Him. But this implies great steadfastness of mind and constancy of heart, and such a fortitude of love as cannot easily be diverted from this divine exercise, either by dissipation of mind or by sadness of heart. The contemplative Psalmist therefore says to God: "Thou art my fortitude"; and "I will keep my fortitude to Thee". But this can be nothing but that fortitude of love that adheres to God with constancy, and endures all things rather than suffer the least separation of the superior mind and the heart from God.

It is a very great thing to have the mind habitually placed in the light of this truth, that the soul has but one Supreme Object, one Supreme Good; that all other things are only so far good as they lead us to that Supreme Good; that we are only blessed in that degree in which we partake of that good; and that the steadfast contemplation of our Sovereign Good, sustained by the fortitude of love, is the nearest approach that we can make in this life to the Living Fountain of all good. For the fortitude of love both loves and endures; loves on the side of God, endures on the side of the creature, which is the perfection of charity.

This strong and ardent virtue may be likened to the furnace that purifies gold; to the root in the fostering soil that upholds and invigorates the tree; to the armour that protects life from hostile weapons; and to the strong pinions upon which the eagle soars into the light of the sun.

As the furnace refines the gold, fortitude purges away the drossy incumbrances upon our spiritual nature, and makes it beautiful in strength. As the Proverb says: "Strength and beauty are her clothing". The wind breathes into the furnace to enkindle its ardour; the Holy Spirit breathes fortitude into the flame of charity; in token of which that Divine Spirit came visibly upon the Apostles in a mighty wind with tongues of fire. The root sustains and invigorates the tree through its stem, branches, leaves, and fruit; fortitude sustains and invigorates the soul in all her powers, virtues, works, and sufferings. The Lord said to Josue before he entered the promised land: "Take courage and be very valiant: that thou mayest observe and do all the law, which Moses my servant hath commanded thee: turn not from it to the right hand or the left, that thou mayest understand all things which thou dost".[28]

The breastplate protects the heart from hostile weapons; fortitude protects the soul from the temptations of every spiritual and carnal enemy. The whole world cannot injure a soul that is fenced with faithful fortitude. Armed with this defence the most delicate virgins, such as Catherine, Agnes, Cecilia, Agatha, and Lucy, were able to overcome the rage of tyrants, and every invention of fear and cruelty. But the wonder grows less when we reflect that "strength comes from Heaven". The eagle soars on his strong pinions against the sun, fortitude sustains the wings of the contemplative soul, and upholds her flight into the regions of light, from which the Sun of Justice shines upon her.

We may consider the ascending degrees of fortitude after the manner of St. Bonaventure. If we view the virtue as it raises us above the things of this world: it is a high degree of fortitude to conquer the world's allurements, and look down upon its transient delights; it is a higher degree to conquer the body, and keep down its concupiscences; it is the highest degree to conquer one's self in the soul, and to change self-love into the love of God.

If we consider the virtue as it resists evil: it is a high degree of fortitude to resist and repel the sins of the body, such as intemperance, sensuality, and uncleanness; it is a higher degree to resist and repel the sins of the soul, such as self-love, pride, vanity, and insincerity; it is the highest degree to resist and repel the first movements and occasions of sin, whether in body or in soul.

If we consider the virtue as it endures adversities, privations, or sorrows with peace and resignation: it is a high degree to endure with contentment the loss of such things as this world can give us; it is a higher degree to endure our personal sufferings and sorrows with a patient and peaceful heart; it is the highest degree to give up our mortal life for God's sake, whensoever He may call for it.

If we consider this same gift and virtue of fortitude as it carries us with cheerful content through the labours of our vocation: it is a high degree to do our work in this world with a view to our salvation; it is a higher degree to do our work in the right way, that is, according to the will of God; it is the highest degree to labour in the interior of the soul, so as to perfect our union with God in time and for eternity.

To sum up the whole doctrine of fortitude in a sentence, it is the strength of God's grace working through the co-operation of the will in the weakness of the creature; and the fortitude of resignation, as the word implies, is the surrender of one's self to God amidst accepted afflictions, that, attached to the cross of Christ, they may perfect our soul. This is the summit of fortitude.

A comprehensive view of fortitude, as the virtue of the virtues, will take us deep into the designs of God, far and wide over the history of mankind, and high into the heavens above. It is the eternal plan of God to draw the greatest possible amount of good out of the evil produced by evil wills, and to demonstrate His power in the weakness of His creatures where their wills are good. These two magnificent demonstrations of His power and goodness are effected by the strength of His grace in the souls that freely and generously co-operate with His gifts. But this involves the conflict of good with evil, a conflict that goes on increasing in intensity, owing to the growth and complication of evil as the world grows older. Contemplate the history of the world from the opening of the Book of Genesis to the last prophecies recorded in the Book of Revelations, and you will see how the combat of good against evil goes on complicating and extending, at one time in violence, at another time in subtleties, until the time our Lord predicted when "you will scarcely find faith upon the earth". Hence, as evil increases, fortitude and patience become still more needful to the servants of God. The rewards of those who overcome in the conflict are set before us for our encouragement in the same Book of Revelations in which those combats are described; and St. John sums up the whole spirit of the conflict in these words: "Here is the patience of the saints, who keep the commandments of God and the faith of Jesus".[29]

When the conflict with evil is ended; when that evil has been compelled to serve for the probation and sanctification of God's elect; when all the good that can be drawn out of evil has been accumulated in the souls of the just; then will come that glorious manifestation of God's wisdom and power before the assembled universe of created intelligences, and the wonders of His grace and providence will be seen from beginning to end. But the most wonderful demonstration of God's love and power will appear in this, that the active, violent, subtle, combined, and most aggressive powers of evil have been all overcome by such gentle virtues as charity, humility, and patience.

Of all material elements fire is the most powerful and the noblest. By its subtle force all things live, grow, and are preserved. It illuminates, invigorates, and fertilizes the powers of nature. Into what it enters, that it expands; and to many things it gives strength and consistency, from the granite bones of the earth to the vessel of clay from the potter's wheel. It has not only the noble property of ascending, as in flame, but also the benignant property of descending, as in the rays of the sun. Having dominion over the weaker elements, it consumes without destroying them, and converts them into more ethereal forms of existence. Fire was therefore the most expressive element in which to manifest to mortal eyes the invisible descent of the Holy Spirit upon the disciples of Christ—expressive of the light of wisdom, the ardour of charity, and the strengthening and transforming power of fortitude.

When the Holy Spirit conveys His gifts to a soul, He infuses the strength of fortitude into the ardour of charity, and this fortitude ignited by this charity passes into our spiritual powers; and if our will is faithful to co-operate with the divine gift, from our powers it passes into the virtues, making the soul strong from weakness and pliant to endure trials and to resist the evils of this mortal life. Then fortitude gives steadiness and strength to that bright flame of charity which aspires to God and to the service of God in His creatures, and gives honour and glory to our glorious Lord and Creator. What is weak or vicious in the creature is consumed in that strong fire, that it may be changed into spiritual good. In descending, that celestial flame consumes what ought to be consumed, and strengthens what ought to be strengthened; and that gift which descended as a flame of grace re-ascends as a flame of love, bearing up the soul along with it into a closer, more constant, and more elevated communion with God, from whom the fortitude of charity descends.

# 5

# ON THE PATIENCE OF THE SON OF GOD

"May the Lord direct your hearts in the charity of God and the patience of Christ."—*2 Thessalonians iii. 5.*

Although the perfection of God is infinitely beyond the comprehension of His creatures, He has not left us in this darkling world without light to know that He is the Fountain of all goodness, or without conscience to feel that He is merciful, compassionate, and just. He has given us luminous revelations of His glorious nature, and has manifested His divine attributes in ways suited to our understanding, that we may rise through that knowledge to the contemplation of His infinite perfection in some degree, and may enkindle our desires for divine communion with Him. He has done more for us, and has manifested Himself through His Divine Son, one with Him in His divine nature, one with us in His human nature; and in the communication of His Holy Spirit, poured forth with love into our hearts, whereby we receive the sense of God, and the power to love Him and feel after Him, even whilst tied to this earth by the corruptible body, that we may have our conversation in Heaven.

But of all that God has taught us, and of all that we have learnt by experience, there is nothing that strikes the reflecting mind with more awe and wonder, or proves more fully His perfection, than His infinite patience with His rebellious and sinful creatures. This is the great consolation of the just; this is the great scandal of the proud. Truly His thoughts are not as our thoughts, nor His ways as our ways. The patience of God is the silence of His power, whilst His mercy speaks to the conscience. He made us all for Himself, every one of the children of Adam. He made us all that we might be happy in Him, who can never be happy in ourselves. But he knows the dust out of which He has so wonderfully made us; He knows how weak and restless is our spirit which He made from nothing, without His help to fortify our nature, and to lead and guide it to Himself. And when we trust to ourselves instead of trusting ourselves to Him, and fall into every kind of sin and misery, our merciful God has patience with us, gives us time, speaks to our conscience, encircles us with His providential mercies, and scourges us with the miseries of our iniquities, that we may have every motive for returning to Him. And when we do return, His mercy and pardon are as perfect as His patience.

What a spectacle to the angels is the patience of God imposing silence on His justice whilst souls are still in the course of probation! When we reflect upon the long endurance of our Heavenly Father with His earthly children, so movingly described by the prophets; and how through the long ages of their blind perversity, He was benignly preparing the way for their Redemption, speaking all the time to their conscience, giving them admonitory warnings, merciful corrections, and visible proofs of His providential care of them; and waiting, still waiting in silence, if perchance, before their final summons from the body to His awful presence, they might acknowledge Him, turn to Him, and repent; we stand transfixed in astonishment at a patience so great and divine. "Thou, our God, art gracious and true, patient, and ordering all things in mercy."[1] So wonderful is the merciful patience of God, that not a few sects of philosophy or creeds of religion, falsely so called, following the instincts of pride, have construed the divine patience into indifference or cruelty, not seeing that the patience that awaits for the conversion of the sinner is of the divine goodness that orders all things in mercy. But, 'o the eyes of faith, this very patience is one of the sublimest proofs of the divine perfection.

When we reflect again upon the history of the ages since God has manifested Himself openly to the world in his Son, since the Gospel of grace and truth has shone with such love to the souls of men; how far more profound has been our insight into that divine patience with which God endures the sins and ingratitude with which so many of His Christian children have repaid his infinite love! Stupendous is the patient love with which our Heavenly Father awaits the conversion of rebellious and ungrateful souls. But when at last the sinful soul returns to Him, and finds the pardon and peace that remove all her miseries, she exclaims in astonishment: Oh, infinite patience of my God and Saviour!

What a profound conception of the mystery of the Incarnation has been given us by Tertullian in this short sentence:—"God placed His Spirit in His Son with all patience"[2]. From the moment that the Eternal Word of the Father was made man by the operation of the Holy Spirit in the womb of the Virgin Mary, His human nature was "full of grace and truth"; and was endowed with a divine patience derived from His Godhead, with whose person that human nature was united, that was perfect for enduring all the conditions of humanity, all its trials, and all those sufferings which He was destined to undergo for our redemption and salvation.

It was through the loss of patience that Adam fell into sin. It is through the loss of the same virtue that his innumerable descendants have sinned after his example. And it was by the power of His loving patience that the Son of God worked out our redemption, by whose sufferings we are healed. As by the loss of that fundamental patience which adheres with constancy to God we fell into pride and self-seeking, and thence into every kind of weakness, sin, and misery; so through the patience of Christ we are brought back to God, and are restored to the possession and consistency of those virtues by which we adhere to God and preserve ourselves from evil. When we consider who He was, and what He was, and all the things that He suffered and endured from the moment of His incarnation to His last breathing on the Cross, and with what gentle love and meekness He endured, we see that His patience was as wonderful as His humility, and that His Incarnation is the amazing mystery of humility and patience. From this we also collect that humility and patience are the true foundations of human perfection. Wherefore, in contemplating the one complete and perfect example of humanity, perfect because united with the divinity, what calls for our most especial attention and imitation is His divine patience and humility; because these are the most difficult as well as the most fundamental virtues, and the virtues which perfect that sovereign virtue of charity, by which we also, in another order, are united with God.

The place in which to contemplate the humility and patience of the Son of God in their supreme manifestation and greatest light is on the desolate hill of Golgotha, where, according to the tradition of the early Fathers, derived from the Hebrews, the body of the sinful Adam was interred. There at the foot of the Cross of Jesus, whose blood falls upon the earthly remains of the fallen parent of our race, as well as upon us, his descendants, we may contemplate the divine patience by the light thrown upon it from Mount Thabor. But let us first raise the eyes of our faith above that dreary hill, strewed as it is with the relics of criminal executions, and contemplate the Eternal Father sending forth His Son upon His mission to this guilty world. "God so loved the world, as to give His only-begotten Son, that whosoever believeth in Him may not perish, but may have everlasting life."[3]

In the instant of His Incarnation His human nature became one with His divine personality; and, through that personal union of His soul with His divinity, Christ held from the Father the plenitude of wisdom and knowledge, and internally possessed the glory of the beatific vision. He called Himself "the Son of man," but on every suitable occasion proclaimed Himself "the Son of God," and asserted His equality with His Father. He says: "He that seeth Me seeth the Father also,"[4] and: "All whatsoever things the Father hath are Mine"[5] Again He says: "I am in the Father and the Father in Me,"[6] and: "I and the

Father are one."[7] And again: "I came forth from the Father and have come into the world; again I leave the world and I go to the Father"[8] He was the light of the world, knew all that is in heaven and earth, and all that is in man.

After contemplating the Son of God in His own unspeakable light, think of the wonderful patience with which He held back within the veil of His corporal frame the fulness of the light and glory within Him, that He might converse with men in humility, and might suffer contradictions and persecutions with unalterable patience. His life was hidden, and He became a "sign to be contradicted". The power that creates and rules the world was with Him, the light that enlightens all created intelligences was within Him, because He was the Son of God. Once, and only once for a brief hour, He revealed to chosen witnesses the glorious majesty which for the rest of His human life was concealed from mortal eyes. Yet He enjoined on those chosen witnesses that they should tell the vision to no man until He had arisen from the dead.

Of the three apostolic witnesses of that glorious vision, St. John declares: "We saw His glory, the glory as it were of the only-begotten of the Father, full of grace and truth"[9]. And St. Peter appeals to the same glorious vision as bearing testimony to the truth of his teaching. "We have not followed cunningly devised fables when we made known to you the power and the presence of our Lord Jesus Christ, but having been made eye-witnesses of His Majesty. For He received from God the Father honour and glory: this voice coming down to Him from the excellent glory: This is My beloved Son in whom I have pleased Myself; hear ye Him. And this voice we heard brought from Heaven when we were with Him in the holy mount."[10]

After realizing to your mind the power, the majesty, and the glory that were hidden in the Son of God from the eyes of men, think to the full extent of your light of that divine patience and fortitude with which, to use the words of St. Leo, "He held back His majesty, that the persecutors might have power to inflict their rage upon Him". With what astonishment must the three witnesses of His glory have observed His humble and patient ways, as, "with looks hidden and as of one despised," He bore in silence the contradictions of hypocrites and the reproaches of sinners! With what meekness He accepted the humiliations, with what gentleness the sufferings, that were heaped upon Him, as though He were the worst of criminals, and the enemy of the people whom He had come to save!

For how many ages, and through how many vicissitudes, had His chosen people waited for Him as their Messias and their Deliverer? Instructed by their prophets, trained incessantly to the expectation of Him by their laws, their sacrifices, and the rites and ceremonies that mingled with their daily lives, that expectation, of whose approaching fulfilment there were so many visible signs, was the ruling thought of their minds. But the veils of pride and sensuality were upon their hearts; and although He proved Himself to be their expected Messias by the lights of His teaching, by His power over nature and His fulfilment of the prophecies, they could not endure His lowliness, or the humble garniture under which He concealed His majesty. He was in the world, and the world knew Him not; He came to save the world, but to save it through His sufferings. Ever imitating the patience of His Father, He bore to be unknown except to a few disciples. After accomplishing the stupendous work of our redemption, He left it to His disciples, after He had departed from the world, to make known that He had saved mankind from eternal death and had brought them everlasting life. Truly Thou art a hidden and most patient God! Thou art concealed from the proud and made known to the humble.

Let us here pause and turn our reflection upon ourselves. We profess to be the patient followers of the patient Son of God. Do we understand how deep that patience goes which rests the humanity of Christ upon the firm foundation of His divinity, and gives to His human will the strength to hold to the will of His Father, unmoved and undisturbed in its peace and self-possession by all that men can say or do against Him? Do we understand the profundity of that patience which refrains from every egotistical self-assertion, however grossly He is misjudged, however ignominiously He is insulted? He only glorifies His Heavenly Father, declares His unity with His Father, and equally declares that he can do nothing without His Father. Yet He calls upon us to be the imitators of His patience, to rest for strength on Him; to take up our daily cross and follow Him; to refrain from our selfish egotism; and in patience to possess our souls.

Contemplate the plenitude of the Godhead dwelling corporately in Christ Jesus, and how nevertheless He only manifested His grace and wisdom by degrees, as men could bear their light, whilst the splendour of His light and wisdom is all reserved within Him, held back by His infinite patience. Although in the person of God, He bore with unspeakable patience the enclosure of the virginal womb; He endured the humbling conditions of infancy, the trials and subjection of youth, the labours of obedience to His earthly guardians, and the toils of labour.

He submissively remained under the law of obedience for thirty years, until the law of Moses permitted Him to teach. Yet He was Himself the master of the law, Himself the object of the law. He came with the new law of grace and love, yet patiently submitted Himself to the hard restraints and rigorous observances of that ceremonial law which was but an irksome and laborious figure of His own mission and sacrifice. But though he faithfully observed its commands to the letter, apart from the corruptions of the Pharisees, that very law was made the pretext for opposing His preaching, and the final plea for putting Him to death. Whoever will apply his mind with diligence to the consideration of these contrasts between the interior spirit of Christ and the exterior law of Moses to which He was obedient, will obtain a new key to His divine patience. By obeying the law of life He was made subject to the law of death.

Severe to Himself, He is gentle, mild, and forbearing to all others. His meekness is the beautiful flower, His peacefulness the sweet fruit of His patience. His doctrine is doubted and disputed; He is charged with being an impostor; He is called a blasphemer; His wonderful works are ascribed to the devil; His adversaries gnash their teeth, burn with rage, and are prepared to stone Him. Yet His equanimity is unmoved, His meek demeanour is not altered, the calmness of His peace undergoes no change. Resting on His union with His Father, the ground of His invincible strength, His divine fortitude is tried at every point, and at every point His patience is invincible.

After submitting Himself to the baptism of John, in obedience to the Holy Spirit He retreats into the savage wilderness, abides among wild beasts, fasting from all food for forty days, and devoting Himself to prayer. Then came His encounter with the enemy of mankind and His endurance of those vile and hypocritical temptations, in which He taught us how like temptations must be resisted by the strength of patience and the word of God. His acts are the seal of His teaching; His patience a great part of His expiation for our sins.

As the Lord of men He became their teacher, and having the perfect knowledge of what brings pardon from the offended patience of God, He taught them how to escape from death to life. Meeting darkness with light and insults with meekness, His voice was not heard in contention, but for revilings He gave back the blessings of compassion. He despised no man's roof, He refused not to sit at any poor man's table. He came not to seek the just, but sinners to repentance. The pretenders to purity brought this very charge against Him, that He conversed and sat at table with publicans and sinners. He was not angry with the city that refused Him entrance within its gates; and when some of His disciples would have Him bring down fire from Heaven, as Elias did, to revenge the insult, He rebuked them in these words: "You know not of what spirit you are. The Son of Man came not to destroy souls, but to save."[11]

He healed the ungrateful. He yielded Himself to His betrayers. Nor was this much, since He took a traitor into His company, treated him with habitual kindness, entrusted him with the common purse, and gave warnings to his conscience; yet all this goodness only proved his hardness and ingratitude. Betrayed by this man to His enemies, and led like a sheep to the slaughter, He opened not His mouth in complaints, but bore all that came upon Him in meek and silent patience. When Peter drew the sword in His defence, He not only rebuked him with that patience which is the mother of mercy, but healed the wound that He had not inflicted.

Was it necessary to heap contumelies upon contumelies, and lay them on His head, when malice deliberately planned had already doomed Him to death? Yet, having power to lay down His life, and power to take it up again, He chose to leave this life full and sated with the dignity and joy of patience.[12]

Falsely accused, and that in the name of His Father's law, He is 'spit upon, scourged, derided, clothed in mockery as a sham king, for the entertainment of Jews and heathens alike, and crowned with thorns that the blood of His brow might exhibit His royalty. Upon His exhausted limbs He carries the cross of the criminal with ignominy unspeakable; and stripped to nudity on Golgotha, He is crucified before the people whom He came to save from hell: crucified with every circumstance of cruelty and torment. How wonderful is the death that has given us life! How wonderful in humility, in suffering, in patience! How sublime this deliverance of souls, rescued from death through the harrowings of the cross! Behold God hidden in the nature of man, and that nature is rent and torn to death without a single sign of man's impatience. From this alone should the Pharisees have known their Lord; for no mere man could have shown a patience so divine.

If we enter into the interior of the Son of God, we shall there find a crucifixion of the soul sustained by a charity most patient because most divine. Nothing can be so helpful to souls under interior trials as to enter in spirit into the interior crucifixion of our Blessed Lord. He thirsts for the salvation of all whom by His Incarnation He has made His brethren; and the resistance that He meets with from the pride of self-seeking wills causes Him the greatest anguish of spirit. To this anguish He gave voice when, approaching Jerusalem, He spoke to her people with lamentations and tears: "Jerusalem, Jerusalem, thou that killest the prophets, and stonest them that are sent to thee; how often would I have gathered thy children as the hen doth gather her chickens under her wings, and thou wouldst not? Behold your house shall be left to you desolate."[13]

If the souls of the Saints suffered intensely from the opposition of sinners to the charity that prayed and laboured for their conversion, how much more did the God of charity suffer in His human soul, when His light, His grace, and all His sufferings for the souls of men were rejected and despised. The fire of His charity consumed Him within, because their hardened hearts would not suffer it to spread abroad.

It is written that "our God is a consuming fire"[14] It is also written prophetically of the Son of God as the spouse of souls, that "love is strong as death, jealousy is hard as hell, the lamps thereof are fire and flames"[15] And St. Justin the Martyr tell us there was a tradition in the Holy Land among those who had seen the disciples of our Lord, that He was wont to say: "Those who are near to me are near a fire". He said to His disciples: "I came to cast fire on the earth; and what will I but that it be enkindled? And I have a baptism wherewith I am to be baptized: and how am I straitened until it be accomplished!"[16] This fire was His burning charity; this baptism His fiery sufferings. He was straitened by His intense desire to accomplish His sufferings that He might spread the living fire of His charity. But His patience held His desires in obedience until the hour appointed by His Father. Thus was His ardent love of souls repressed and restrained within Him, until, brought to His baptism of blood, His love was crucified within Him; and then by His death He purchased the descent of the Holy Ghost in flames of love upon the souls of men.

Throughout His mortal life His cross was always before Him, and He looked upon its nearer and nearer approach not only with an enduring but with a desiring fortitude and patience. From time to time, and by degrees, He brought the passion that He should suffer before the minds of His chosen disciples, not only showing that His sacrifice was before His mind, but preparing them for its tremendous realization. He thus commended to their hearts His supreme love of their souls; and taught them, what they only after His resurrection understood to the full, to return love for love, blood for blood, and death for death. What else did He teach in His admonitions but that they should take up their cross daily and follow Him? On His last journey to Jerusalem, going direct to His sacrifice, "Jesus went before the disciples, and they were astonished; and following were afraid". And taking the twelve, He began to tell them the things that should befall Him, saying: "Behold we go up to Jerusalem, and the Son of man shall be betrayed to the Chief Priests, and the Scribes and Ancients, and they shall condemn Him to death, and shall deliver Him to the Gentiles, and they shall mock Him, and spit on Him, and scourge Him, and kill Him, and the third day He shall rise again".[17] And the Gospel records the amazement of the disciples at the ardour with which He went to His sufferings.

The cross is the furnace of love. The patience of the cross demonstrates the perfection of love. "Greater love than this no man hath, that a man lay down his life for his friend."[18] What was the patient love of Christ, that suffering love of His Father, that suffering love of our souls, to what did it all tend, but to the full and firm surrender of His human nature to His Father, through those mortal agonies, endured with supreme resignation, in the absolute certainty that He who accepts the sacrifice will glorify the Victim, and make the oblation of patient love most fruitful? In the words of St. Leo, that ignominious death became "the fountain of all benedictions, the cause of all graces, giving strength out of weakness to believers, glory out of ignominy, and life out of death".[19] Of this we have a prophetic figure in the riddle of Samson, who extracted honey from the jaws of the lion he had slain.

The Sacred Scriptures teach in many places that the patience of Christ is the principle of His glory. For by patience He perfected His sufferings, by patience He perfected His work of love, by patience He perfected His merits, infinite because He suffered in the person of God. This great truth is entitled to profound consideration; for the sufferings of Christ were perfected by His patient resignation to His Father's will. And this throws the greatest light upon the value and reward of all patient suffering, under whatever cross or trial, endured with Christ for the love of God.

Our Divine Lord quoted the 109th Psalm in proof of His Divinity. It is a magnificent prophecy of the prerogatives of Christ. Its conclusion gives the cause of the exaltation of His humanity in glory. "He shall drink of the torrent on the way: therefore shall He lift up His head." The Fathers unanimously assign this verse to His humiliations and sufferings as the cause of His exaltation. The torrent is the rapid course of human events, that rush into the current of time with the impetuosity of a flood, loud-sounding, turbid, and unpeaceful. But death steps in, and man leaves no vestige of his troubled path. Into that torrent the Son of God descended, and on the way of His mortal life, He drank of the turbid waters and endured their bitter flavour with most loving patience. He suffered the griefs of humanity in their severest form; He went into the depth of the torrent in His passion. He was not refreshed with the sweet waters of delight, for sin and misery were all around Him; but drank of those dark and bitter waters, of which it is said in another Psalm: "The waters have come in even unto my soul. I am stuck fast in the mire of the deep: and there is no standing place. I have come into the depths of the sea: and the tempest hath overwhelmed me."[20]

"Wherefore He hath lifted up His head," and the same psalm proclaims His exaltation and power. "The Lord said to my Lord: Sit Thou on My right hand, until I make Thy enemies Thy footstool. The Lord will send forth the sceptre of Thy power out of Sion; rule Thou in the midst of Thy enemies. With Thee is the principality in the day of Thy strength: in the brightness of the Holies: from the womb before the morning star I begot Thee. The Lord hath sworn, and He will not repent; Thou art a priest for ever according to the order of Melchisedech."

On the very day of His resurrection the Son of God taught this principle to the two disciples on the way to Emmaus. To their fears caused by His sufferings and death He replied: "O foolish, and slow of heart to believe in all things which the prophets have spoken, ought not Christ to have suffered these things, and so enter into His glory?"[21]

In his Epistle to the Hebrews St. Paul has also shown that it was by His patient sufferings that Christ was perfected a high priest, and received the power to save mankind: "Who in the days of His flesh, with a strong cry and tears, offering up prayers and supplications to Him that was able to save Him from death, was heard for His reverence: and being consummated, was called by God a high priest according to the order of Melchisedech."[22] In another and most memorable passage the great Apostle exhibits in a most striking way how the humiliations and obedient sufferings of the Son of God were the principle of His exaltation; and that with the express object of impressing upon us that if we suffer in a like spirit of patient and humble obedience we shall be glorified with Him. "Let this mind be in you, which was also in Christ Jesus; who, being in the form of God, thought it not robbery to be equal with God; but emptied Himself, taking the form of a servant, being made in the likeness of man, and in habit found as a man. He humbled Himself, becoming obedient unto death; even the death of the cross. For which cause God also hath exalted Him, and hath given Him a name which is above all names; that at the name of Jesus every knee should bow of those that are in heaven, on earth, and under the earth. And that every tongue should confess that the Lord Jesus Christ is in the glory of God the Father."[23]

We are thus divinely taught that the humility and the patience which subject our wayward nature to the will of God, and keep us steadfast in that subjection through all that we must suffer, are the preparation, and already contain the seed of the glory that is promised us. For this reason our Lord exhorts us to take up our daily cross, and to follow Him with patience. And the two great Apostles give us each of them a solemn exhortation in the same direction. St. Paul says: "Let us run with patience to the fight proposed to us; looking upon Jesus the author and finisher of our faith, who, having joy set before Him, endured the cross, despising the shame, and now sitteth at the right hand of God".[24] And St. Peter tells us: "If doing well you suffer patiently, this is thanksworthy before God. For unto this you are called: because Christ also suffered for us, leaving you an example that you may follow in His steps."[25]

These high instructions all go to one point, that as the patient sufferings of our Lord were the cause of His glory, the like patience in sufferings will bring us to His glory. Everything points to patience as the perfecter of the soul. For charity is patient. If not patient, it is very imperfect; it has not brought our weak and irritable nature into full subjection to the grace and will of God. We may mortify the body, but of what avail is that if the soul is not duly mortified. Charity will be left without its firmness and stability; nature will reign where God should reign. Hence St. Paul advises us that we should not look to ourselves, but to God, for the power of patience, and should exercise it in Christ by bearing our cross with Him. Let us again hear the ardent Apostle: "God who commandeth the light to shine out of darkness hath shined in our hearts, to give the light of the knowledge of the glory of God in the face of Christ Jesus. But we have this treasure in earthly vessels, that excellence may be of the power of God and not of us. In all things we suffer tribulation, but are not distressed; we are straitened, but are not destitute; we suffer persecution, but are not forsaken; we are cast down, but we perish not: always bearing about in our bodies the mortification of Jesus, that the life of Jesus may be manifested in our bodies."[26] And so he prays for the faithful that they may "be strengthened with all might, according to the power of His glory, in all patience and long-suffering with joy".[27] The great difficulty in instructing those good people who live mostly on their own sensibilities, and who obtain the name of being devout, is that they do not realize to themselves in what devoutness consists; for devoutness means devotedness, and devotedness means being given to something which is not one's self. The true sense of devoutness is the being given to God, and not to our own sensibilities and feelings—the feeling after God, not after one's self; for our good is in God, not in ourselves. But we have to bear with ourselves, and cease being occupied with ourselves, that we may feel after God. Those pious persons who are attached to their own soft sentimentalities, that mere milk for babes, cannot enter into the strong things of the patience of Christ or of His saints. They will accept it for a truth that patient charity is the cause and the principle of the future glory, but will mainly look upon it as the enduring of bodily sufferings when they come, whether by persecution or by the visitation of God. They will not realize to themselves that fundamental patience which rests the soul on God, and establishes order, strength, and peace within the soul. Engaged with their sensibilities and the troubles that arise from them, they seem to expect that patience is to come to them without either effort or combat with themselves. They never seem to understand in a practical way that this patience is chiefly concerned with their own interior trials, and that they can only obtain that perfection of charity, which brings uniform cheerfulness and peace, by enduring with constant patience and true resignation both their trials and themselves.

Let us now ascend to the contemplation of the interior pains and sufferings of Jesus Christ the Son of God. They as far exceed His exterior sufferings as spirit transcends body. But let us take with us the light of the principle, that patience proceeds from charity.

"I will go up into the palm tree and take hold of its fruits."[28] The palm is the symbol of victory and peace. The cross of Jesus is the most fruitful of palm trees, bringing the greatest peace after the greatest of victories, won through unspeakable pains and sufferings. For if Jesus was what the prophet Isaias predicted of Him, "a man of sorrows, acquainted with infirmity," He was always victorious by the force of His divine patience. His spiritual sufferings were incomparably greater than His corporal sufferings. For in His innocence He was the victim and vicarious penitent for all the sins of the children of Adam, and so became the model of all true penitents, as well as the example of resignation to all who are afflicted with interior desolation. "Surely He hath borne our infirmities and carried our sorrows, and we have thought Him as it were a leper, and as one stricken by God and afflicted. But He was wounded for our iniquities, He was bruised for our sins; the chastisement of our peace was upon Him, and by His bruises we are healed. All we like sheep have gone astray, every one hath turned aside into his own way; and the Lord hath lain upon Him the iniquity of us all."[29]

The griefs of our Divine Lord were not the griefs of sadness; for sadness is the most selfish of human passions. His sorrows were the sorrows of love and compassion. He grieves over the multitude and magnitude of the sins by which God is offended; He laments over the calamitous condition to which the offending race of Adam has been reduced. His love of those innumerable souls, whom the Father created through Him, the Word of His glory, and of whose reason He is Himself the illuminator, is the cause of all His grief. He beholds those souls, whom no man can number, gone astray from God into misery and darkness, and leading a dying life that is in bitter conflict with their instincts for good and with the light of their conscience, and He pleads with a strong cry and tears for their return to peace.

Hanging on the cross before His Father, and loving the sinful world that is crucifying Him with a love only second to the love of His Father, whilst every sense and fibre of His mortal frame suffers exquisite and ignominious torture, His afflicted soul is overwhelmed with grief and desolation. Bearing the vast accumulation of the sins of human nature upon His own most pure soul for their expiation, He not only sees in His pure light, but feels through His pure nature, all their foulness, their hideous deformity, their unceasing accumulation, and their unspeakable malice. The mockeries and insults heaped upon His languid head are but the concentrated expression of that pride, uncleanness, and insolence with which the ungrateful creature has insulted his Beneficent Creator throughout the history of the human race.

As only divine eyes can penetrate the secrets of human hearts, the Son of God beholds the miseries of souls whilst their hearts ferment in wickedness. He sees the blindness of His chosen people, deaf to the voice of the prophets, deaf to His own voice, and blind to His light. He sees mankind at large immersed in idolatries, sunk in vices, dead to the cry of conscience, ignorant of the stupendous work of mercy that is being accomplished for their redemption.

Thus, whilst the Divine Victim enters into the evils for which He suffers, He mourns and grieves over the crimes that rise in filthy floods against His Father, and over the destruction of innumerable souls. But as by reason of His patient charity, the sufferings of His spirit were in perfect conformity with the Divine Reason, they were only equalled by His love of souls. Who can fathom that immense love of the souls for whom He suffered? Who can search the abyss of that grief which fills up the chasm between those fallen souls and God? Who can explore that divine compassion with which His grieving soul is moved over His erring brethren? Who can divine the ardour of his desire to save them from that everlasting ruin into which their perverted wills have driven them? "I have a baptism wherewith I am to be baptized, and how am I straitened until it be accomplished!" Oh, what a baptism of blood, of grief, and desolation!

The Son of God is more deeply wounded in His spiritual than in His corporal nature. The first wound inflicted is the contempt and dishonour offered to the Divine Majesty in His person. The second wound inflicted is the malice with which every grievous sinner crucifies the Son of God in himself, and makes Him a mockery. The third wound of His spirit is inflicted by the hideous deformity of each mortal sin, destroying as it does the good order and beauty of God's noblest creation. The fourth wound of His spirit is from the destruction that He foresees of a great part of His kingdom of grace and of glory by the dark pride of heresy, and by malicious habits of sin. The fifth and deepest wound is inflicted on His spirit by the deliberate fall of so many souls from grace into the eternal abyss of darkness and punishment, although to save them from that abyss He is crucified.

We have yet to enter into that awful dereliction and desolation in which the soul of Jesus is steeped, when He reaches the last degree of spiritual suffering with the last degree of patience. His soul endures the last penalty due to the sins He is expiating in the abandonment of God. This may be looked upon as the atonement for that pride which is the root of all sin and the cause of all malice. It may be looked upon in another light, as the occasion of the divinest patience and of the most absolute resignation, and as the perfect example to which every soul should be conformed that suffers the interior pains of desolation. The beatific vision recedes to the extreme summit of His spirit, whilst all else of His human soul is invaded by darkness, withered in dryness, and drenched in bitterness; and He exclaims to His Father: "My God, my God, why hast Thou abandoned me?"

In the Garden of Olives the Divine Penitent for our sins breathes forth the agonizing cry: "My soul is sorrowful even unto death". On the cross the Divine Victim of our sins sends forth the cry of utter desolation. Yet, in that last stage of desolation, with what a divine fortitude and resignation He surrenders Himself to the will of His Heavenly Father! "Yet not My will but Thine be done." And resting His weary and exhausted soul upon the Divine Strength for support, He sighs out His life in those words of oblation and surrender: "Father, into Thy hands I commend My spirit".

In the Garden of Olives the Son of God is in an agony of soul so fearful, that tears of blood gush from His earthly frame. On the dolorous way, we behold His patient spirit bending down His shattered body under the load of the cross, and bearing it along with invincible fortitude to the place of execution. On Golgotha, in His cruel denudation and atrocious suspension, we hear His prayer for the pardon of His executioners. In His interior crucifixion and desolation we contemplate His love for all disconsolate souls, for whose strengthening He is preparing grace and consolation. In His death He teaches all of us in the midst of our last sufferings how to surrender up our souls to God. He is the model of the living and the model of the dying; the grace of the living and the grace of the dying; the love of the living and the love of the dying; and all who die to this world in patient love live through Him for ever and ever.

Were we to contemplate the sufferings of Christ with our whole mind and heart all the days of our lives, we could not reach the hidden depths of His patient sufferings and loving sorrows. Nor could we exhaust the light and consolation which flow from that contemplation. God alone knows what He suffered for our sins. God alone knows all the love and patience with which He suffered. God alone knows the depths of the tenderness of His divine compassion for our souls.[30]

What men desire to have in this world, and to have above all things else, is power. If they love money, they love it as an instrument of power, and as the means of having their own will and way. But all power is from God; and the greatest power is the charity of God. For charity can do all things. It unites earth with heaven and the soul with God, and gives to the soul peace in herself and power of well-doing. But the highest power that we weak mortals can possess is the fortitude of charity, which adheres with constancy to God, conquers evil, and fills the soul with good. By the fortitude of charity Christ conquered death for all, and redeemed the world. It is the power of Christ; and if we imitate His patience we shall come to His power. Open to Him your soul, and with His patient charity He will come to you, and will fortify you against His enemies and yours.

It has been a maxim of the world for some ages that knowledge is power. Knowledge is not power, but a condition of power. Knowledge is of the mind, power of the will. It is one thing to know, and another to do. If we act on human knowledge we shall accomplish human things; if we act on divine knowledge we shall come to divine things. But unless the light to know is accompanied with strength of will to act according to our knowledge, that knowledge is in vain; and to act upon divine knowledge requires a divine strength. The knowledge which is given us of the most dear Passion of Our Lord and Saviour, intimate in proportion to our love, is the revelation to our souls of the divinest love in the divinest patience, enriched with heavenly fruits for all that hunger for them. But this revelation is a most solemn invitation to us, that we should imitate His patience as much as His charity; and for this very reason, that without patience charity never can be perfect, and can never bring us perfect fruits. "He that taketh not up his cross, and followeth me, is not worthy of me."[31]

The grandeur of the patience of the Son of God is a great argument of faith. It demonstrates His divine power as much as His miracles, and must be construed with them. It is not the reason but the pride of the infidel that is scandalized with a suffering Redeemer of the world. To put on our nature, to stand in our place, to gather all the sufferings due to sin upon His own divine person, to endure them with the divine patience of an infinite charity, is the loving action of a most merciful God, who thus teaches us how to convert all our sufferings into virtue, and how to make them fruitful to eternal life. Bridging over the vast gulf between heaven and earth, which sin had rent asunder, through the marvellous union of God with man, He has opened the way through His own sufferings and death to our resurrection. He has sanctified all sufferings by His own, and has given us the power, by uniting our sufferings with His, and by acting with the grace of His patient charity, to share in His everlasting glory.

Nor is this all; for not only have the patient sufferings of Christ opened Heaven to us; but whenever we draw near to the suffering Son of God, and put our heart into that furnace of love and patience, we receive a light, an affection, and an unction that soothes all sorrows into peace, cleanses the soul from evil, and comforts her with a cordial strength and an ever-increasing desire of the Eternal Good. The world is full of mysteries; the soul is full of mysteries; Heaven is all mystery to us earthly creatures. But whoever embraces the Cross with open heart finds therein the explanation of a thousand mysteries.

# 6

## ON PATIENCE AS THE DISCIPLINE OF THE SOUL

"In your patience you shall possess your souls."—St. Luke xxi. 19.

We have come to the great problem of our moral nature. What is it to hold our soul in our own possession? As we have not our resources from ourselves, because we are not created for ourselves but for God, we cannot possess our soul except in God. We possess our mind in the light of His truth, and our will in the grace of His love. Hence when Adam fell from God he lost the possession of himself. So long as our mind adheres to God in His truth, and the will adheres to God in His love, we are in possession of ourselves. But if we follow the seductions of error we lose the possession of ourselves. And if we follow the unreasonable impulses of temper, of passion, or of sensuality that spring up in our inferior nature, we lose possession of ourselves. As the body depends for its life and health on the light and air and food, which by the ordinance of God this visible world provides, the soul depends for life and health on the truth, the love, and the food of grace which, through the merciful mystery of our Redemption, the gracious goodness of God provides. And as our mortal life is only free and self-possessed when we live in light and air, our spiritual life is only free and self-possessed when we live in the truth and love of God.

But that we may be able to abide in the truth, the grace, and the love of God, and to abide in these life-giving gifts with constancy, God has given us the grace of patience, that by forming it into a virtue we may abide in these gifts with stability, and so hold possession of ourselves. By patience we hold our soul in the grace, truth, and love of God. By patience we resist and repel the invasions of error, of passion, of temptation, and of vice. By patience the will commands and rules the powers of the soul and the fascinating sensibilities of the body. Patience is the possession of the soul, enabling the will to keep the soul in peace, and to regulate her actions and desires by the light of truth and justice, with a constant view to her final end. But only those who have a great love of God can have great patience. It is in vain to seek this invincible virtue for our interior regulation outside of charity. Even the pagans, with eyes too blind to see the true God, could discover that patience was the Christian's strength; and when the Emperor Titus condemned the Holy Bishop Ignatius of Antioch to torments and death, he exclaimed: "There is no people who endure so much for their God as these Christians". They endured much for God because they possessed their souls in God. Impatience is the beginning of every movement that takes away the soul from God, and so from her self-possession. For every evil begins by yielding to some irritation, provocation, or seduction that breaks into the fence of patience, which guards the good and peace of the soul; and so the way is opened for the soul to wander away from the light of truth into the delusions of the imagination, from the law of justice into the base ways of sensuality, from peace of conscience into the whirlpools of passion, and from the love of God into the saddening pits of self-love. Patience is the fence of the soul; and within the fence of patience the whole choir of the virtues flow in harmony and peace, and unite in the praise of God. But impatience is the destroyer of that securing fence.

St. Gregory may be here invited to assist our explanation. "The soul," he says, "holds possession of herself by patience, because patience is the root and guardian of the virtues. In learning to govern ourselves, we begin to possess that very thing which we are. This patience must not be looked for in any visible display, but in the heart. But by the vice of impatience even that light of learning is dissipated by which the virtues are nourished; for, as it is written in the Proverbs, 'The learning of a man is known by his patience'."[1] We know, then, that when a man is less patient he is less instructed. Solomon has also taught us to what a height this virtue should be carried, where he says: 'The patient man is better than the valiant, and he that governs his spirit than he that taketh cities'. [2] A victory over cities is the less of the two, because it only brings into subjection what is outside of us. There is a great deal more of victory in the patience that conquers one's self, because when the soul establishes herself in humble endurance, she commands herself, and is the subject of her own will."

The great Doctor of morals then proceeds to illustrate his teaching by the example of Abbot Stephen, who had governed a monastery close to Rieti, and whose life and death were well remembered and much talked of in his time. Of rude speech b'it learned life, this holy man despised all things here below for th' love of Heaven, and would have nothing in the world of his own, but gave himself to long and frequent prayer. The lov': of patience grew to such a vehemence in his soul, thct he looked upon any one who gave him trouble as his friend. Contumelies he repaid with thanks; and if any one injured him in his deep poverty, he reckoned it among his gains. He welcomed every adversary as a helper to his soul. When the day of his death drew on, numbers of people hastened to him, hoping to commend themselves to that holy soul before it quitted the body. Some with their mortal eyes saw angels visit him but dared not speak; others saw nothing. But such a fear came over all that, they dared not remain to interfere with his recollection at the peaceful hour of his departure. [3]

But the law of patience is one thing, the practice is another. God gives the law and the grace to fulfil the law; the exercise depends on the resolution of the will. He who commands us to love God above all things commands us to possess our souls in patience, that we may be in a condition to love God above all things. And as it is the work of patience to establish the soul in order, unity, and peace, it needs little reflection to understand that such a state of soul can only be acquired by observing certain rules and following certain methods of self-discipline. In this respect virtue is a certain art that calls for the judicious regulation of our powers. Those who are trained to exhibit their physical prowess with a view to victory have to abstain from many things, to command their temper amidst the greatest provocations, and to go through severe exertions regulated by fixed rules; and St. Paul has more than once brought forward this example to illustrate the spiritual combat with ourselves. It is an arduous struggle in which everything depends on self-denial, self-command, and well-directed efforts, according to the rules delivered by the saints. The prize is our present well-being and eternal happiness.

But when we come to examine individual souls, many who have the grace of patience have no method worth speaking of for its exercise. To speak plainly, they strive at random, a sure sign of habitual impatience. Their patience is little better than a vague sentiment hanging loosely in their souls, and is easily blown aside by the breath of provocation or temptation. Some will tell you that they never can follow any definite rule, but do their best in their own fashion. If they have a way, they must have some sort of rule; but this commonly means that they have but little knowledge of what real patience is, or of what it is able to do for the soul. Let them adopt but one rule and do their best to follow it, and they will soon feel the want of more. It is lamentable to see how many souls there are desiring the better things of virtue, who yet never put themselves under effective regulations for obtaining them. There can be no great progress in any virtue without progress in patience. But these good people, so good in desire, waste their lives in a romance of unshaped wishes instead of striving by rule for the solid realities of virtue.

There must be light before there can be reasonable action; and therefore certain principles should be fixed as lights in the mind to enlighten and animate the will in the regulation of its conduct. We shall first give the principles and then the rules of patience.

**FIRST PRINCIPLE**—There is an order in patience which is the same for all persons, because all souls are made alike, and all have the same nature to overcome, and that order gives the rules for its exercise. It is a primary truth that human nature is weak and irritable, and that it has become much weaker in its moral powers through sin; but patience is the virtue that strengthens this weakness. How does it strengthen us? What is weak is made strong by being united with what is strong. As the body cannot put forth its energies unless it have a firm ground on which to rest and from which to put forth its powers, neither can the soul put forth her powers of virtue without a firm foundation on which to repose and from which to act. Without such a foundation of repose the soul is restless, unquiet, and changeable. It is revealed to us that God is our patience and our fortitude ; He is the firm, immovable, and unchangeable patience, on whom resting we shall not be moved. It is therefore the first and essential rule of patience to adhere with constancy to God, and to rest ourselves upon His divine and unchangeable strength for our foundation. Another great reason for adhering to God is that we may receive from His goodness the grace that breathes strength into our nature. "The Lord is my firmament, my refuge, and my deliverer,"[4] sings the Psalmist. And again: "I have lifted up my eyes to the mountains, from whence help shall come to me. My help is from the Lord, who made Heaven and earth. May He not suffer thy foot to be moved."[5]

**SECOND PRINCIPLE**—The will is the spring and originator of all our free and responsible actions. The action of all the other powers, even that of the mind, depends upon the action of the will, which is the prime mover of all. It must therefore be remembered that the patience of the other powers, and of the whole soul, depends on the patience of the will. But, as we have already explained in a previous lecture, the will has two kinds of action ; it either puts forth its action to what it desires, or refuses to put forth its action to what it does not desire, and therefore concentrates that action within. For example, the will puts forth the hand to receive something that is good or useful, or turns the mind to some beautiful truth, or puts forth the affections to something worthy of affection. But the will gathers up its strength within when it refuses to act in any evil or disorderly direction. For example, when it refuses the eye to temptation, or to give the affections to what is unworthy of them. It was the will of Eve that touched the forbidden tree and plucked the forbidden fruit. Had she kept her will in her own power, she would have kept her patience, and therefore kept her will at one with the will of God.

But that movement of the will by which it refuses to enter into irritation, provocation, or temptation, and refrains itself from them, is the principal sphere of patience. By patience also the will refuses to enter into sadness, that miserable slough, which is nothing but the dregs of defeated self-love.

On its more active side patience sustains the will from wavering in its good purposes, so that its good actions may be calm, reasonable, resolute, and complete; neither distracted on the one hand, nor weak through hastiness or irritability on the other. This is the type of patience which we see in our Blessed Lord, and by imitation in His saints. At this we have to aim; and though we may have many failures before gaining habitual steadiness, patience comes in here to endure those failures, and to turn them into useful lessons.

**THIRD PRINCIPLE**—It will greatly help us in managing our interior if we clearly understand and keep in view that our spiritual faculties have two sides, a superior and an inferior side, or we may call them an interior and an exterior side, in virtue of which they look in opposite directions. All our spiritual faculties are united in the essence of the soul, and meet in the will, where the light of God illuminates them, and His grace strengthens them. On their superior or interior side, therefore, they look towards God. The more, therefore, we are recollected interiorly, the more we can look towards God, and be united within ourselves through His light and grace. But on their inferior or exterior side our powers divide like the fingers of the hand to their exterior offices, and communicate with the body, with its senses, appetites, and passions, and through them with the exterior world. But in communicating with them, our spiritual powers communicate with the weakness of the unregenerated body, through which the temptations of the world, the devil, and the flesh are apt to irritate, trouble, and pervert the powers of the soul, to weaken her spiritual force and defile her.

The chief, then, or superior side of the Christian soul is rooted and grounded in the light, grace, and strength of God. But the exterior or inferior side of our powers is expanded like the branches of a tree into manifold communication with the sensual body and the sensible world. But as the sap and life of the tree spring from the root which is hidden and nourished in the ground, so the soul, having her spiritual root in God, is by Him nourished with life. The more, therefore, the spiritual powers are opened and concentrated on their interior side upon God, be it mind, will, or desire, the more they receive of that divine light and grace which ground the soul in fortitude and patience, and the more able is the will to resist the incursions of evil.

We may strengthen this exposition by the words of Albert the Great in his explanation of the fortitude and maturity of the soul.

"True and perfect fortitude," he says, "consists in the internal government of the soul; so that whenever she is tempted to pride, envy, vainglory, self-complacency, or sensual delight, the mind withdraws its attention and the will its consent. The office of this virtue is to strengthen the understanding in the knowledge of God, and the affections in the love of God, and, consequently, of our neighbour. When the soul is thus fortified, she neither fears adversity nor is softened into weakness by prosperity."[6]

Showing again how patience and fortitude are brought to maturity, the same great religious thinker says: "That true and perfect maturity of soul consists in collecting the forces and affections of the soul upon God with a unanimous recollection. By this means the soul is kept from vanity, and the five senses are held aloof from intruding their allurements upon the soul. But when the soul recoils from this blessed union with God, she is caught in the net of vanity; for, as Ecclesiasticus says, 'all things that are under Heaven are vanity'."[7]

This collecting of the spiritual powers on the centre of the soul looking towards God, and obtaining the sense of God, is properly called recollection. It is founded in prayer, and carried by patience from prayer into the active duties of life. But so far from interfering with those duties, it gives a mental clearness, a prudence, and a force that render those duties most efficient.

**FOURTH PRINCIPLE**—As the strength of Christian patience is the gift of God, and the virtue results from our industrious exercise of that strength, it is essential that it should be united with humility. First, because without humility we cannot be subject to God so as to receive from Him the strengthening gift of patience. Secondly, because God gives His grace to the humble, and not to the proud. Thirdly, because without humility we shall trust to some imaginary strength of our own, and so be deceived. For the proud are hollow-souled, and, whilst making an exterior show of self-possession that is altogether fictitious, are inwardly restless, irritable, and impatient.

The Fathers teach from their great experience that humility and recollection are essential to patience. St. Gregory calls patience the humility of endurance; St. Ambrose gives patience as the evident sign of the presence of true humility. Abbot Piomon says in the Conferences: "True patience and tranquillity are neither obtained nor preserved without deep humility of heart".[8] St. Bernard says: "We must always hold that humility is the guardian of purity and the mother of patience".[9] St. Francis of Assissium proclaims that "where patience is, there is humility; there is neither anger nor perturbation".[10] And St. Bonaventure teaches that "the patience which ordains the soul to eternal life is born of charity and humility".[11] We might quote many other authorities, but these will suffice to fix this important principle in the mind.

**FIFTH PRINCIPLE**—The last principle to be inserted in the mind is of equal importance with those already set forth. Every virtue is perfect in proportion to its patience; every act we do, whether interiorly or exteriorly, be it act of mind or act of will, is perfect in proportion to its patience, and every work we accomplish is perfect in proportion to the patience we put into it. "Patience hath a perfect work," says St. James, "that we may be perfect and entire, failing in nothing."[12] But, as St. Zeno observes, patience is chiefly concerned in perfecting the virtues. It perfects both the workman and the work. Nature is hasty and inclined to hurry; light and grace, like their Divine Author, are calm and deliberate.

The temperaments of constitutions are different. some are quicker and some slower; but we should never run before our light, or we shall be left to our natural obscurity; nor should we hurry on before the movements of grace, under penalty of being carried away by self-will into rashness and imprudence. In other words, in whatever we say or do, we must not lose our self-possession. We must not let the busy imagination carry off our attention and desires from our present work and present duty. If we do, we fall into an impatience that confuses the mind, troubles the will, injures our tranquillity, and blemishes the work in hand. With our Christian light, we ought never to be the victims of that delusion, so common in the world, that only things of a certain visible bulk, show, and dignity are worthy of patient care and solicitude. For the perfection of the workman is far more important than the perfection of the work. The greatest thing for us is the perfection of our own soul; and the Saints teach us that this perfection consists in doing our ordinary actions well. But we do them well when we do them patiently and lovingly, a method which, though at first laborious, with custom becomes delightful.

To put the whole relation of patience with charity theologically, it is not the habit or exercise of patience alone that gives perfection to our actions, but it is patience proceeding from charity, and working in the spirit and abundance of charity. In short, it is charity bearing all things and enduring all things. All aversions that have impatience or passion in them are contrary to the love of God, and the patience of charity casts them off by refusing to entertain them. Sufferings have to be endured for the love of God, but it is the patience of charity that endures them. We have to perfect our ordinary actions for the love of God, that we may be perfect in our human way before our Heavenly Father, as He is most perfect in His divine way. But it is the patience of charity that makes our actions perfect.

**FIRST RULE**—The first rule for acquiring this virtue is to hold its value in great estimation, and to have a great desire of it. This desire will be best entertained by reflection and meditation on its inestimable value, both for removing evil and obtaining good. It is for this reason that we have enlarged so much upon its indispensable necessity for the perfecting of charity, and for making real progress in perfection of life. The mere reading of a book will do little, however, towards generating this desire, unless its truths be well digested by reflection and assisted by prayer. Another great help to this desire will be to observe how much we fail from our best intentions and best endeavours after the virtues, solely because of our want of patience. A virtue so precious can only be perfected by sustained and vigorous efforts, and these come of earnest desires and strong motives.

**SECOND RULE**—The second rule is to begin the exercise of patience with our own interior, and to direct our chief attention to the controlling of our interior powers. For this virtue must be strong at home before it can be strong abroad. By its very nature, as resting on the internal strength of the will, it can only proceed from the interior to the exterior. The whole secret of it lies in the government of the will: if the will is patient the whole man will be patient. This is what spiritual writers call the custody of the heart, and what St. Ambrose calls the temperance of the heart. The heart is the seat of the affections and the organ of the will. So long as the tremulous heart is kept in the custody of the will, and is recollected in the sense of God, outward provocations will have no power over it, whether they come from the irritation of the senses or from external troubles. In a word, by the heart the Sacred Scriptures signify the interior and central spirit of life, which looks to God and adheres to God.

The Proverbs says: "With all watchfulness keep thy heart, because life issues out from it".[13] Upon this custody of the heart the Psalmist never ceases his song. It would be tedious to crowd these pages with references; but whoever is familiar with the sacred psalmody will remember that God is there represented as watching the heart of man. And the heart of the just man watches unto God. He maketh the heart of each one separately. That is, God maketh the good which every single heart possesses. He is also called the God of my heart and my portion for eternity. His law is in the middle of the heart; and they who return to the heart return to God. He says to each one: "My child, give me thy heart"; and when it is given to Him He speaks to the heart, enlightens the heart, searches the heart, proves the heart, heals the contrite of heart, and saves the humble and just of heart. The meditation of the heart is in His sight: the hope of the heart is set upon Him: the prayer of the heart ascends before Him, like incense in His sight: and the sighs of the heart go up to Him, seeking His mercy and His love.

The just man under trials is exhorted to expect the Lord, to do manfully, to let his heart take courage, and await with patience the coming of the Lord. When prepared to hope in the Lord, his heart is strengthened, and shall not be moved until his enemies are vanquished. In meditating with the heart the fire of love is enkindled, the heart is liquified, faints from itself and flows unto God, and exults in the living God. Then is the heart disposed to make ascensions, until the God of gods is seen in Sion.

But all this exercising of the heart under the custody of the will is the movement of life towards life, and is the work of that interior and fundamental patience of charity, with which our central life adheres to God, and protects the divine good within the soul from the disturbing intrusions and burglarious thefts that are perpetrated by anger, concupiscence, or sadness. The more the heart is recollected in God, the more sensitive will it become to the least intrusion of things tending to disturb its peace, and the more firm in refusing them an entrance within the soul, whether they come in movements of irascibility or of inordinate desire; so that by gathering up the will, that inordinate movement may drop defeated for want of entertainment.

**THIRD RULE**—The surest test of the custody of the heart will be found in the government of the tongue. Let thought go before speech, not speech before thought. This is an admirable discipline of patience. For that small member the tongue, full of nerve and sensibility, is rooted close to the brain, the magazine of our animal sensibilities, fancies, and passions, and is as touchy and inflammable as a magazine of powder. It is therefore quickly set on fire by the inferior instincts, sensibilities and passions, before reflection and judgment intervene with their control. For unless by patient watchfulness the animal man is kept under the strict control of the superior man, under its restless and misguided influences the tongue will break out into all sorts of irritabilities, vanities, and follies. It is by the patience of recollection that the will restrains those blind, vicious, and silly emotions that become acts through the ready pliancy of the tongue. Quick are the motions of fancy and sensibility, quick through the electric sympathy awakened by the tolling of other tongues, and rapidly they find expression, making revelations of the vanities within. Where the soul is undisciplined by watchful patience, the mind in conversation is soon thrown off its guard; the emotions that start before reason or judgment get the ascendency, and the will becomes involved in vanities, irascibilities, detractions, and scandals.

Hence St. James compares the ungoverned tongue to a fire that once enkindled makes a great conflagration. It catches one inflammable material after another that lurk within the speaker, sets his neighbour's house on fire, and the contagion spreads from tongue to tongue in exaggerations far and wide. Not satisfied with this figure to express so great an evil, the Apostle says again: "It inflameth the wheel of our nativity". He compares the tongue to that birth in evil that like a wheel whirls away the man from God; for a restless tongue, like a rapid wheel, whirls him anew into the evil from which he has been regenerated by a better birth. Again he calls the tongue "an unquiet evil". It is the great disturber of our peace, and of the peace of other souls. But the remedy of unquietness is patience. Observe the careful method of St. James. First he lays down the principle that "patience hath a perfect work". Next he gives the test of this principle in the government of the tongue. "If any man offend not in word, the same is a perfect man. He is able also with a bridle to lead about the whole body."[14] The bridle is the instrument of restraint; it figures the restraining power of patience. The man who can bridle his tongue with patient charity can govern his whole person.

Silence is strength, and the proverb calls it golden. Much talkativeness is the sign of a feeble mind, and an undisciplined will. Stobaeus tells us that when that acutest of philosophers, Aristotle, was asked the question: What is the most difficult thing for a man to master? he replied: To keep silence on things on which it is best to be silent. St. James says that no man can tame the unquiet tongue. He thus leaves us to Solomon's conclusion: "It is the part of man to prepare the soul, and for the Lord to govern the tongue"[15]. Man prepares his soul by subjection to God; God gives the grace of patience by which the tongue is governed. "Be thou, O my soul, subject to God: for from Him is my patience."

The tree is known by its fruits, and man by his speech. Hence the saying of the ancients: Speak that I may know thee. Our Divine Lord has therefore given us this rule: "Out of the abundance of the heart the mouth speaketh. A good man out of a good treasure bringeth forth good things: and an evil man out of an evil treasure bringeth forth evil things. But I say unto you, that every idle word that men shall speak, they shall render an account of in the day of judgment."[16] From this it follows that the evil tongue comes from evil dispositions, and consequently that the watch over the tongue should be directed to the heart. A light, foolish tongue, careless of another's feelings, is the proof of levity in the heart. A vain, conceited, boasting tongue is the sign of a vain heart. A flattering tongue betrays the spirit of hypocrisy. An impatient, irritating tongue is the sure token of an intemperate heart. A calm, sincere, and prudent tongue is the clear indication of a heart that is patient from self-discipline.

**FOURTH RULE**—The fourth rule of patience is to keep all things in their just and due order. That order should first appear in our own interior and our interior exercises; next in our exterior and our exterior duties; then in our personal surroundings. Justice is another name for moral order, that order which God has established in His laws. Hence the proverb that order is Heaven's first law. All the virtues are the servants of justice, that is, of order. The soul says of Christ in the Canticles: "He hath set charity in order within me"[17]. There is no beginning of order in the soul without charity, which orders the soul towards her final end. Every other kind of order is subordinate to this first principle of order. Where charity is begun, observes St. Augustine, order is begun; the perfection of charity is the perfection of order. But charity is perfect when all the affections are in their due order and subordination to the love of God. The object of patience is to keep the soul from disorder and her acts from disorder; and of that external order which reflects internal order, St. Paul says: "Let all things be done decently and according to order"[18].

Order, again, is that primal law by which God regulates His works, adjusts them to one another, establishes harmony among them, and makes them good, useful, beautiful, strong in their kind, and suited to their ends. Order is therefore the perfection of the creature. The type of all order is in the mind of God; and God has placed a law of order in the mind of man, following which he may perfect himself, and whatever depends on his will. If he neglects this law of order, he is weak, confused, and less happy, or altogether at discomfort; because disorder is always feeble, always irritating, even though it reach not the deformity of sin.

"Order is defective," observes St. Augustine, "when there is less of order than there ought to be; for when order is not where it ought to be, and in the manner in which it ought to be, there is still disorder. Where there is some order there is some good, but where there is no order there is no good."[19] The absence of all order belongs to that land of darkness and misery, where, says holy Job, "is the shadow of death, and no order, but everlasting horror dwelleth"[20].

To quote St. Bonaventure: "The soul that is wisely disciplined should observe a well-regulated order everywhere and in all things. To the well-regulated mind the beauty of order is not only most becoming but delightful. To be careless about the order of external things is the sign of an ill-regulated mind."[21] What patience is to our individual actions, order is to the whole chain and succession of our actions, giving them their completeness, perfection, and as much merit as they are capable of receiving. But who does not know that to keep to this good order is the work of patience? To lose patience is the beginning of disorder. True order is the result of that disciplined thought and deliberate self-control in which patience is the chief and the ruling element.

It takes a great deal of patience to keep our own interior in order, and not a little of that virtue to do everything in its proper place and time, and in the best way of which we are capable. Some persons have a natural love of seeing everything well-disposed around them; but if anything becomes deranged, their fretting shows that they have not the same love for internal order. They love exterior more than interior beauty, and take a pride in it, as something that may give them credit in their neighbours' eyes. The true order of the interior man is to ascend from sensible to spiritual things, and, when engaged in external duties and affairs, still to keep an internal hold of those spiritual lights and motives that give value to his external works. The due ordering of the interior soul is to keep her centre recollected in God, and so to use her powers and her corporal members that they may be the instruments for the performance of her duties. She ought never to throw out the central soul upon anything, that there may be no departure from the basis of her strength. If we lose that calm and collected centre for a time, it must be recovered as soon as possible. For when the will is united with the light and will of God it becomes easy, with a little patience, to restore order everywhere else. A good interior order will produce a good exterior order, for when the will is well regulated it can regulate everything else well.

Of exterior order the most beautiful examples are to be found in the Church of God, where a divine order of things is externally expressed under the guidance of the Holy Spirit. Much the same may be said of the well-regulated condition of religious houses, when they reflect the rule in the lives of their inmates. Such external order is very helpful to interior order, because it engages the senses on the side of order and law. The same may be said in its degree of every other kind of external order.

**FIFTH RULE**—The fifth rule is to bear patiently with those whose tempers are infirm, and to endure their tempers with charitable kindness. This rule is given us by St. Paul: "Now we that are stronger ought to bear the infirmities of the weak, and not to please ourselves. Let every one of you please his neighbour unto good, to edification. For Christ did not please Himself, but as it is written: 'The reproaches of them that reproach thee fell upon Me.'"[22]

It is shrewdly remarked by Cassian that weak spirits are quick to imagine wrongs, and prompt to inflict insults and injuries, whilst never suspecting that they are themselves in fault. Having but little knowledge of themselves, they use the licence of offence without misgiving, yet cannot endure the least rebuke themselves. Their irritability and impatience is like a painful malady, which gives them great disturbance, the cause of which they cannot see. It never enters their mind that in charging their sufferings to their neighbours they make themselves a pitiable spectacle. Yet, not unconscious of the pain they inflict, they mistake their weak complainings for a kind of power over others, careless of self-respect, careless of charity.

Such infirm spirits are the victims of sadness, and have need to be borne with in great patience, prudence, and charity, like the sick in body or mind. To retort upon them would be to mistake their case and increase the infirmity. To avoid them would be to abandon charity, and to forfeit a gain to one's own soul, because they offer an opportunity to the virtues of patience, charity, and self-conquest. It will not do to answer them in words of affected gentleness, which instead of appeasing will only enkindle a greater conflagration. Nor will it do to let them know that you look upon them with compassion, and bear with them patiently: this would be to assert a superiority provocative of indignation. But in your heart keep patience and in your voice cheerfulness, and let your words be prudent, few, and kind. Think not of your own, but of what may be profitable to that infirm spirit. Remember how that heart is suffering in secret, and will suffer more when the excitement has passed away. So shall you reap the fruits of patience in charity, and help to heal that suffering soul. Saints have sought to be the servants of such irritable souls with a view to their self-discipline and perfection, and have finally brought them to meekness and peace.

When we are associated with the sick or infirm of body, their sufferings and complaints awaken no bitterness in us; we know that we are liable to the like infirmities. Hence we have a tender and charitable care of those who are thus afflicted. Why, then, should we be irritated with weak and infirm souls, unless we wish to catch the contagion of their infirmity? The needs of their condition call for charity. God endures them; and they suffer from their infirmity. If in His mercy He has given to us a greater self-control, the gratitude of our patience requires that we should endure what we cannot cure; and whilst bearing the trial we should ask Him to heal what is beyond our remedies.

**SIXTH RULE**—The sixth rule is to manage our own infirmities of temper wisely. The provocation may arise within ourselves, or may come from the voice or conduct of another. Whichever it may be, the true cause of evil temper is always in one's self. It arises from want of control over our inferior nature, that is to say, over our imagination and sensuous emotions. The imagination, moved by self-love, generates fears and suspicions of wrong or of humiliation that are hateful to our pride; the untamed blood swells into excitement, the nerves become agitated, and self-love adds its sting; then our reason becomes clouded, the folly of the sensual man is predominant, and passion has its sway. Anger is a brutish thing, and has been rightly called a transient insanity. It corrects nothing, it protects nothing, it accomplishes nothing but disorder and evil.

Quick temper has a double sting: it stings the heart and stings the tongue. It suffers a double loss—loss of sense and loss of peace. Just and deserved rebuke moves from right reason with authority to correct pride and persistent disobedience or wrong. But anger moves from offended self-love, in which our own deluded imagination is commonly the chief offender. When another is the real offender, not anger but patience is our true protector.

One who is habitually recollected in God cannot easily be moved to anger. Resting the soul on her divine foundation, he enjoys a peace which makes the soul quickly sensible of the first movements of disturbance, and quick to turn from them, so that they cannot take hold of the superior soul. But in less recollected souls the true method of self-management is this: the moment that irritation and disturbance are felt to rise up in the inferior or animal nature, let the mind turn to God and the will follow the mind: you will then keep your soul in your own possession, and that brutal commotion, left to itself, will sink and die for want of encouragement. You may then look upon it, and even suffer it to appear again, and see by the light in your mind what a contemptible thing it is, and how happy you are to be free from it. Thus by the habit of looking on your evil temper with contempt as a brutal weakness and a vile deformity, you will become the master of it.

The Psalmist gives this rule: "I was troubled, and I spoke not,"[23] which he thus expands in another place: "I said, I will take heed to my ways: that I sin not with my tongue. I have set a guard upon my mouth, when the sinner stood against me."[24] This guard is less the silence of the lips than the patience of the heart, until the will obtains the mastery. The power of the will over the movement of the senses is immense, provided we look to God, and dwell on some high motive on the first appearance of rising temper.

**SEVENTH RULE**—This rule of patience is given by St. Paul: "Be not overcome by evil, but overcome evil by good."[25]</h2> The evil that conquers our patience may come of our own ill-nature, fancying wrong where it does not exist, or from brooding in melancholy self-discontent, a base feeling that makes us displeased with every one and everything around us; or it may come of actual provocation or wrong inflicted; or, what is most common, of wrong imagined to have been inflicted upon us. In any of these cases the first thing is to recover our temper and good spirits, and return to charity. The second is to be kind and generous, whether we have only injured ourselves or another has injured us—to overcome evil by good.

There are no worse evils than sadness and melancholy, because they reject the cure of every other evil. Sadness is a malady that unhinges the spirit, contracts the heart, and brings down the powers of the soul into the caverns of self-love, where their light is obscured, and the virtues are buried in sensuous slime. A dark shadow hangs over the mind, and in that shadow self-love paints melancholy images of herself, that flatter her as if she were some great victim of wrong. The will is chained a captive to this self-love, and the soul is unnerved by illusions that exhale from the malignant humours thrown up from the oppressed and saddened spirit of wounded and defeated pride.

But it is amazing with what a little effort this illusion may be dissolved. It seems to be an immense, unconquerable, immovable nightmare seated on the soul. But when the eyes open the nightmare melts away. It requires but an effort of the awakened will to disperse the whole illusion; and the Poet of the Spleen has found a re-echo from the common sense of mankind to his famous sentence: "Throw but a stone, the giant dies". Some little effort to expand the contracted heart will dissolve the spell. The malady consists in the collapse of the powers upon the bitter ground of egotism and self-love: the cure is effected by breaking out of that corrosive shell in which the spirit has become enclosed, just as a puncture draws off the humours of a dropsy. The first effort may be little more than mechanical, still it is an effort of the will, and, followed up, will soon become an act of reviving charity. A smile, a kind look, a gentle word will suffice to open the cloud, and admit a ray of light that will dispel the delusion, and show that it was but an idle dream of mischievous self-love.

When we are exposed to provocation or offence, then is the time to hold back the will with firmness until we are sure of our self-possession, and that we can proceed untouched by the fire of anger. The Proverb of Solomon gives us the plainest language on the subject: "A fool immediately showeth anger: but he that dissembleth injuries is wise"[26]. When another contradicts you or exhibits resentment, it is time to remember the apostolic admonition: "Give place unto wrath,"[27] the sense of which is explained in the Proverb: "A mild answer breaketh wrath: but a harsh word stirreth up fury"[28]. To reason with anger is to show a light to the blind; it is taken for reproach, and will only increase irritation. But mild looks and gentle words subdue the fire of wrath as with a spiritual charm, and will save us from catching the contagion. If you can follow this up with benefits you will overcome evil with good. In mastering yourself you will master evil as well.

**EIGHTH RULE**—The eighth rule of patience is to bear your internal trials, crosses, and aridities with peace and resignation. These are far more trying than external tribulations, because of the fears which they awaken respecting our eternal interests; as also on account of the sadness which they will give rise to, if not borne with patience, and which, if it does arise, will greatly unnerve the soul, and impede, if not injure, the spirit of prayer. Few souls, when under trial, take sufficient account of the injury they do themselves by those disquieting fears and that disturbing sadness. Consider then how important it is to be patient when you are dealing with God Himself. When you are inwardly tried or made desolate, for the purification of your soul, the whole profit depends on your patience and resignation. You have to be patient with God, who is patient with you. But of this we shall speak at large when we come to the subject of patience in prayer.

**NINTH RULE**—The ninth rule of patience, and one of very great importance, is to bear patiently with one's own faults and failures. Faults call for regret, and sins for contrition and repentance. But they ought not to awaken the impatience of pride, or the fear of not being forgiven upon true repentance; for this is to mistrust the goodness of God, and to open the door to new faults and graver offences. Unless we bear our failings with patience they will lead us into numberless faults. It is extraordinary how many spiritual faults may be committed over one material fault. That one fault may be indeliberate and devoid of malice, but if it humiliates one's pride and vexes one's self-love, it will annoy us, make us impatient, disturb our peace, and thus lead us into a number of spiritual faults.

We either know something of our natural weakness or we do not. If we do not, it is time we learnt it, and our faults and failures will be our instructors if we can only bear them patiently. But if we do know something of ourselves, we ought not to be surprised, and still less disturbed, when we fail, but should ascribe it to our having trusted too much in ourselves.

But if instead of being humbled and corrected by our failures, we turn them into temptations, and nurse our offended self-love upon them, these accidental failures will be turned into positive offences through the spiritual disorder to which they give occasion. We thus put the soul into a disturbance and disorder that never came of the original fault, but of the trouble of self-love. To be patient with one's self after a fault is to keep in the right disposition to correct and repair it. To lose patience over a fault is to part with the remedy by which it can be repaired. There are moments when we cannot bear the recollection of a self long past. Who has not experienced those quick flashes of mortified pride at the sudden recollection of some long-past act of indiscretion or folly? They reveal what lurks hidden and untamed in the soul.

If through weakness of nature or wandering of mind our self-possession is lost for a time, a sense of privation and discomfort begins to be felt, and then patience must be called upon to recover us to recollection. Yet it is not by turning upon one's self, not by dwelling upon one's failures, as they are displeasing to self-love, not by indulging impatience that any failing can be cured, but by turning to God, who is patient with us, who knows our frame, who remembers that we are dust, who is compassionate of our weaknesses, and has mercy on our follies: it is by turning to Him as a child to a father, simply, and without prudery, that we find the medicine that our weakness requires: "Be thou, O my soul, subject to God, for from Him is my patience".

**TENTH RULE**—The last rule is that of the perfect, who find a cheering joy in trials, contradictions, and sufferings; not only because they are great helps for advancing towards God upon the groundworks of humility and patience, but because they can find nothing more conducive to detachment from all that is not God, nothing more effective in subduing their nature to the reign of grace. They delight in bearing upon them the marks of Christ crucified, in carrying their cross after Him, in suffering with Him, for the exceeding love of God. St. Paul rejoiced in all his tribulations, and gloried in nothing save Jesus Christ crucified. St. Francis found the perfection of holy joy in contempt and humiliations. These are but examples of the ways of the Saints. But this is a degree of fortitude more than human, a singular gift of the Holy Ghost, by which the superior will is so closely united with God as to remove all repugnance to suffering; and that hallowed will embraces things that are even contrary to nature with a cheerfulness to which the sensuality of nature can make no effectual opposition, even though they come suddenly and without preparation.

# 7

## ON PATIENCE AS THE PERFECTER OF OUR DAILY DUTIES

"That on good ground are they who in a good and very good heart, hearing the word, keep it, and bring forth fruit in patience."—S. Luke viii. 15.

That perfection of life consists in doing our ordinary actions well is one of the wisest maxims of the Saints. Those duties make up the chief sum of our lives during the time allotted to us in this world. As we owe our life and time to God, the good Christian has duties at all hours; even the time which is properly given to recreation and health-bestowing repose requires to be regulated by the virtues, and therefore comes under the name of duty; and that all the more, because it is the time most exposed to insidious temptations. It is seldom that we are called upon to do great actions or to endure great sufferings; but when the hour arrives for them we shall be able to go through them in a great and generous spirit in proportion to the perfection with which we perform our daily duties.

The perfection of our ordinary actions depends on high motives, good will, and cheerful patience. High motives give them their value before God; good will makes them vigorous; cheerful patience makes them orderly, peaceful, effective, and pleasant. For what gives our actions their value before God is not their visible magnitude, their publicity, or brilliancy, but the purity and elevation of their motives, and the generosity with which they follow the light and comply with the will of God. They are ennobled by the sacrifice of nature to grace. Hence the poor man who goes to his daily toils with good will and cheerful patience for the love of God is a much nobler person in the sight of God than the man who, from mere human motives, shines with splendid actions in the sight of the world. The one acts on a divine principle, the other on a human one; the one has his heart with God, the other with the world; the one has God for his friend, the other has the applause of men; the one may have a rude exterior, but is inwardly refined by converse with God and His Saints; the other may have the outward polish of social life, whilst his interior is a moral chaos.

The love of God dignifies the humblest work and the humblest workman. What a breadth and elevation belongs to the soul that can unite the lowest work that is done on this earth with the highest motive that reigns in Heaven! By His Incarnation and human life the Son of God has glorified the lowest things of human life and labour that are undertaken for God's sake. Labour thus motived has received a special dignity from the patient toils of the Son of God in the workshop of Joseph. How the humble things of God confound the proud judgments of the world! That pagan philosopher was not far wrong, who, when asked what God was doing, replied: "He is putting down high things, and lifting up low things," words that remind us of the whole tenor of the sublime Magnificat.

We may accept it as a principle that whatever we do is perfect in proportion to the self-possession with which we do it, and that self-possession is proportioned to patience. Let us first take the labours of the mind. St. Zeno observes, with great truth, that without patience we can neither learn nor teach. It will even compensate for certain deficiencies in the power of apprehension, and will greatly help the power of memory. Whether we learn from men, books, or things, it is the virtue of patience that steadies attention, and frees the mind from what interferes with or disturbs attention. Painstaking, in short, is patience. It is patience that gives to insight the ability to penetrate through the details of a subject to its principle. And this is the act of study, first to reach the principle of the subject through the details of its statement, and then by the light of the principle to understand the details, and hold them in the mind as they stand related to that principle. For to learn a subject thoroughly is to possess it in the mind in that order in which it exists, and to know it by the principles on which it depends. For it is the first principle of each subject that sheds light upon all the details that belong to it, and when that is possessed by the mind it is not difficult to understand and remember the whole. But without a good deal of patient attention it is impossible to ascend from details to their principle, and so carry the light of that principle throughout the details.

Understanding is proportioned to attention and reflection; memory is equally proportioned to attention and reflection. In his celebrated treatise on man, Buffon insists that patience is the foundation of genius. Some undiscovered truth looms obscurely and as from a distance on the mind. Thus far it is little better than a vague and indistinct conjecture; the mind looks and looks, waits and waits, in patient expectation of more light. At last light suddenly flashes on the understanding, and your pen cannot go fast enough to record the discovery. We should rather say with Plato that genius is an original power of apprehension, and that patience is the discipline in virtue of which that power of apprehension obtains its success. Sir Isaac Newton ascribed his success in discovery to the protracted patience which enabled him to think longer on a subject than other men had done. When asked by what means he had arrived at his discoveries, he replied: "I keep the subject constantly before me, and wait till the first dawning opens slowly, by little and little, into a full and clear light". Again, in a letter to Dr. Bentley, he says: "If I have done the public any service in this way, it is due to nothing but industry and patient thought".

The greatest defect in modern teachers of science even in our own schools is the neglect to teach their pupils the right use of their faculties. This was done in the college where the writer was trained some sixty years ago by occasional visits of professors to the students in their rooms, when both logical and moral methods were explained in a kindly way and adapted to each one's capacity and progress. Such kindly visits were always an enjoyable relief as well as a friendly help.

The patience required of a good teacher is proverbial. Such a teacher requires a double patience—patience with his pupils and patience with himself. Unless he have patience with his pupils he will never get at the measure of their capacity or attainments—will never put them at their ease, secure their attention, or control their restlessness. He must have patience above all with dull and irresponsive heads, leading them step by step as far as they can go, and not expecting from them what is beyond their power. He must also remember that where their will is good they often suffer much from the consciousness of their deficiencies and require encouragement rather than further humiliation. But when pride accompanies superior intelligence, it is apt to be unjustly harsh and discouraging. The quick-witted oftener require the bridle than the spur to save them from overrunning their subject or turning their minds into devious paths.

Unless the teacher have patience with himself he will be unable to secure the respectful attention of his pupils, and will commit notable errors against method in his teaching. He must keep back much of his knowledge and not let it come before its time, that is, when his hearers are prepared for its reception. Knowledge communicated before it can be knitted into the knowledge already possessed perplexes and confuses the mind and gives occasion to discouragement. Hence great thinkers are seldom well suited to teach the elements of knowledge, their own last thoughts occupying them much more than the first thoughts of their pupils.

Both kinds of patience are essential to sound judgment in teaching. A cheerful patience conciliates attention and awakens interest; a kind and genial patience inspires affectionate confidence, and is the best means of securing a loving and industrious response to the labours of the teacher. Young people are quick to discern where strength of will is covered by a kind and sympathetic interest in their progress; and on both sides attention and painstaking are proportioned to the kindly patience which the teacher possesses and inspires. In those higher branches of study, where abstruse science is concerned, the true professor will not confine himself to his lectures, but will take a kindly interest in each one's progress, and give him those private helps which may enable him to use his mind to the best advantage. It is wonderful how much a slow mind may be encouraged by such help and sympathy.

In every occupation and pursuit success depends on taking pains. But painstaking is only another word for patient and persevering industry, which always costs more or less of pain to our nature. This pain arises from the restraint imposed upon the restless senses, from the resistance that attention gives to the tendency of the mind to wander, and from the fatigue resulting from the tension of the nerves and faculties after a certain length of time. Whatever may be the aptitude for any special pursuit—be it study, art, teaching, management, government, or manual work of whatever kind—the chief moral ingredient of painstaking is patience. It may therefore be taken as a maxim that every work is perfect in proportion to the amount of patience put into it. Here we have all the difference in art between mechanical and manual productions. Beyond the original design of the inventor, what is produced by machinery is as dead as the machine itself, whilst manual work vibrates with the life, mind, and imagination of the artist, and offers some expression of the loving patience given to the work. The one is a material, the other a moral production, and what delights us in the last is the expression which it conveys to us of mind, will, and feeling.

In his description of the virtue of patience, St. Bonaventure includes the willing and unconquerable endurance of labour with a view to the eternal glory. This implies the putting of the Christian virtues into our work in their due proportion to its character. Nothing, however trifling, can be done well without good judgment. There are fifty ways of doing anything, but only one perfect way. Judgment is an act both of mind and will—of mind considering, of will deciding what is best. But nothing is rightly judged where personal fancies or selfish feelings are allowed to mix in the consideration of it; they warp the judgment and confuse the object under consideration. Whether in work, in employments, in the management of affairs, in doing justice to others, or in the offices of kindness and charity, patience is required to secure sound judgment. Nature is always inclined to hurry, to run before judgment, and avoid the least pain of suspense. But grace is deliberate and conscious of responsibility, keeping down selfish feelings and excitements that deliberation may be just and prudent.

To work with judgment is to work with intelligence; but this implies thinking before acting, and delaying when needful, until the right way of acting is understood. To work fruitfully is to work with a patient will; fretful haste damages both the work and the workman. There is no healthy energy without endurance. Haste is waste; and there is much truth in the adage: "The more haste, the less speed". Lord Bacon gives the saying of a shrewd old man of business, who, whenever he saw any one in restless hurry over his work, interposed with the remark: "Wait a little; there is no time to lose." All good work bears upon it the impress of judgment, painstaking, and patience; and everything we do reacts upon our own moral character. What we do well is embalmed with the motives and virtues with which it is done; what we do poorly or reluctantly leaves us personally all the poorer.

Patience is especially needed where some knot or entanglement comes up in our work. For when we are in the swing and content of our employment, such interruptions are apt to worry and tease the mind, and put us out of time and temper. The very triviality of such unexpected impediments becomes a cause of annoyance, and will interrupt our calmness with irritation and impatience. It offends our self-complacency to be stopped by trifles in the full course of action, and calls for a little more patience than at the time we are willing to give. But let this be observed, that those rubs and teasing impediments are valuable moments for self-discipline, and that to use them well is no trifling thing. They who are patient with obstacles will be patient when the work runs smoothly. Such hindrances are in the nature of the work, and there is no reason for being offended with them, although many people, like unreasoning children, get angry over the innocent work when the fault is in themselves.

What has been said of work, whether mental or manual, is equally applicable to persons. Their interruptions, interferences, and meddlings are often trying to human nature, and require the patient management of the will to save us from inward perturbation. When unexpectedly interrupted in matters of gravity, or in which we are interested, we require no little patience to save us from being internally annoyed and vexed; and to be thus suddenly called off from one thing to another, or from one unfinished duty to another, is often trying to an undisciplined temper. There are few greater proofs of a well disciplined interior than to be able to break off at any time with cheerfulness from one duty and to turn with equal cheerfulness to another, however unexpected the interruption may be. It is an effect of that detachment of will that comes of patient charity.

The management of affairs embraces the prudent guidance both of persons and of things, so as to keep right order in things, and observe justice to all persons concerned in them. But to establish right order in things confused, and to keep right order in things that tend by their nature, or through human negligence, to disorder, demands much patience as well as judgment. Where affairs are complicated or obscure to the mind, owing to want of information, impatient haste will only augment the difficulty, and prudent delay will bring them sooner to an end; whilst consultation will greatly contribute to their elucidation. For when we have recourse to consultation, it is not only the light we obtain from others that helps us to see more clearly, but the greater light we elicit from our own minds, by speaking the subject out, than we are able to get from merely revolving it within the mind. Whenever the interests of others are mixed with our own, unless patience is there to withhold the mind from selfish motives and restrain the will from selfish emotions, justice can scarcely be fairly dealt to all concerned. The same interior rule will hold good in the distribution of kindness and attention to those who have claims on our encouragement; patience must withhold the will from all preoccupations, prejudices, and preferences of favouritism.

Lord Bacon has wisely said that "patience and grave hearing are essential to justice". When a superior has to deal with accusations or complaints, the first thing to be done is to put the mind in a judicial position, so as to hear the statements on both sides with a mind divested of all colour and bias, and thus take a purely objective view of the case until the matter is investigated and the facts are made clear. This is the patient charity of justice, which acts not from passion but from reason, and makes large allowances for human limitations and weaknesses where there is an absence of malice and scandal. For mercy should ever be exalted above judgment where the heart is submissive to authority.

That our offices of kindness and charity may have all their sweetness, beauty, and consolation, they must proceed with direct simplicity from the love of God in the heart. The love of God is the most earnest and practical of all things; and when it is devoted with sincerity to the service of our neighbours it places us in a sublime position that has more of Heaven than of earth in it; and the value of our kind actions is greatly heightened by that patience which conquers every repugnance in our own nature. In its principle the love of God embraces the love of all mankind; in practice it embraces all with whom we come in contact, and whom therefore we call our neighbours. But its most fruitful exercise is towards those who, owing to their ignorance, sufferings, or distress, stand most in need of our loving help. God loves each and every soul with an eternal love so great that He has constituted Himself the supreme object of their love and happiness; and when, with great cruelty to themselves, they seek not their happiness in Him, He still continues to be to them the sovereign good that they ought to seek. Then what nobler charity can there be than to help their return to their sovereign good? God is patient with all souls and good to all souls; and we enter into His charity when we imitate His patient love towards all that come within our sphere of action.

By nature our affections are attracted to some persons, are indifferent to others, and are drawn back with dislike and repulsion from others, often on slender grounds. But our Divine Lord makes His gift of charity as expansive as His own, that it may embrace every creature that He loves, and for whom He died. That the gift of charity may be extended to all, He has added to it the gift of patience, that by its aid we may conquer every repugnance that might otherwise rise up in our nature to hinder the expanse of charity. And that through patience we may carry our charity to its full extent and raise it to its most ennobling height, He has given us this law: "You have heard that it has been said: Thou shalt love thy neighbour, and hate thy enemy. But I say to you, love your enemies, do good to them that hate you: and pray for them that persecute and calumniate you: that you may be the children of your Father who is in Heaven, who maketh His sun to shine upon the good and the bad, and raineth upon the just and the unjust."[1] But this law of supernatural charity invites us to a triple conquest and a triple triumph over the hardness of our nature; a conquest by endurance over the wrongs inflicted upon us; a conquest by patience over the repugnances of our nature; and a conquest by generous love over those enmities of nature which contract the heart, that it may expand in charity to those who love us not.

That this sublime love, which raises the soul to God and makes us like to Him, may have its generous sway, unimpeded by our irritable nature, unopposed by the repugnances of pride, unchecked by the loathings of self-love, God has placed the strength of patience within the fervid gift of charity, as the pith and marrow of this heavenly virtue; that whenever nature rises with its selfish fears and disgusts against the expansion of the heart in charity, patience may be ready to resist the swelling repugnances of pride, and leave to charity its generous sway.

Every duty calls for more or less of care, that is, of attention and consideration proportionate to its nature. Matters of graver importance, especially if they present difficulties, call for solicitude, that is, for a wakeful and watchful attention and thoughtfulness. In a mind well regulated by patience these are peaceful operations that cause no disturbance to the soul. There is indeed a care and a solicitude for the things of this life against which our Lord gives us solemn warning, because they choke the divine seeds of life and grace implanted in the soul, and reverse the due order of things, which requires that we seek first the kingdom of God and His justice. But this is a solicitude that belongs more to anxiety than to peaceful watchfulness of mind.

Beware of anxiety. The very sound of the word anxiety is painful. Next to sin, there is nothing that so much troubles the mind, strains the heart, distresses the soul, and confuses the judgment. It is worthy of remark that the words anxiety and anger come from the same root; they are both derived from the Latin verb angere, to overstrain or strangle, which in its substantive form is angor, which means anguish or vexation. Anxiety is the uneasiness and trouble of mind to which we give way because of some difficulty of which we cannot see the solution, or because of some uncertainty respecting oneself or another, or because of some future event of which we are uncertain. It is more than uneasiness and disturbance, more than solicitude and trouble; it is attended with fear and perplexity, and inclines the soul to sadness. It has a certain paralyzing influence, compressing the soul with the ligaments of fear, suspense, and uncertainty, that impede and stifle the freedom of her powers. St Gregory describes it by a strong figure as "strangling the throat of the mind". A modern writer has described it as "fright spread thinly through the soul".

Anxiety is not in the things about which we are anxious; it has its existence in a combination of passions raised up in the soul. It is caused by taking our solicitudes and uncertainties into our own interior, and there making them the subject of our troubled, disquieted, and overstrained feelings; the result of this being that the mind is obscured and the heart made restless, so that no clear judgment can be formed on the subject of our disquietude. In some respects anxiety has a considerable resemblance to scrupulosity: it produces a like obscuration of mind, a like torturing pain of heart, a like fear and suffering from uncertainty, and a like troubling of the soul's peace. Scrupulosity, is in fact, one of the most painful and disturbing kinds of anxiety. Some persons are by nature anxious, as others are by constitution scrupulous; and in both cases there is a tearing and a wearing of the spiritual man, and what St. Gregory in a strong figure calls "the strangling of the throat of the mind". Hence St. Francis of Sales has observed that anxiety is the most injurious of all things to the soul, next to sin.

There is but one remedy for anxiety, and that is by using the firm force of patience to keep the objects of our solicitude in their proper place, and that place is outside of the feelings and before the mind. For it is not the feelings but the mind and will that are the true judges of things. When the feelings get mixed up with any subject of solicitude, they turn into passions, and become eager, excited, and restless; they confuse the mind and blind the judgment. We know when we are thrown into this state of anxiety through the trouble and disturbance of the soul and the obscuration and uncertainty of the mind. When we find ourselves in this state of troubled uncertainty and indecision, the subject of our anxiety should be dismissed altogether from the mind for a time, that it may be resumed when the feelings have subsided and the mind is clear. This, again, is the work of patience, and one that requires no little firmness of will, because if the eagerness, curiosity, fear, and restlessness which stir up anxiety are not altogether suppressed, it will be impossible to recover serenity of mind and tranquillity of soul. Then suspense itself is painful, and especially when assaulted by any of the above-named passions; and this, again, demands enduring patience.

But when we have obtained a calmer temper and a better control of our feelings, on returning to the subject, it will be for patience to keep the feelings in subjection whilst the will puts forth the attention of the mind without disturbance. When things external to us are thus kept in their external and proper position outside the soul, they are much more capable of being seen through, understood, and dealt with. What is not seen through on a first consideration will be seen through on a second, or on a third, provided the mind is not troubled with the passions of anxiety. But if difficulties still remain, it is then time to have recourse to some prudent adviser, who, from his more independent position, may be able to see into the case more clearly.

Besides the anxieties which fret and injure souls on account of external persons and things, there are but too many that have their origin in internal troubles, owing to the want of interior self-discipline, and of that interior patience which is the keeper of peace. But for this kind of anxiety we have given rules in various parts of these lectures; and they not unfrequently require obedience to a wise director. All that we shall say further at present is this, that every advancement in humility and patience removes the causes of anxiety and trouble, because they all have their roots in the restless impatience of sensitive self-love.

St. Francis of Sales has written so wisely on the spirit in which we should manage our affairs that nothing so good can replace his maxims. He observes that the care and diligence which we owe to our duties are things very different from anxiety and eagerness. Our Guardian Angels have diligent care of us; this belongs to their charity. But they are not anxious, they are not eager with excitement, for this would interfere with their peace and happiness. Be careful, be diligent in all that is committed to your charge. God has entrusted these things to you and expects you to manage them with great care; but avoid as far as possible all disquietude, anxiety, eagerness, and hurry, because these disturb the soul's peace, trouble the reason and the judgment, and hinder things from being well and successfully done.

Our Lord did not rebuke Martha because she was diligent in His service, but because she was "solicitous and troubled about many things". Nothing done with eager excitement can ever be done well. Flies are not formidable by their strength, but by their multitude: so great affairs give us less trouble than smaller affairs when they are numerous. Take them up in peace, and in their order, one by one; for if you try to take them altogether, or in a disorderly way, they will oppress you, they will dishearten you, and you will do nothing that is effective and satisfactory.

In all your affairs and responsibilities rest wholly on the providence of God, who alone can bring your plans to a happy conclusion.

Yet do your own best in a peaceful way to follow the guidance of God's providence; and then be assured that if you trust has been in God, whatever success you may obtain will be all the more profitable to yourself whatever you yourself may be inclined to think of it.[2]

The reverse of eager solicitude and disturbing excitement is found in sadness and sloth. These corrupt and corrupting vices are directly opposed to patience as well as to charity; they stagnate the soul and corrupt its fruits.

The Fathers and the Divines of both the Eastern and Western Church include these two vices under the one name of *acedia*, thus intimating that sloth and sadness go together. St. Bonaventure gives another reason why they are both expressed by the same word: because they are both enemies of religious devotion. In its primitive sense the word *acedia* signifies a fainting or failing through weakness. But here it signifies a fainting of the soul through the weakness and languor that is caused by the vice of sadness. Charity delights in spiritual and divine good; but slothful sadness sinks the soul into self-love and egotism. There it breeds an antipathy to all divine and interior good, and the soul, whilst adhering to sensual self-love, is unwilling to rise from it to seek the divine good and adhere to it with love; so that there is even a certain loathing of that good, owing to the corruption of the spiritual appetite by the disease of self-love. Hence this vice is opposed to charity as well as to patience. When it destroys charity in the soul it is mortal; when it only weakens charity it is venial. But even in its venial form this vice of sadness is very enfeebling, and so subtle in its movement, that pious souls are often deceived by it, and mistake sadness for regret over their failings and deficiencies. But sadness proceeds from self-love; regret from the movement of grace.

Sloth is defined to be a torpidity of soul neglecting to begin what is good; sadness is defined by St. Thomas to be a weariness of, and a moroseness with respect to, internal and spiritual good, to which these words of the Psalm are applicable: "Their soul abhorred all manner of food"[3]. In our catechisms it is placed as one of the capital sins under the name of sloth, and is called a capital sin or vice, because it is the head or immediate cause of other sins or vices. For, as the effect of charity is spiritual joy, the effects of sadness or spiritual sloth are malice, spitefulness, pusillanimity, despondency, torpidity, and wandering of the mind from good to evil thoughts. Such is the fertile brood of brooding sadness; all its offspring partake of its moral deformity.

If we put together what the Fathers say of sadness, it is an unnerving grief and a wearing anxiety of soul that hinders cheerfulness, extinguishes spiritual joy, makes prayer insipid, and spiritual duties distasteful, whilst it issues in a sluggish and impracticable temper, and produces the immoral and unhinging disease of sloth. What we are told of St. Gall is equally applicable to all the saints: "He was joyous in action and bland in speech, because sadness was a stranger to his heart". We are informed by St. Gregory in his *Life of St. Benedict* that one of the disciples of that patriarch of religion had given himself up to Satan through the vices of sloth and sadness; but the Saint applied such a prompt and severe correction that the disciple was delivered from both vices at once.

The cause of sadness is either wounded pride, or disappointed self-love, or unreasonable anxiety. Cassian distinguishes two kinds of sadness, one of which follows upon exhausted anger, or upon some injury received or imagined to have been received, or upon having been hindered or defeated in something that we desire. The second kind descends as a distressing load upon the heart from unreasonable anxiety or despondency of mind. Like a worm within the soul this miserable vice gnaws and consumes the joy and strength of the virtues, whilst the soul herself contracts and shrivels up like a leaf attacked by blight. To quote its accurate description from Cassian: "Sadness makes the spirit on which it seizes bitter, impatient, obdurate, full of rancour, full of pain, grief, affliction, and despondency. It breaks down exertion, stands stupefied against the entrance of healing sorrow and repentance, destroys the efficacy of prayer, and empties the soul of the fruits of the Holy Ghost."

Under the influence of this morbid languor loneliness is preferred to the converse of society, so that self-love, which is the loneliest of things, may be fostered in brooding melancholy. For, notwithstanding the pain of the malady, a gloomy pleasure is extracted from the intense egotism that sadness generates. The mind swarms with unpleasant fancies and delights in odious comparisons. The bright cheerfulness of others is looked upon with sinister eyes, as if it were an insult to the misery which the sad one loves to cherish. Whilst sympathy is longed for, it is felt to be odious, because pride predominates, and to pride the sympathy of others takes the shape of commiserating our weakness. Peevishness and sullenness are the first steps into sadness, and already partake of its obstinacy and gloom.

Sadness is opposed to spiritual joy, and patience is opposed to sadness. The sorrow which is according to God has nothing of sadness in it; it is a healing sorrow, that, as St. Paul says: "You may suffer damage by us in nothing," because, as the Apostle continues, "the sorrow that is according to God worketh penance steadfast unto salvation".[4] Like convalescence after sickness this sorrow is full of comfort and consolation; the vital powers are reviving under its influence and restoring the glow of charity. "Blessed are they that mourn, for they shall be comforted."[5]

But whilst the sorrow of repentance expands the soul into life, the sorrow of sadness contracts the soul and closes her in upon herself, swathes her with the bandages of bitter self-consciousness, and shuts out all generous movements. There she feels herself, tastes herself, loves herself, and is unhappy on that which feeds her. The remedy for all this misery is to break out by some resolute act of will from the delusion to which the soul is bound by the clammy unction of self-love. A puff of wind breaks the soap-bubble, and an act of kindness breaks down sadness.

It is justly observed by St. Bernard that a diversity of occupations is a great remedy for sadness. This is happily provided for in the rules of religious life. But in every state of life the principle of variety should be consulted. Variety refreshes both mind and body, and prevents too much self-absorption. Change of occupation and change of surroundings bring change of mind, relieve the system, and restore its balance.

One cannot too much insist upon the duty of keeping all cares and solicitudes outside the heart and feelings, of holding them firmly in their objective position, and of making them solely the objects of the mind and judgment. It requires a good strong habit of interior patience to withstand their seizing on the affections, but this shows the extreme value of interior patience. For unless we have this interior patience, so that we can take them up and lay them down at will, our solicitudes and cares will become anxieties, will harass, wear, and obscure the mind, and greatly disturb the peace and serenity of the soul. How many persons have suffered both mental and moral derangement owing to this want of patient method in managing their cares!

There is one form of sadness which is criminally prolonged by dwelling persistently on the memory of some great affliction, loss, or disappointment, to the unhinging of the soul and the neglect of present duties. The image of that event is kept before the mind with all its circumstances, and is allowed to oppress the heart until the features bear the fixed stamp of a cherished sorrow. What is worse, that fond entertainment of saddened memory prolonged through the years is mistaken by the mourner for virtue, as it seems to imitate the virtues of constancy, endurance, and perseverance. The understanding is misled, as well as the heart, by this enduring strain of self-love and sadness. But this is a sin against the providence of God, whose hand is in all events; against the soul herself, whose powers it unnerves and depraves; and against that cheerful performance of our duties, for which the soul loses her freedom by brooding on events past recall.

It may be taken as a maxim that whatever fosters selfishness disposes the soul to sadness. There is a habit of self-introspection, too much indulged in by many well-meaning persons, that is disastrous to the spirit of religious cheerfulness and generosity. Self-knowledge is invaluable; yet it is not obtained by peering into our own darkness, but by seeing ourselves as we are reflected in the divine light. We shall never find what we are by dwelling in our own troubles, and making them whilst we are dwelling in them, but by getting our mind above them, and dwelling on the goodness of God, when that divine goodness will teach us what we are by comparing ourselves with Him. But when we dwell upon ourselves alone, and dwell in ourselves apart from the view of God, the truth is hidden from us, and we feel nothing but discouragement. Souls that act thus cling to themselves, discouraged, saddened, and disheartened. With their eyes bent upon their own breasts they see but themselves, and that in the shallowest way; it is only by looking to God that they can see themselves truly. "Know yourself," says St. Catherine of Siena, "not in yourself, but in God, and God in you." Then will you find what in the sight of God you are.

Much and solicitous occupation with one's self produces much consciousness of one's self, and this breeds a sense of self that greatly interferes with the sense of God. It gives not the true but a fictitious sense of one's self through means of the imagination, so that we alternately hug our self-complacency and our miseries, instead of looking with cheerful confidence to God for their remedy. For instead of cleaving with the heart to God, such souls cleave to themselves with self-love, and suffer more from the subtleties of sadness than they know, They are afraid to quit the sandy shores of their nature, and to leave the sense of themselves behind them, that they may launch forth in generous faith and confidence upon the ocean of God's goodness and mercy.

Moreover, this incessant self-introspection and consciousness of self greatly impedes the spirit of duty as well as of devotion. These laborious self-inspectors cannot have that "very good heart which, hearing the word of God, keeps it, and brings forth fruit in patience". For that very good heart is unselfish, open, loving, patient, cheerful, generous, "seeking not her own, but what is profitable to many," and diligent in all duties for God's sake. This clinging to self-consciousness leaves patience defective, humility defective, and charity defective; for how can one be subject to God, or adhere to God, when internally engaged with the feeling of one's self? Rolled up into one's self like the snail in its slimy shell, the soul can neither open herself to God nor to her neighbour. She is too much engaged with her selfish feelings to look to God with serene eyes, or to feel after Him with a loving heart. And that soul suffers: suffers from internal corrosion, suffers from depression and sadness, suffers from irritation and impatience, suffers from the want of a diviner air to breathe in, suffers from anxiety and loss of cheerfulness. But the cheerfulness of patient charity, better than all those anxieties of self-introspection, better than all those cleavings of self-love to self, would keep away temptations and evil, and purge the fancy of its megrims. The irritability which in idle and self-conscious persons produces so much disorder would find its legitimate escape in useful works and services, consulting the health both of body and soul.

Labour disciplines the will to patience and endurance. Endurance! what a power is expressed in that word! Endurance holds the will with firmness to God despite of every discouragement that moves in our nature. Endurance bears up the will in patience against every pressure of disagreeable and mortifying things. Endurance holds the soul intent on her good works, and resists every temptation to quit good for evil. Endurance holds high the will above the movements of irritation, fear, or disheartenment, and by its solid strength repels the degrading solicitations of our animal nature. Endurance stands firm and loyal to the love of God amidst trials, disgusts, and sufferings. Endurance holds back the soul from the grasp of sadness. In a word, endurance bears all things that must be borne with, regardless of the pain and pressure of the time. And by the virtue of patient endurance, the gift of God, we possess the government of our souls, and keep our peaceful recollection in the face of all our adversaries.

But, as we have so often repeated, and cannot too often repeat, because it is the fundamental principle of all that we are teaching, this patient endurance entirely depends on the adhesion of the soul by her centre to God, which must be maintained amidst the duties of life and in our combats with our trials. The soldier, well drilled in the use of his weapons and the movements of the field, is always ready for battle. Confirmed by the strengthening grace of the Holy Spirit, we are the soldiers of Christ; and by the daily exercise of patience and endurance we are prepared for the hour of trial, which for us is the hour of combat. To be unprepared is to ensure defeat. When passion has swollen to its height, it will listen neither to rule nor reason. Pride and folly are its only counsellors. To use Plutarch's illustration, a man in the swell of passion is like a house on fire, full of smoke, noise, and confusion; he is deaf to everything but the din and clatter of the flames that rage within him. But when, like the falling wrecks of that fire, his passion sinks down into sadness, it fills his soul with choler, bitterness, and moroseness; the will is displaced and does dismal things.[6] But whoever is well disciplined in interior patience will detect and quell the irritation before it can develop into passion.

The great remedy for sadness is prayer. For as sadness arises from a morbid clinging to one's self, prayer is the most effective way of detaching one from that inordinate self-adhesion, and of drawing us off from one's self to God; whilst it obtains the grace to overcome this vile clinging to one's own disorder. "Is any one of you sad," says St. James, "let him pray."[7] But as it is in the nature of sadness to loathe the remedy of prayer, this can only be begun by an effort, and by beginning with vocal prayer, which, as the soul becomes freer and more detached from self, will lead to mental prayer.

There is a quality of endurance which, owing to its great value as a discipline of the soul, calls for special remark. That quality is the power of waiting. Whenever the mind is anxious, or in a state of suspense and uncertainty, it finds that state painful and restless, and has a disposition to rush out of it into action. But as this action is without due light and is unreasonable, it is sure to commit us to some folly. A soul that is patient waits with calm endurance for light before acting, and in virtue of this calm and patient endurance suffers no pain or anxiety, because the soul possesses herself and waits for light; and when the mind waits patiently for light, sooner or later it is sure to come. Trials of mind affect us more deeply than pains of body, and if we give way to anxiety such trials become troubles, and are immensely increased. But this cannot happen to those patient souls, who, regardless of human respects, feel that they are in the hands of God, and are encircled with His fatherly providence, and that all things are in His disposal. When we see not our way through some trial or difficulty, we have only to look to God, and to wait in patience, and in due time His light will come and guide us. This very attitude of waiting, this very patience of expecting, will dispose the mind to receive, and the will to rightly use, the needful light.

Whenever you are perplexed as to what course you should take, if you go blindly into action, you will be sure to repent of it. Wait for light, wait with patience, and light will not fail you. But to delay where you ought to act is the very opposite to the spirit of patient waiting. When you put off until to-morrow what you ought to do to-day, and can do to-day, this is not the waiting of patience, but an unwillingness to exercise the patience required for the duty.

When placed under some trial that afflicts and pains the soul; patient charity will recognise the will of God, sent in this shape for the discipline of the virtues. Seek not to escape from it, but remember the words of our Lord: "Take My yoke upon you". Wait with patient endurance the deliverance of God, and this will greatly augment your virtue. To abide under the trial with cheerful resignation will strengthen and sweeten your soul. "My yoke is sweet, and My burden light." The cross that is heavy to impatient anxiety is light when borne with patient love, because He who gives the sensible burden gives the secret strength to bear it sweetly.

There are trials laid on devout souls from which every drop of sensible sweetness seems to be extracted. The one sense left is the sense of desolation. In this most purifying trial the suffering soul shares her Lord's desolation on the cross. Yet is there a way still left to see the will of God, to acquiesce in the trial, to understand its justice, to wait with patient endurance the coming of God, and meanwhile to see the hand of God. Great is the pain, the privation, and the pressure, yet the soul can desire and pray, and feel her poverty, abiding in the resigned attitude of waiting and endurance; and she is conscious of the divine wisdom expressed in the words of Ecclesiasticus: "Wait on God with patience; join thyself to God and endure, that thy life may be increased in the latter end"[8].

Magnificent is the patience of faith under such a trial well endured; and the more so because the sufferer sees not the virtue of his endurance; it is only beheld by the helping angels. What the soul sees is her naïve poverty; what she desires is the Divine Goodness. What she feels in the depth of her spirit is an infusion of the gift of endurance. Then will the heart say to God with the Psalmist: "Hear, O Lord, my voice, with which I have cried to Thee. Have mercy on me, and hear me. My heart hath said to Thee: My face hath sought Thee. Thy face, O Lord, will I still seek. Turn not Thy face from me. . . . I believe to see the good things of the Lord in the land of the living. Expect the Lord, do manfully, and let thy heart take courage, and wait for the Lord."[9] See how the soul is drawn to God by the trial that only seems to take her from Him. The voice seeks Him, the heart seeks Him, the face seeks Him, the wants of the soul seek Him, the desolation seeks Him; patience pleads, endurance pleads, the expectant waiting of the soul pleads, and love pleads in them all. And when all these pleadings have purified the spirit, and drawn every purified desire from self to God, then God shows His face to that soul in the great benignity and sweetness of His visitation.

# 8

## ENCOURAGEMENTS TO PATIENCE

"He that is patient is governed with much wisdom: but he that is impatient exalteth his folly."—*Proverbs* xiv. 29.

There are two Christian virtues whose names sound unpleasantly to the sensual man. Humility is one of them, and patience is the other. If the cross is an offence to him, it is because it is the expression of these two virtues sanctified and enforced by the divine example of God in man. Sensuality of life breeds self-love in the heart, and weakens the whole man with irritability. By their fretful pressure on the soul these two disorders produce an immense amount of self-consciousness, and bring down the life of the spirit to a feeble state. Humility relieves the spiritual system from those evil humours, and patience restores it to strength. But self-love and impatience are cowardly vices, that shrink with insane fear from the health-giving labours of humility and patience. A child dislikes the medicine that gives him health, and the tasks that give him understanding; and the sensual man is little better than a child: his sensual feelings rule his mind; he has neither the inward sincerity that humility gives, nor the inward strength that patience gives. Nothing but the strong grace of God can give him heart to conquer his weaknesses, and courage to embrace the patience that will strengthen him. Yet, if he will only ask, this will be given him, and then the cross will become to him the consoling sign of life.

What is this Christian patience that any man should be afraid of it? It is the defensive armour of the Christian soul. Unlike the stiff armour of pride, it is pliant as well as strong, flexible but impenetrable, not cumbrous by its weight, but light as air to carry, bright from its celestial origin like the armour of angels, not of earthly metal but of spiritual power, not covering the body but woven through the soul. It is a divinely given habit that gives the soul her security, and is only formidable to her enemies. Obtained of God, it gives the Christian man his character.

So completely does the habit of patience form and perfect the character of the Christian man, so thoroughly does it furnish the test of his faith as well as of his charity, that St. Paul has not failed to point this out in his own example to his favourite disciple Timothy. "For this cause," he says, "I have obtained mercy: that in me first Christ Jesus might show forth all patience, for the information of them that shall believe in Him unto life everlasting."[1] And the great Apostle appeals to his patience as one of the chief signs of the power of God working in his infirmity. "The signs of my apostleship have been wrought on you in all patience, in signs, and wonders, and mighty deeds."[2]

The wonderful character which their patience and constancy gave to the early Christians under those privations, afflictions, and sufferings which their faith brought upon them, was something so new and so surprising, that it struck the mind of the pagan world, and led many to enquire by what divine power this marvellous change of character had been effected. It was a fact so notorious that, in his Apologia for the Christians addressed to the authorities of the Roman Empire, Tertullian makes it the subject of his final appeal. "That constancy," he says, "with which you reproach us as though it were obstinacy, is the Christian teacher. Who, when he reflects on this constancy, is not struck by it? Who in thus reflecting is not led to enquire, what can be the cause of it in these Christians? Who, when he has found out the cause, does not join them? Who, when he has joined them, does not wish to suffer the same things? And that with the view of obtaining the whole grace of God, and complete forgiveness in exchange for his blood. For all sins are forgiven to the patient work of suffering; and for this reason, the moment you pronounce your judgments upon us, we give thanks to God. Your conflict with us is that of human with divine power; when you condemn us God absolves us."[3]

"The sum of the Christian character," we repeat with St. Maximus, "is to return love for love and patience for injury.

Whoever is most patient will be the greatest in the kingdom of God."[4] This law of perfection our Lord introduced when He taught us to love our enemies, and to pray for our persecutors, that we may be like to our Heavenly Father, who overcomes evil with good. That patient suffering brings the highest of all rewards our Lord also taught us on a special occasion. When the mother of James and John asked that her two sons might sit on His right hand and His left in His kingdom, He asked: "Can you drink of the cup that I shall drink?"[5] Plainly intimating that those who suffered most with Him in the most patient charity would be the greatest in His kingdom. And He crowned His Beatitudes with the declaration, that those who suffered most for His sake were to rejoice and be glad, because their reward should be very great in Heaven.

Divinely helped and divinely motivated, this virtue of patience is a sublime imitation of God, all the grander because it is a combat for life against the death-working frailties of nature. It gives power to the will to keep the way of justice, serenity to the mind to see the way to God, regulation to the powers, and discipline to life. Fortitude is the gift of the Holy Ghost, and patience trains the power of fortitude, giving unity, consistency, and harmony to the soul, and conquest over everything in our nature that lifts itself against the will of God. The gifts of knowledge, understanding, counsel, and wisdom are brought into vital action through patience. Whatever possibilities of good have been planted by God in our nature, they are brought into act and duty by that charity which is patient.

The patience of God is most wonderful. It belongs to His goodness and wisdom. How can creatures so weak and impatient as we are understand that sovereign patience? It belongs to the moral power of Omnipotence. It is an element of that Eternal Charity which is the life of God. How infinite the goodness which made such weak and inconstant creatures, knowing that only through His infinite patience with them can they be brought out of their misery to His happiness! Consider with what patience He upholds every creature, lest through its inherent weakness it fall back into nothingness. Be astonished when you consider that patience with which God endures, sustains, and endows with benefits those myriads of intelligent creatures, who, made for Him, have turned His bounties against Him, and have given themselves up to vice and folly.

If, from the remote and obscure point of view at which we are placed, our wonder at that sovereign patience is so great, what would be our amazement were we placed in the full light of God, and in that light could see the hearts of the multitude of His dependent creatures as God beholds them, and the divine patience with which He deals with them! How profoundly significant of that merciful patience are the words which God spoke to Noe after the subsidence of the deluge. "I will no longer curse the earth for the sake of man: for the imagination and thought of man's heart are prone to evil from their youth: therefore I will no more destroy every living soul as I have done."[6] God spoke the word of His eternal patience in view of the redemption and salvation prepared in His Son, the Word of His bosom. Having made man free to be the author of his own acts, He saw that sin would abound; He joined His patience with His mercy that His grace and justice might more abound.

His patience delays His justice that His mercy may have its course; and that enduring us whilst plunged in evil, the magnificent grace and cross of His Son may raise us out of our malice, and make us the inheritors of His glory. We could never be the children of His mercy if we were not first the subjects of His patience. In refraining from punishing our iniquities God reserves His justice; and, sending His merciful grace, awaits our return to better things. He has not even removed those good things far from us, but patiently keeps them at our doors, always waiting for our repentance, always ready for our acceptance. In our mind He leaves the precious light of reason, in our Christian mind the far more precious light of faith, that when we return to them from our wild wanderings, we may find His truth, and come back to His patient mercy. Behold with what silent patience our God endures the abuse of His magnificent gifts, the perversion of reason, the neglect of faith, the swelling pride, and the corrupting sensuality that blot and defile those luminous blessings with dark ingratitude!

From His high Heavens the most patient God of mercy sends those healing and restoring graces, the purchase of the patient sufferings of His Son, to cleanse us from errors and evils, and fill us with the virtues of a holy life. The complement of those spiritual blessings are the gifts of His Holy Spirit enveloped in the fire of charity; the gift of fortitude, that we may adhere to God, and by imitating His patience we may resist sin, and may suffer with great reward; and the gift of wisdom, whereby we may both know and feel the value of things eternal as compared with the things of this sublunary world. Yet, notwithstanding all that God has done for us; notwithstanding all that Christ has suffered for us; notwithstanding the celestial gifts with which He has endowed us; we have still great need of the infinite patience of God, waiting and helping, still waiting and helping, long waiting our conversion and helping our infirmity, that we may turn from the weak elements of the world, and come to the divine things of our peace. For "the Lord is compassionate and merciful; long-suffering and plenteous in mercy. He knoweth our frame; He remembereth that we are dust."[7]

If we have not those divine things in abundance it is because we have not courage to imitate the divine patience, that charity may be perfected and evil kept at a distance. What evil have we ever known, experienced, or heard of, that did not demonstrate the patience of God and the loss of patience in man? Whilst the unbeliever affects to be scandalized at the patience of God, and blind to the truth that His patience belongs to His goodness, and uses His patience profanely as an argument against His goodness, that most merciful and blessed patience is a profound instruction and unbounded consolation to the faithful soul. For God bears with all this evil to exercise the patience of the just, and to give the unjust time to return to justice. Though silent to the senses He is not silent in the conscience; there His voice is heard; there He rebukes the ungrateful; there, through their own reason, He judges them; through their fears He binds them; through their remorse He torments them. "Say not," says the wise man, "I have sinned, and what evil has befallen me? For the Most High is a patient rewarder."[8] O sinner, look within thee, and thou wilt find thyself desolate. Listen within thee, and thou wilt find that the patient God is thy terror. Absent from thy heart, He speaketh to thy conscience: "Despisest thou the riches of His goodness, and patience, and long-suffering? Knowest thou not that the benignity of God leadeth thee to repentance?"[9] Yet if the sinner will not repent, but will abuse the merciful patience that waits for him, then the words of holy Job come home to him: "God hath given him place for repentance, and he abuseth it unto pride: but His eyes are upon His ways".[10]

As the reason of man is no measure of the revelation of God, the patience of man is no measure of the patience of God. His infinite patience is one with His inexhaustible goodness and mercy. All things of time with all their times are all equally present to His undivided and eternal life, "with whom there is no change nor shadow of alteration". What is perfect is unchangeable. The patience of God is unchangeable. But we, with our little patience, are the subjects of time and change; and impatience always changes us for the worse. Change, like death, destroys what went before; if the change come from God, it is a happy change; it makes us better than before. If it comes from impatience, it makes us worse than before. But whoever by patience adheres to God is saved from the changes that make us worse by union with the unchangeable good, whereby we always change to better things. This truth inspired St. Paul when he wrote these remarkable words: "To them who, according to patience in good works, seek glory, and honour, and incorruption, eternal life".[11] Which words St. John Chrysostom interprets of the constancy and perseverance that calmly pursues what is good, resists temptation, endures trial, and refuses the will to every disturbing element, awaiting in patience the coming of eternal life.[12]

The good which the Divine Majesty contemplates in His patience with sinners is magnificent, but awful. St. Paul has gone into the profound depths of the divine patience in the following sentences: "What if God, willing to show His wrath and make His power known, endureth with much patience vessels of wrath, fitted for destruction, that He might show the riches of His glory in the vessels of mercy, which He hath prepared for His glory".[13] It is not God who makes those vessels to be vessels of wrath; they make themselves to be such when they fill themselves with the filth of sin, and God endures them with much patience. He endures them that, if they turn to Him, He may make them vessels of mercy. Meanwhile they become instruments to try the patience of God's servants, and so to perfect them. But if during the time that the much patience of God allows them, they will not return to Him, then says the Apostle: "According to thy hardness and impenitent heart, thou treasurest up to thyself wrath, against the day of wrath and revelation of the just judgment of God".[14] Most consoling to the penitent, most terrible to the impenitent, are the ways of God's patience.

Wherefore the Almighty Father gave all patience to His Son, who put it to full exercise, and carried it to the utmost for our salvation, and then gave it to us in grace with His example. And He enlightened the power of the gift with the precept: "In your patience you shall possess your souls". Every man is a man in so far only as he holds the free possession of his soul. Every woman is truly a woman only in so far as she possesses her soul in peace. The Christian is so far a true Christian as he possesses his soul in God, so that the world cannot take hold of him. And the secret of this self-possession is in the patience which gives him a beautiful resemblance to Christ. But there is a much deeper resemblance to Christ in the patient endurance of evils, and even a much greater participation with Christ in His work of saving souls, than appears on the surface. Conscious of this in the depths of his inspired soul, the great Apostle boldly says: "I rejoice in my sufferings for you, and fill up those things that are wanting in the sufferings of Christ, in my flesh for His body, which is the Church".[15] The Apostle does not say that there was anything wanting in the sufferings of Christ; on the contrary, in another place he teaches that God "perfected the Author of our salvation by His passion".[16] He says that by his sufferings he fills up those things that are wanting to Christ in His body the Church. This opens a grand view into the whole economy of suffering as well as into the profound significance of patience.

Christ is the Head, the Church His body, united with the Head; into which the truth, spirit, and life of Christ descend, and are diffused through His members, giving to the Church one organic life with Christ, animated by His spirit, living by His virtue. And although every member is not equally animated with His spirit, but some more, some less, yet all who are in the unity of His body partake in some degree of His spirit, by faith if not by charity. He is present with His Church, and teaches through His Church; His grace animates the Church, and produces those divine virtues which imitate His own. The sufferings which He endured, the Church in her members endures, that in all things the Church as His body may exhibit His own life and death to the Father. For this cause the Church seems always dying to the world, whilst always living unto God.

For Christ our Lord not only perfected His own patience by His sufferings, but He receives all the sufferings endured by His members for His sake, incorporates them with His own, endows them with His merits, and thus gives them a communion with His own proportioned to their loving patience. For in virtue of His grace and love they are made holy and sacred. Through these patient sufferings the Church is propagated and defended, her members perfected, and she herself is made like to Christ in His patient life and passion, and especially in His endurance of the Cross; and when as the Head of all He shall offer all that He has redeemed and sanctified to the Father, among the richest offerings will be the patient sufferings of His saints united with His own.

As the Head and body of the Church are mystically one, one is the passion of Christ with the sufferings of the Church borne by His grace and through His presence in her members. In her apostles, martyrs, saints, and faithful members, the Church suffers in Christ, through Christ, with Christ, and for Christ. He sanctifies those sufferings, and makes them fruitful. Not only what is suffered externally, from His enemies, and in the sight of men; but what is endured internally with patience for His sake, and for the sake of the virtues, is united with the interior sufferings of Christ, and is sanctified by His grace and acceptance, an offering to God. How completely Christ makes the patient sufferings of His members His own, He has Himself taught us in most touching terms. To those who feed the hungry, clothe the naked, harbour the harbourless, comfort the sick, or console the afflicted, He says: "Amen I say to you, as long as you did it to one of these My least brethren, you did it to Me"[17]. And when Saul raged against the Church, and persecuted her members, Christ said to him: "Why persecutest thou *Me*" making the sufferings of the members of the Church His own.

In her deep sense of the divine things within her bosom, the Church therefore takes a grand and lofty view of the benefits that spring from the patient sufferings of her children. Our whole redemption and salvation rest on sufferings. United with the patience of charity they have a most mysterious power of destroying evil and producing good. The Book of Revelations is the prophetical history of the sufferings of the Church through the ages, in which the suffering faithful look up in adoration to "the Lamb who was slain, and who hath redeemed us in His blood"; and the whole history of the Church militant is finally summed up in this sentence: "Here is the patience of the saints, who keep the commandments of God and the faith of Jesus"[18].

As there is a great communication of evil in the world, there is a great communion of good in the Church. We neither pray, suffer, nor do good works for ourselves alone. From patient suffering, when it is endured in Christ, there is a diffusion of expiatory good beyond what we can fathom. St. Paul suffered exceedingly for the Church at large, and this generous motive gave him joy and consolation. Explicitly or implicitly all the servants of God suffer for the Church as well as for themselves. For, as the Apostle teaches, we are all of us the body of Christ, "and if one member suffer anything, all the members suffer with it; or, if one member glory, all the members rejoice with it"[19]. And as all the members are united together in Christ, whoever lays his sufferings with patient humility on the Cross of Jesus, obtains from His Blood a rich merit not only for himself but also for the needy members of the Church, which the Vicar of Christ distributes in His name.

In their hardness of heart the communion of the wicked "treasure up wrath against the day of wrath". But the communion of the just treasure up good works and patient sufferings for the day of reward. The wicked with their selfish vices spread the communication of evil far and wide: the just spread far and wide the communication of their good, and are generous with their prayers and unselfish sufferings to all who stand in need of mercy. What a contrast between these two communions! What an opposition between these treasures! The evil treasure is from evil hearts; the good treasure from good hearts. The one flows from selfishness and malice, the other from charity and patience. The one is the dark subterranean treasure of wrath, that must be finally sepulchered in hell; the other the bright treasure of patient love laid up in Heaven, where Christ unites the glorified sufferings of His servants with His own.

Many things are wanting to the sufferings of Christ's body, the Church, before its glory is completed; they are wanting to perfect its likeness to Christ; they are wanting to perfect His virtue in His members; they are wanting to draw unbelievers and sinners to His mercy; they are wanting to complete the sanctification of His elect; they are wanting that He may present His Church to God the Father glorified with victory, and bearing on her members the scars and wounds of the fight of patience. These the Apostles and servants of God fill up by their preaching, suffering, and patience. But, according to the divine plan, there are also other sufferings wanted, that the sufferings of Christ may be daily and more plentifully applied to souls. For the sufferings of patient souls are a great prayer, pleading for souls with a deeper voice than tongues can utter. Every one of the faithful whose soul is in charity applies to himself the satisfaction of Christ by his prayers, by his good works, and by his sufferings, but in a more special manner by his sufferings; and so satisfies for the penalties due to his sins. But after he has received the pardon on his sins, and has satisfied for their penalties, all of which rests on the satisfaction of Christ, and is commingled with that divine satisfaction, what remains of good works and patient suffering is applicable to other souls that stand in need of assistance. This belongs to the communion of saints and to the members of the Church. But they are applicable only through the sufferings and satisfactions of Christ, as of the members through the Head.

Thus, as a king honours his faithful servants by giving them a share in his power and government, Christ honours His devoted servants, associates them with Himself, and gives them a share in the service of the Church, and in the great work of satisfaction. Not indeed as primary but as secondary and subordinate causes, working through His power, and through the merits of His sufferings. It is in this sense that St. Paul says: "I fill up those things that are wanting in the sufferings of Christ, in my flesh for His body, which is the Church".[20]

There is nothing that we suffer for the honour of God, however little it may be, that is not more serviceable to us than if we possessed the dominion of the world. But suffering must be unselfish, and when suffered for God it must be sacrificial. Wherefore in repayment for what little we endure with loving patience God will give us nothing less than Himself. Knowing as we do how much and how cheerfully the saints suffered for God's sake, we should equally remember that they were frail mortals like ourselves. The arm of God is not shortened; He is as ready to help us as He was to help them. But if we shrink from the pain and patience of suffering, let this reflection confound us, that it is not because we cannot, but because we will not suffer for God's sake. For God is not less powerful or less willing to help us than He was to help them.

Reflect again, that God would not have us suffer anything for His sake that is not both useful and fruitful to ourselves. Reflect once more, that however great our trial or affliction may be, and our interior trials are the greatest, the Son of God bore them first, and permits them for our good. They are easy to bear when we once understand that they come from the hand of God. No adversity can befall us that is not in a certain way repugnant to the divine nature; and this makes it all the more certain that God would never permit adversity to come upon us, were it not that He sees the great fruit that we may obtain from it. For affliction does not please God because it is affliction, but only because of the incorruptible good to which it brings us, a good that He has ordained from eternity. As the providence of God sends the burden that we bear, and as He who endured all things for our sake bears the burden of every one's trials who is resigned to Him, the cross with its affliction is made sweet and divine, and the sufferer learns from it to be indifferent to contempt or honour, to the experience of bitter or of sweet things, and by his likeness to Christ becomes divine through the Spirit of God that moves within him.[21]

It would be long, and beyond the scope of these lectures, to enter upon the history of the patience of the Saints. Whoever loves this essential virtue will not fail to trace that history in the Holy Scriptures and the Lives of the Saints. But we must not pass over what we can learn of the patience of the greatest and most perfect of the Saints. Every act and word of the Blessed Virgin Mary that has reached us breathes the most exquisite meekness and tranquility, through which the most perfect patience is revealed.

There was a tradition in the early Church that she was very silent, and spoke only at the call of charity. Of this habit of silent recollection St. Luke gives us some intimation. Contemplate that silent chamber with Mary in modest recollection; the sudden presence of the Archangel, and the trouble in her heart at the salutation. The heavenly messenger dispels her maiden fears; and however mighty, however awful the mystery in which she is invited to share, in calm simplicity of heart she bends herself down to the divine will in the words: "Behold the handmaid of the Lord, be it done to me according to thy word". Yet upon that stupendous mystery of which she was the subject, she is silent to Joseph and to all the world, leaving its revelation to God in His own good time, and patiently in the meanwhile enduring misconstruction and reproach.

Her profoundly contemplative spirit, of which fortitude is the moral basis, is made known to us through her sublime canticle the Magnificat. There we read the clear profundity of her humility in the enraptured sweetness of her gratitude. There we see the sublime height of her intuition into the ends contemplated by the Divine Incarnation already accomplished in her bosom. She is full of God, and in a few burning sentences sums up the light of the Prophets of all past ages. After that burst of humility and gratitude, all melted into praise, that moved her pure soul in ways unspeakable, we see in her words the Word Incarnate putting the mighty down from their seats, dispersing the proud, and lifting up the humble. We see Him filling those who hunger for justice with good things, and sending away empty those who glory in their riches. We see the promises of God to the Patriarchs fulfilled, and the true Israel received to mercy. The whole mission of her Son is unrolled before our eyes.

After the birth of her Son St. Luke tells us: "All that heard wondered; and at those things that were told them by the Shepherds. But Mary kept all these words, pondering them in her heart. All are talking and wondering around her; she is thinking in God. As the Archangel proclaimed her full of grace, and prepared her for the full presence of the Holy Ghost, we are not left to conjecture her fortitude and patience. Besides, we see it all in the rude cave of Bethlehem. What a trial was that sudden command in the night to fly to Egypt, with all her solicitude about her infant Son; there to dwell in poverty in that strange heathen land; there to wait in all patience and uncertainty for the divine command to return! What a touching incident was that of her three days' sorrowing at the loss of her Son and what a consolation when she found Him in the Temple! There was already a shadow from the three days of His passion upon her soul.

She piously follows her Son throughout His travels, labours, ministry, and sorrows; and whatever contradictions, insults, and persecutions He endured in His person, she suffered in her heart. For the prophecy of Simeon was fulfilled from first to last. "This child is set for the fall, and for the resurrection of many in Israel, and for a sign which shall be contradicted... And thy own soul a sword shall pierce."[22]

The whole strength of her patience and fortitude is expressed in one sentence of the Gospel. St. John tells us: "There stood by the cross of Jesus His Mother, and His Mother's sister, Mary Cleophas, and Mary Magdalen"[23]. There, close by the cross, *stood* the Mother of Jesus. In the midst of the most awful scene of sacrilege and violence that the world has ever witnessed; among the rough executioners and coarse pagan soldiers; surrounded by the maddened crowd, mocking, jeering, with loud clamouring and rude gestures scoffing; close by the cross *stood* the Mother of Jesus. The Apostles had fled in terror; John alone remained, bound by his love of Jesus and of Mary. Nailed upon that cross, with the thorns around His head, torn by the stripes, worn with protracted sufferings, was Jesus her son and the Son of God. He was pierced with five wounds: she through all her senses to the soul. Yet she *stood*. Her fortitude and patience are divine, and reveal the whole virtue of her innocent life.

Her sister, Mary Cleophas, and Mary Magdalen stand by her, the faithful companions of her sorrow and distress. They cling in great faith and constancy to Jesus, and would not desert Him in His tremendous day of sacrifice. They stand by His Mother pierced through all her being with that great agony, the Mother by the Son, making her oblation with His sacrifice, and receiving His dying words, until He expires between two criminals. "And thy own soul a sword shall pierce, that out of many hearts thoughts may be revealed."

Nothing strikes with such a depth into the soul as the passion of our Lord and Saviour. Nothing cuts into our follies so effectually. Nothing implants in us a wisdom so divine. Through the sufferings of Jesus we see straight into eternity, and behold the compassion of God for us miserable sinners. There we see the cost of sin and the value of immortal souls. To love the sufferings of Christ and His patience is to bring His spirit into our heart with great energy and light. From His cross He reveals the grand truth to our soul that patience hath a perfect work. From the cross He inspires us with the love of patience. From the cross He grants us patience. When we contemplate the Son of God with His spirit exalted above all His sufferings, and see the heart of the Mother exalted to Him above all her sufferings, we feel the healing power of patience. And through the patience of the Son we see the patience of the Father, who permits these cruelties for our salvation.

Both in the Son and in the Mother you feel the divine power of resignation. These words—*Thy will be done*, when they spring from the surrender of all to God, bring to the soul a peace and courage that are not without a tasting of the goodness of God. Why are great trials allowed, except to bring the soul to devout acts of resignation? "This pure resignation," as the experienced Taulerus observes, "brings the soul straight to God, establishes her in God, and makes her conformable to God; nor can that soul seek the pure honour of God without respect to her own enjoyment, or without a sense of God in her own spirit, however hidden it may be." True devotion therefore consists in true and most humble resignation, and this includes self-abnegation, whether we abound in consolation, or are left in penury and desolation, so that whatever befalls we always abide with God in peace. It was thus St. Paul knew how to abound and how to suffer need, secure in God who strengthened him.

When temptations come that are neither sought nor desired, be neither alarmed nor disheartened. The virtues are perfected by their conflicts with evil. It is useful that God should leave us those evil propensities, that we may manfully resist them; not by facing them, not by prying into them, not by giving them countenance in any way, but by turning away from them and patiently adhering to God. They thus drive us to God when we are the least disposed to seek Him; and for this lawful striving a great reward is prepared. When the crops of the field have endured the rigours of winter, they become stronger and more fruitful; and it is not every one who can come to perfection without rude conflicts with temptation. The words of Eliphaz were not applicable to holy Job, but to many weak souls they come home with too much truth. "The scourge is come upon thee, and thou faintest; it has touched thee, and thou art troubled. Where is thy fear, thy fortitude, thy patience, and the perfection of thy ways?"[24]

These are the soft and tender souls that have lived in sensible devotions, who stand in need of trials not only to strengthen their virtues, but to drive them out of themselves, that by stress of trial they may draw nigh to God. Without such trials they never can be perfected.

It is quite certain, as the devout Blosius observes, that persons who have a natural propensity to vice, and consequently find it a labour to keep the imagination free from vain and foolish images that imprint their colours on the inferior soul, when they strive in earnest to mortify themselves and get rid of those intrusions, become much more vigorous in virtue than those who are not troubled with such propensities, or besieged with such imaginations. A statue that has been carved with laborious patience and perseverance into perfect form out of a block of marble is far more precious than the same figure moulded with ease from a lump of soft wax. The more difficult the material out of which the soul is perfected, the more glorious will be the work when completed.

Hence those who have striven the most vigorously against themselves, though they may leave this world imperfect and have to be purified in the next, will obtain a much higher place in Heaven than those who have not striven with the same energy and patience, even though these last should reach Heaven without any need of purgation.

Sometimes even souls that are more perfect will feel inordinate movements in their inferior nature or animal senses, to which their whole reason and will is opposed. A tempest may rage in the inferior nature whilst the superior man is at peace. Such things do occur, and are displeasing to the will; but let not that soul imagine that the grace of God has left her. For God often promotes the salvation of His elect by things that to the sufferer seem contrary to salvation. Hence He sometimes permits those foul and infernal temptations that are a horror to the soul. Amidst such involuntary trials, the devout soul will resign herself to God, adhere to God, and abide in her superior nature, and will omit neither her good works nor the Holy Communion; for as long as the soul refuses her consent she suffers no injury. The imagination may be beset even with blasphemies and other absurd follies, suggestions of the evil one, and they may almost seem to speak with a human voice; still let the soul not trouble herself any more than if they were so many flies buzzing about the face, and let her turn to God. If they grow urgent and vehement, sign the cross, look to our Lord's Passion, and say to Him: "Keep my heart immaculate, that I may not be confounded".

There may be even a yet more terrible trial. In your hour of desolation it may seem to your fancy that God has abandoned you, and that to your feelings He would seem to say: "You please Me no more, and I quit you". Yet even then must you not abandon your patient trust in your Heavenly Father, but must say with holy Job in full faith: "Even though He slay me, I will trust in Him; but yet will I reprove my ways in His sight".[25]

For why has this trial come but to strengthen your faith and your hope, and to awaken a deeper sense in you of your nothingness apart from God? Why has it made you desolate but to bring you into the exercise of that fundamental patience, and draw out of you that profound resignation, which, searching your nature deeply, will enable the grace of God to penetrate, secretly indeed, but into the very essence of your soul?[26]

We may now sum up the value of patient and resigned suffering in the language of the devout and learned Blosius.

1. Nothing more valuable can befall a man than tribulation, when it is endured with patience for the love of God; because there is no more certain sign of the divine election. But this should be understood quite as much of internal as of external trials, which people of a certain kind of piety are apt to forget.

2. It is the chain of patient sufferings that forms the ring with which Christ espouses a soul to Himself.

3. There is such a dignity in suffering for God's sake, that we ought to account ourselves unworthy of an honour so great.

4. Good works are of great value; but even those lesser pains and trials that are endured with peace and patience are more valuable than many good works.

5. Every sorrowful trial bears some resemblance to the most excellent Passion of our Lord Jesus Christ; and when it is endured with patience, it makes him who endures it a more perfect partaker of the Passion of his Lord and Saviour.

6. Tribulation opens the soul to the gifts of God; and when they are received tribulation preserves them.

7. What we now suffer God has from eternity foreseen, and has ordained that we should suffer in this way, and not in any other way. Would He allow the least adversity to fall upon His children, or to come within them, or the least breath of wind to blow upon them, that He saw was inexpedient for their salvation? Heat and cold, hunger and thirst, infirmities and afflictions, all these and each of them, whenever they befall the servants of God, come not only to purify but to adorn their souls.

8. The artist lays his lines and colours in lights and shades upon the canvas, to set forth some beautiful production of his genius. The noble maiden is adorned with rich garments set with gold and jewels for her nuptials. So God adorns His elect, whom He separates unto Himself, investing them with the magnificent virtues produced by sufferings, like those with which he adorned His well-beloved Son. Wherefore all affliction and bitterness must be borne with cheerful patience, as they are so much better than the pains of purgatory or the eternal flames.

9. One of the friends of God has said: When any one feels affliction or sorrow, and is humbly resigned to God, this resignation is like a harp that gives out sweet-sounding notes, and the Holy Spirit brings out a canticle that resounds melodiously, though secretly, in the hearing of our Heavenly Father. The lower chords, strung in the inferior nature of the man, send forth low and mournful notes of grief; but the higher chords, strung in the superior powers of the soul,

are full of devotion, and resound with the free and soaring notes of patient resignation to the glorious will of God. The sensible nature is crucified, and sighs over its sufferings; but the rational spirit praises God in peace. For those fiery afflictions that consume the marrow and the bones prepare the soul for close union with God; and as fire prepares wax to receive new forms, these trials prepare the soul to receive a better likeness of God. Nothing can receive the form of another until its own form is put away; and before the Divine Artist can imprint the most noble image of His glory on the soul, that soul must give up the image of the old Adam with pain and suffering, that she may be supernaturally changed and transformed. The Almighty prepares her therefore for this happy transformation by severe adversities. Having decreed to adorn her, after this divine transformation, with the divinest gifts, so great a change cannot be effected by soft and soothing baths, but by plunging her into a sea of bitterness.

Yet all are not brought into the same depths of interior trial, nor are all subjected to the like accumulation of external afflictions. These are God's special favours to souls marked out for great perfection, and consequently for a large share of the cross and glory of Christ. To these divine purifications it may be truly said that "many are called, but few are chosen". Feebler souls are treated in gentler ways. Some God conducts more in the way of consolation than in the way of the cross. Others, because of their stronger nature, require greater purification. Others, again, because faithful to the gift of fortitude, can endure more for the love of God. But in this world or the next must every soul be perfectly purified before her admittance to the open glory of God.

It by no means follows that the strongest natures, whether strong in body or in mind, have the greatest share assigned them of the cross and sufferings of Christ. These favours are granted to those who are faithful to the strongest graces. Hence we often see them bestowed on persons of feeble frame or of simple mind, in whom, as true lovers of the cross, grace triumphs over nature in admirable ways. St. Gertrude was divinely instructed, that sometimes when God would favour a soul by abiding with her, when she is not constant in abiding with

Him, He sends her troubles or pains of body or soul to change her spirit, that she may be able to abide with Him. These are the mysterious ways of God's grace and goodness. For "the Lord is nigh to them who are of a contrite heart"[27]. And of such He says: "He shall cry to Me, and I will hear him: I am with him in his trouble"[28]. There is one instruction more, and of great importance, that may be given in the words of St. Catherine of Siena. The pains that people suffer in this world are chiefly inflictions because the will is inordinate. If the will were in its right place, in its just order, and in due accordance with the will of God, the soul with such a will would be in a certain manner free from pain. For although one endowed with a will so holy and well regulated still feels labour and sorrow, yet he bears all this just as if he had no pain; because he endures it most willingly, and with clear knowledge that he is suffering by the holy will and permission of God. His mind is free, he has no anxiety about what he so well understands, and his will is united with the will of God. Affliction and pain depend upon how we take them; a man is only afflicted through having what he is unwilling to have, or through not having what he desires to have. Take his self-will away, and his spirit becomes tranquil and enjoys peace.[29]

We cannot better conclude this lecture than with the commendations given to the virtue of patience by St. Cyprian, the holy Bishop and Martyr of Carthage. "After carefully weighing the goods of patience and the evils of impatience, let us hold fast to the full discipline of patience, that we may abide in Christ, and come through Christ to God. This virtue is so abundant and so manifold that it cannot be kept within narrow bounds or be forced into shrunken conditions. It is a far-reaching virtue, whose large abundance proceeds from one divine fountain, but the streams thereof spread through many paths of glory. In our actions and praises nothing can be complete unless the firmness of patience be there to give it perfection.

"Patience is that virtue which commends us to God, and keeps us with God. It smoothes down anger, keeps the tongue obedient, governs the mind, maintains peace, and upholds us in good discipline. It breaks down the assaults of concupiscence, holds back the soul from the swellings of pride, and extinguishes the hidden flames of hatred. In the rich and the mighty it restrains the abuse of power: in the poor it fosters content with their lot: it protects the blessed integrity of virgins, the laborious chastity of widowhood, and the united charity of married life. It makes us humble in prosperity, strong in adversity, and mild against insults and injuries. The patient one is prompt to forgive, and ready to ask pardon where offence has been given. By patience we are made strong to resist temptation, to endure persecution, to consummate suffering, to perfect martyrdom for justice' sake. This virtue gives to faith its firm ground and strong foundations, sublimely elevates the growth of hope, and directs our energies to follow on the path of Christ in imitation of His long endurance. It gives the spirit of perseverance to the children of God, whereby we imitate the patience of our Heavenly Father."[30]

# 9

# ON THE GIFTS OF THE HOLY GHOST

"The Spirit helpeth our infirmity."—ROMANS viii. 26.

Fortitude is one of the seven gifts of the Holy Ghost: it is the strengthening gift, and patience is included in fortitude. These instructions would therefore be incomplete without some exposition of the divine gift of fortitude. But as the seven gifts of the Holy Ghost are united with each other, this again requires that we should explain the whole of the divine gifts, first in their union, and then in their distinctions.

God the Father was especially manifested in the work of creation, God the Son in the work of redemption, and God the Holy Ghost in the work of sanctification. But even in the work of creation there was a certain manifestation of the Son and of the Holy Ghost. The Father spoke His creative will through His Eternal Word, and the Spirit brooded like a divine bird over the chaotic elements to fertilize the creation, and bring it into order and completeness. He also breathed the breath of living grace into the newly created Adam. In the Old Testament He was equally promised with the Son, was manifested in the benedictions of the Patriarchs, spoke through the Prophets, gave fortitude to God's heroes, and sanctity to the just.

In the Prophet Ezechiel the Holy Spirit of God is especially promised as the sanctifier of souls cleansed in the blood of Christ. "I will pour upon you clean water, and you shall be cleansed from your filthiness, and I will cleanse you from all your idols, and I will give you a new heart, and a new spirit within you: and I will take away your stony heart, and will give you a heart of flesh. And I will put My Spirit in the midst of you; and will cause you to walk in My commandments, and to keep My judgments, and do them. . . . And you shall be My people, and I will be your God."[1]

In the Creed the Holy Spirit is especially distinguished by what He does for us as "the Lord and Giver of Life". This office of Life-giver He has revealed in one of the most striking figures of Holy Scripture in the prophecy of Ezechiel, where he restores life and vigour to the vast multitude that lay slain and reduced to dry bones upon the field of battle.

"The hand of the Lord is upon me," says the prophet, "and brought me forth in the Spirit of the Lord: and set me down in the midst of the plain that was full of bones, and He led me about through them on every side: now there were very many on the face of the plain, and they were exceedingly dry. And He said to me: Son of man, dost thou think these bones shall live? And I answered: O Lord God, Thou knowest. And he said to me: Prophesy concerning these bones: and say to them 'Ye dry bones, hear the word of the Lord. Thus saith the Lord God to these bones: Behold I will send spirit into you, and you shall live. . . . And I prophesied as He had commanded me: and as I prophesied there was a noise, and behold a commotion: and the bones came together, each one to its joint. And I saw, and behold the sinews and the flesh came up upon them: and the skin was stretched out over them, but there was no spirit in them.

"And He said to me: Prophesy to the Spirit, prophesy, O son of man, and say to the Spirit: Thus saith the Lord God: Come, Spirit, from the four winds, and breathe upon these slain, and let them live again. And I prophesied as He had commanded me: and the Spirit came into them, and they lived: and they stood upon their feet, an exceeding great army. And the Lord God said: You shall know that I am the Lord, when I shall have opened your sepulchres, and shall have brought you out of your graves, O my people: and shall put my Spirit into you, and you shall live."[2]

But although promised as the Giver of life in the Old Testament, the Holy Spirit was not completely manifested as the Third Person of the Holy Trinity until the accomplishment of the divine mystery of the Incarnation, when the Father revealed Him through the Son. As "the power of the Most High," He was manifested to Mary at the Incarnation. To John the Baptist and His disciples He was manifested at the baptism of Jesus, when He appeared in the form of a dove resting upon the Son of God, whom a voice proclaimed to be the teacher of mankind. He was manifested when the Son of God proclaimed His mission in the Synagogue of Nazareth. "The Spirit of the Lord is upon me, wherefore He hath anointed me, to preach the Gospel to the poor He hath sent me."[3]

He was manifested in the preaching of Christ, who promised Him as the enlightener and strengthener of souls. He was manifested in the glorious Transfiguration of Christ, when His interior glory streamed forth to chosen witnesses, and the Holy Spirit was in the bright cloud above, and His voice came from the cloud. He was manifested after the Resurrection, when the Son of God breathed on His Apostles, and said: "Receive ye the Holy Ghost; whose sins ye shall forgive, they are forgiven them".[4]

He was manifested in splendour and glory on the day of Pentecost, when as in a mighty wind He came down from Heaven, and rested in tongues of fire upon the heads of the Apostles, "and they were all filled with the Holy Ghost".[5]

Through the Apostles the Holy Spirit was manifested to the world in the inspiration of their preaching, the fortitude of their sufferings, and the wisdom and sanctity of their lives. He is incessantly manifested in the Church through her wonderful unity, the unchangeableness of her teaching, the divine gifts of her ministering, and the number of her saints.

What a mighty Creator is the Holy Spirit! exclaims St. Gregory. He has only to touch the soul and all is taught. He fills the youthful

David with His spirit, and he becomes the Psalmist. He fills the rustic Amos with His spirit, and he becomes a prophet. He fills the child Daniel with His spirit, and he judges the elders, and proclaims the coming destruction of princes and powers. He fills the fisherman with His spirit, and he becomes an Apostle. He fills the persecuting Pharisee with His spirit, and he becomes the Doctor of the Gentiles. Quickly is it done, for the grace of the Holy Spirit knows of no tardy delays.

What are we to understand by the gifts of the Holy Ghost?

In what do they agree with the graces of the virtues? In what do they differ from them? What, again, are the effects which they produce in souls that are faithful to them?

The attribute of the Holy Spirit as "the Lord and Giver of life," deserves prolonged meditation, and what follows will be but the exposition of that attribute. Spiritual life implies light, love, freedom, power, and union with God through His Spirit dwelling in us. The Holy Spirit is the principle of love and union in the Holy Trinity. He is also the gracious principle of our union with God. His sanctifying grace gives the first principle of supernatural life to our soul in baptism; and in this sanctifying or justifying grace we receive the habit of the theological and moral virtues. These habits are the operations of the Holy Spirit within our souls, giving us dispositions and inclinations to believe in God, to hope in Him, to love Him, and to fulfil the law of God in the exercise of the other virtues.

Sanctifying grace comes with charity, and is charity; this charity gives life, and by it we receive the beginning of the gifts of the Holy Ghost. But this sanctifying or justifying grace is a supernatural and divine principle implanted by the Holy Spirit in the soul. How it is received into the soul so as to reach all her powers St. Thomas will explain. "As the powers of the soul flow from her essence, and these powers are the principles of her actions; so from sanctifying grace the habits of the virtues flow through the essence of the soul into her powers, and through these habits of virtue the powers are moved into action."[6]

But this sanctifying grace is more than a divine principle; it is an actual partaking of the Holy Spirit of God, of which St. Peter says: "Grace to you, and peace be accomplished in the knowledge of God, and of Christ Jesus our Lord: as all things of divine power, which appertain to life and godliness, are given to us, through the knowledge of Him who hath called us by His own proper glory and virtue. By whom He hath given us most great and precious promises; that by these you may be made partakers of the divine nature."[7]

And St. Paul teaches that "the charity of God is poured forth in our hearts, by the Holy Ghost who is given to us".[8] These words, "the Holy Ghost who is given to us," and "we are made partakers of the divine nature," require careful explanation. St. Thomas observes that, although the light and power of grace are partakings of the divine nature, and the sanctifying grace of the Holy Spirit establishes in us a holy union with God, yet this is by a created participation, and not a partaking of the substance of God. It comes of His divine presence in the soul, and of His operation, and is the result of His divine action. Nor is it the substance of the soul, but it is given to that substance, and may be taken away from the unworthy. For which reason St. Paul says: "Know you not that you are the temple of God, and that the Spirit of God dwells in you? But if any man violate the temple of God, him will God destroy."[9]

We owe it to the supreme condescension of God that His Holy Spirit attaches Himself to His gifts of sanctifying grace and charity. By so doing He dwells in us, imparts life to us, adopts us, establishes us in dignity, makes us like to God, and moves us towards God. But the Holy Ghost is never without the Father and the Son, with whom He is to us the bond of union. This truth our Lord expressed to His disciples in the words, "If any one will love Me, he will keep My word, and My Father will love him, and We will come to him, and will make our abode with him"[10] After which words He promises His Holy Spirit that we may love Him.

The sanctifying grace of the Holy Spirit establishes us therefore in a supernatural state of life, raises the image of God within us to His likeness, makes us God's children, inheritors of His kingdom, and temples in which He deigns to dwell. So great, noble, and precious is this grace, exalting the soul above the order of nature, and bringing her into such union with God, that the good of this grace in one single soul is greater than all the natural good of the whole universe.[11]

What an inexhaustible subject of meditation and gratitude! The presence of God in the soul gifted with charity is a divine fact, to be realized by the mind to the utmost. It places the possessor of grace in a divine order of things, that leads up to God and points to His glory. Take the whole circle of created nature, where grace is not; that nature is powerless to ascend to God. It follows of necessity that there can be no proportion of value between grace and nature.

But the gifts of the Holy Ghost have a higher excellence, a superior force, and more powerful efficacy than the habits of the virtues; they have immediate reference to the Holy Ghost as dwelling within us, from whom they proceed as from their direct cause and their most bountiful Giver. For it is one thing to have divine movements in the soul and another to have the Divine Mover present, and acting immediately within the powers, and perfecting their action.

St. Thomas defines the gifts of the Holy Ghost to be certain habits that perfect the soul to obey the Holy Spirit with promptitude[12]. These habits attract the soul to follow the divine inspirations or inbreathings with ease and freedom. The Holy Spirit Himself is called *Altissimi donum Dei*, the gift by excellence of the Most High God. The seven gifts are called the seven spirits as well, that is to say, the seven radiations of divine light, flowings of spiritual unction, breathings of power, that attract and draw the will to comply with the inspirations of the Holy Spirit. St. Paul says, "There are diversities of graces, but one Spirit". And St. Thomas justly remarks, that we ought to follow the language of Holy Scripture which calls these gifts spirits: "The spirit of wisdom, the spirit of knowledge," and the rest. The seven spirits are seven divine qualities inbreathed. It may be a question whether the Seven Spirits before the throne of God may not each represent one of these seven gifts of the Holy Spirit in an eminent degree. The breathing of the Spirit into Adam gave him the breath of spiritual life upon his creation. The breathing of Christ upon the Apostles conveyed to them the power of the Holy Spirit to heal the fallen Adam in his descendants: "Receive ye the Holy Ghost, whose sins ye shall forgive, they are forgiven them". But the Holy Spirit dwelling within the soul is the fountain of the seven gifts; which truth we express in the hymn of the Church, in which we invite Him to come and fill our souls; in which also we call upon Him as "the living spring, the living fire, sweet unction, and true love"; and we ask Him to confirm and strengthen us with constant power.

There are two principles of movement then in the Christian soul; one is the movement of the man, the other is the movement of God. The mere human virtues move from natural reason; the Christian virtues move from grace, the free will works with them, and they perfect the man towards his salvation. But the gifts of the Holy Ghost give a higher perfection to the faculties than the grace of the virtues, raising our spirit to higher things, and rendering it prompt, vigorous, and readily responsive to the divine influences.

Four of these gifts—knowledge, understanding, counsel, and wisdom—refer to the illuminating and elevating of the mind; the other three—fortitude, piety and the fear of the Lord—refer directly to the strengthening, sweetening, and exalting of the will, because they affect the heart or will with the sense of divine things. But the four gifts to the mind are also gifts to the will, because they are not only the greatest illuminators and guides of the will, but give freedom and strength of action to the will, whether in contemplation or in the conduct of life. For the gift of wisdom, which includes the other three, is of the heart as well as of the mind, giving a sensible relish of those heavenly things which the truth presents to the mind, and which we feel through the unction of the Holy Spirit.

Of this divine illumination of the Holy Spirit our Lord says: "He will teach you all truth," and again: "He will bring to your mind whatsoever I shall have said to you."[13] And St. Paul tells us: "We have received the Spirit that is of God, that we may know the things that are given us from God",[14] And commending the Colossians for their "love in the Spirit," the Apostle asks for them the whole perfecting operation of the Holy Spirit. "That you may be filled with the knowledge of His will, in all wisdom and spiritual understanding. That you may walk worthy of God, in all things pleasing: being fruitful in every good work, and increasing in the knowledge of God: strengthened with all might according to the power of His glory, in all patience and long-suffering with joy, giving thanks to God the Father, who hath made us partakers of the lot of the saints in light."[15]

In this inspired passage we have presented to us the whole illuminating and strengthening power of the Holy Spirit, perfecting the virtues with His gifts. With respect, again, to the gifts of fortitude and piety, the Apostle says: "If we hope for that which we see not, we wait for it in patience. Likewise the Spirit also helpeth our infirmity. For we know not what we should pray for as we ought: but the Spirit Himself asketh for us with unspeakable groanings. And He that searcheth the hearts, knoweth what the Spirit desireth: because He asketh for the saints according to God."[16]

When the divine gifts coincide with the virtues, they are only distinguished by their greater splendour and fruitfulness. The virtues are given in the grace of Baptism; the gifts are given in greater strength and abundance in Confirmation; and are afterwards augmented in proportion to the humility and charity of the receiver. Of this we have divine assurance: "If you love Me, keep My commandments, and I will ask the Father, and He will give you another paraclete, that He may abide with you for ever. The Spirit of truth, whom the world cannot receive, because it seeth Him not, nor knoweth Him; but you shall know Him; because He shall abide with you, and remain with you."[17]

We must therefore understand that the spiritual movements of the soul are imperfect and inadequate to reach their end in a perfect way, without the immediate presence, inspiration, and operation of the Holy Spirit, moving us according to the light and sense of His eternal wisdom. Yet He only moves us so far as we are disposed to be moved, and when we do not oppose Him with the dull resistance and unbending tenacity of our self-will, clinging to unworthy or defiling things. But when the will is open, pure, and free, we may confidently say with the Psalmist: "Thy good Spirit shall lead me into the right land"[18]. And we may feel the assurance given us by St. Paul, that "whosoever are led by the Spirit of God, they are the sons of God".[19]

Let then the soul understand this thoroughly, and reflect upon it earnestly, that it is the presence, charity and action of the Holy Ghost within us that makes us acceptable to God, when we are faithfully obedient to His light and inspirations. For what pleases our Heavenly Father in us is His own Divine Spirit, given to us through the merits of His Son, working in our nature, and drawing our will and mind to work with Him. When our Heavenly Father beholds the Blood of His Son upon our soul, His Gospel in our heart, and His Spirit within our spirit, moving us towards Him; when He sees His own Spirit spreading out His gifts in our powers, and hears that Spirit pleading for us through the prayer that He inspires with His own unspeakable utterances, our Heavenly Father is propitiated by the great presence within us, and is pleased to accept us for the sake of the divine good that has come into us, and which is the bond of union between the feeble creature and her Omnipotent and all-pure Creator. The Holy Ghost is also our protector from our enemies. For, quoting St. Thomas once more, when the gifts of the Holy Ghost are combined with the virtues, they are sufficient to exclude the sins and vices, and to protect us both in the present and in the future from sin. But with respect to past sins whose guilt is not yet removed, we have a special remedy in the sacraments.[20]

Yet the movements of the Holy Ghost are so far from impeding the freedom of the will, that they promote that freedom as nothing else can. For they raise the will out of its material fetters, repel the obstacles to that freedom interposed by self-love and by the other clogging vices, and give greater freedom by giving greater power to the will. Hence St. Paul says: "Where is the Spirit of the Lord there is liberty"[21] St. Basil compares man to a ship under sail. The ship may be well constructed and provided, but without the impulse of the wind it cannot move towards its destination. So man may have sanctifying grace and the habits of the virtues, but without the moving power of the Holy Spirit he cannot advance towards God. Without the wind the ship is not at liberty: without the breathing of the Holy Spirit the soul has not her spiritual freedom.

The Prophet Isaias gives the seven gifts in the order of their dignity and excellence, placing wisdom first and the fear of God last. This is a usual method in the Scriptures, and we have it in the ten commandments. It is the precedence due to what is nearest to God, and to what brings us nearest to God. But when we consider the gifts as they come to us we must reverse the order, and place the fear of God first and wisdom last. This has been pointed out by St. Augustine, and explained by St. Gregory. In his allegorical style the great Doctor of Morals attaches his instruction to the vision of the new Temple as seen by the Prophet Ezechiel. Describing the gate of the Court that looked to the North, the Prophet says: "And they went up to it by seven steps; and a porch was before it"[22].

By seven steps, says St. Gregory, we ascend to the door, as by the seven gifts of the Holy Ghost we come to the kingdom of Heaven. These gifts, as enumerated by Isaias, rested on the head of Christ, and they rest on His body, which we are. The Prophet speaks of these degrees in their descending rather than in their ascending order. For undoubtedly we ascend from fear to wisdom. In our mind the first step of ascent is by fear, the second by piety, the third by knowledge, the fourth by fortitude, the fifth by counsel, the sixth by understanding, and the seventh by wisdom. But what is fear without piety? What is piety unguided by knowledge? What, again, is knowledge without the power to will? Our knowledge therefore must pass into fortitude, that what we know, that we may do without fear or alarm, and may defend the good that we have. But fortitude is unsafe without foresight and circumspection, which saves us from rushing into presumption, and coming to a fall. Fortitude must therefore ascend to counsel, that we may see what is best to be done, and may do it with magnanimity. But there can be no counsel without understanding, teaching us the evil to be avoided as well as the good to be sought and consolidated. For counsel therefore we must ascend to understanding. Yet even though understanding be watchful and well informed, it will still need to be matured and applied by wisdom. We must therefore ascend to wisdom, that what understanding discovers wisdom may ripen and bring to its proper ends.

As, then, we rise from fear to piety, and are led through piety to knowledge, and go from knowledge to fortitude, and tend from fortitude to counsel, and through counsel advance to understanding, and through understanding ascend to the maturity of wisdom, we go up by these seven steps to the door that opens into eternal life.

But it is written that there is a porch before the ascent; for unless a man have humility before he ascend, he cannot go up those spiritual steps, nor reach those spiritual gifts. As it is written: "To whom shall I have respect, but to him that is poor and little, of a contrite spirit, and that trembleth at My words?"[23] And it is said in the Psalm: "In his heart he hath disposed to ascend by steps in the vale of tears, in the place which he hath set".[24] This vale is a lovely place, where the sinner afflicts his heart with tears whilst advancing towards the virtues. Again it is written: "Thou sendest forth springs in the valleys; the waters shall pass between the midst of the hills".[25] These are the streams of living water of which our Lord speaks, that spring from the Holy Spirit unto eternal life. They spring in the valleys, and they flow through the valleys, because the gifts of the Holy Spirit are given to the humble.[26]

Through this diversity of gifts from one Spirit we dispose ascensions in our heart from the lowest to the highest: yet whoever has received the perfection of wisdom has received all these gifts in that one. Because the Holy Spirit is the Eternal Wisdom, and He imparts the gifts that belong to wisdom in proportion to the dispositions of the receiver. Hence it is said in the Proverbs: "Wisdom hath built herself a house, she hath hewn out seven pillars".[27] This house is the sanctified soul in which the Holy Spirit dwells, and the seven pillars are the seven luminous and strengthening gifts that in the living house aspire to God. But wisdom is the chief, giving us both the knowledge and the sense of divine things, and from it there come the purest piety and the firmest fortitude, whereby we both adhere to God and reject what is opposed to God. And the fear of God that belongs to wisdom is not a predominant dread of punishment, but such a vivid sense of God instilled into the heart, as to fill us with the sense of our own unworthiness.

"The fear of the Lord is the beginning of wisdom," because, as St. Bernard observes, "the soul obtains her first sense of God through fear, and not through knowledge. When you fear the justice and power of God it is because He gives you a vivid sense of Himself as He is just and powerful. But fear affects our inward sense, and just as knowledge gives us understanding, fear gives us sensibility. When therefore we begin to feel God we begin to enter into His wisdom, because wisdom comes of the sense of God."[28] But that fear of God which is perfect wisdom is the fear of love and reverence, and it arises from an all-pervading feeling of the Infinite Goodness, the sublime Majesty, and the eternal Glory of God, in contrast with our nothingness before Him. Wisdom, therefore, as the Scripture teaches, "is an infinite treasure to men: which they that use become the friends of God, being commended for the gifts of discipline"[29].

The seven gifts are opposed to the seven deadly sins; and they are the life of the eight beatitudes. As the heart sends the life's blood through all the veins and limbs of the body, the Holy Spirit sends His living fire and unction through all the powers of the soul. The Master of love and sanctity, He descends into creatures unworthy of His presence through the condescension of charity, and fills the mind with His light, the heart with His sense, and the will with His strength; removing evil, bringing good. To sanctify is to purify and to unite with God, and He purifies with fire, and unites with unction the soul that He embraces with charity.

In various forms were the seven gifts prefigured in the prophetic ages, but in none more completely that in the seven-branched candlestick that stood burning day and night in the holy sanctuary of God's Temple. The stem of pure gold was a figure of Christ's humanity, which, hypostatically united with His divinity, ascended erect towards Heaven. The seven branches proceeding from the stem were lilies of pure gold, united with the stem as the Spirit of God is united with Christ, whose seven gifts embrace His pure humanity. The seven golden lamps, ever burning with pure oil, symbol the seven gifts of the Holy Ghost, burning in souls to the honour and glory of God in the flames of charity, according to the mind and sense of Christ. As the Apostle says: "Let this mind be in you, which was also in Christ Jesus"[30]. The three lamps on the right hand are the lamps of illumination; they are knowledge, understanding, and counsel. The three lamps on the left hand, the side of the heart, are the lamps of spiritual sense and power; they are fear, piety, and fortitude. The lamp in the middle crowns the whole; it rests on the stem, which is Christ, and this is the lamp of wisdom.

The first lamp lighted in the soul is the lamp of fear; not of servile fear, for that precedes the divine gifts, but of child-like fear and reverence. This fear moves from charity: it is the chaste and venerating reverence that flows from the touch of the Holy Spirit on the will, moving the soul to revere our Heavenly Father with ease and promptitude, and to dread offending Him. This fear despoils us of our own will, and makes us conscious that we belong to God and not to ourselves. The beginning of this fear casts a certain holy horror over the soul from the sense of the awful Majesty of God, and makes us feel how little we are in His sight, how feeble before His Infinite power, before whom the angels tremble, and whom nothing can resist. This fear strikes down the folly of conceit, and humbles us into our nothingness. It shows that we have no foundation in ourselves, and moves us with humble and awe-struck reverence to seek our foundation in God. It strikes a new sense into us, and gives birth to new resolution that makes us obedient and patient, caring for little beyond the will of God, and prompt to confess our failings and unworthiness.

This child-like fear is the true beginning of hope as well as of wisdom; for in detaching us from trust in ourselves, it sets us free to trust in God. It is neither servile, worldly, nor carnal fear, but the reverence of God in the fear of ourselves. Servile fear is the dread of the slave under the lash of his master, although the master's goodness may change that fear into loving reverence. But so long as fear is servile, it places the love of self before the love of God, and dreads His punishments more than it fears to lose Him. Worldly fear is the dread of losing temporal advantages or social reputation. Carnal fear is the dread of corporal privations, sufferings, or death. The power of the gift of the fear of God is to conquer these fears of the creature, to absorb them, and so banish them from the soul; and to restore us to our freedom and dignity, because the gift of the fear of God delivers us from every other fear.

The fear of the Lord expels pride, which is the radical deformity of man. As St. Bonaventure observes, it introduces God through the humility which it brings, because the man is brought under the mighty hand of God. Wherefore, as St. Anselm justly concludes: "The fear of the Lord is the beginning of the divine gifts, and the Holy Spirit gives this fear for a foundation on which to build the other gifts"[31].

The second lamp, with its golden vessel, oil, and flame, is the gift of piety. Piety is that gift of the Holy Ghost which fills us with childlike affection for our Heavenly Father, and inclines us to love, honour, and worship Him. It is far more excellent to honour God with a child's affection as our Father, than only to honour Him with fear as our Creator, Lord, and Judge; and therefore the gift of piety rises much higher than the virtue of religion. By natural piety children love their parents; by that piety which is the fruit of grace the Christian tends to the love, honour, and worship of God. But the gift of piety is infused from that same Eternal Fountain of piety in which the Holy Spirit loves the Father and the Son, and is loved by them; and this divine infusion of piety softens the hardness of our nature, enlarges the soul by the ardour which it enkindles, sweetens her with unction, and draws her with tenderness towards God, to serve Him with joy, and to worship Him with all her powers.

Hugo of St. Victor has beautifully described this gift as an affection and a devotion poured from the sweetness of the Divine Benignity, that is both grateful in itself, and helpful to mankind.[32]

For these rays from the Sun of divine piety attract the soul into which they enter to the Fountain of all beauty and sweetness, whilst they devoutly incline us to the help of our brethren. Writing to St. Timothy, St. Paul takes this large view of the gift: "Exercise thyself unto piety. For bodily exercise is profitable to little, but piety is profitable to all things, having promise of the life that now is, and of that which is to come."[33]

Piety is also called godliness, as bringing all our affections unto God; for when endowed with this gift we cannot be contained within ourselves, but must go forth, carried by the flame of piety towards the Divine Unity, and moved by love of the Divine Unity to works of mercy and compassion. Wherefore our Blessed Lord in His piety was wholly given up in His interior to the Divine Unity, and wholly given up in His exterior to us, in word, in life, in death, and in the Holy Eucharist.

Piety is the sweet refreshment of a soul filled with the sense of God, and with the consciousness of His friendship. It inspires a disposition to expend the mercy received in works of mercy, both corporal and spiritual. "This piety," to quote Hugo of St. Victor again, "invites us to leave off despondency; the love in it draws us from our own will; the mercy in it pacifies our irritability; the cheerfulness in it makes us feel secure; the affability in it leads to familiarity, and familiarity reveals the divine secrets. When those divine secrets are opened they produce friendship; friendship is preserved by having one spirit, and humility brings us near to God."[34] For, according to St. Paul, "He who is joined to the Lord is one spirit".[35]

The third lamp on the left of the golden candlestick is the gift of fortitude. Fortitude is that gift of the Holy Ghost which infuses strength into the will, that it may control the irascible appetite, and give force and courage both to do and to endure great things with the confidence of succeeding in the face of difficulties, according to the will of God. It is also the work of fortitude to repress the solicitations of concupiscence, and to repel the false allurements of self-love, so as to remove the fears arising from adversities and calamities.

Between the virtue and the gift of fortitude St. Antoninus has drawn these four distinctions. First, the virtue of fortitude acts within the limits of human nature, but the gift has its measure from divine power. The Psalmist says: "By Thee I shall be delivered from temptation; and through my God I shall go over the wall".[36] That is, I shall overcome obstacles that my natural strength could never master. Secondly, although the virtue of fortitude gives courage to brave dangers, it has neither the force nor the confidence to overcome them all; but the gift of fortitude enables us to brave all perils that come in the way of duty, and to surmount them every one.

Thirdly, the virtue of fortitude does not extend to all difficulties, because it rests too much on human strength, which is greater in one faculty in one person, and less in another faculty in another person. Thus one person will have strength to conquer concupiscence, and another to die for God's sake. But the gift of fortitude rests not in our own power, but on the power of God; and consequently it extends to all difficulties, and suffices for all. This was magnanimously declared by holy Job: "Deliver me, O Lord, and set me beside Thee, and let any man's hand fight against me".[37]

Fourthly, the virtue of fortitude will not bring every undertaking to a happy conclusion, for it belongs not to man to carry all his works safely through the evils and dangers that oppose their completion. Death may interrupt them though nothing else should interfere. But the gift of fortitude accomplishes all that God directs us to do, and then brings us to eternal life, the happy ending of our undertakings as well as of our dangers. St. Paul therefore says of this gift: "I can do all things in Him that strengtheneth me"[38].

We must add another important distinction which the devout Gerson has drawn from St. Thomas. When we are so placed that we must either encounter great dangers or sufferings or else abandon the good of virtue—the declaring of our faith, for example, or our adhesion to the cause of justice—the virtue of fortitude will enable us to suffer or to endure; but the gift of fortitude will go much farther, and will enable us to perfect our actions, as they embrace the divine counsels or the state of perfection. It may be objected that this would limit the gift in its abundance to those who are perfect: this however by no means follows; because it is one thing to have the gift as it exists in habit, and another to have it in action through faithful cooperation. As a habit the gift is given with charity, so that even the imperfect who are in charity have the habit of fortitude; but through neglecting to exercise the gift, they have it not in action. But the perfect have brought the habit of the gift into action, and have greatly increased it in reward for their fidelity[39].

The spirit of fortitude includes patience as a component part of the gift; and it is this gift of patience that "hath a perfect work," whereby we possess our souls in God. Much therefore that has been said in these lectures of patience belongs more to the gift than to the simple virtue. The gift demands that we rise in spirit above all that is unlike to God; that we account our native powers but of little worth in comparison with the gift; and that we freely give up our will to the divine power and virtue to make us secure in every combat. If we generously give up our will to the influence of the Holy Spirit, it will take away all doubting, diffidence, fear, shrinking, inconstancy and changeableness, wherever the will of God shall manifestly appear. Hope will spring up that the gift will preserve us from mortal sin; and that noble part of the virtue called magnanimity will arise in a straightforward spirit, will allow of no compromise, will despise whatever is vicious, and will make but little account of what is earthly and therefore fluctuating. Taking small care for these things, the magnanimous soul fears no one but God, looks to no one as great or mighty except God, and puts no great trust in any one but God.

The honest soul, and as no soul is honest without humility, the humble soul then, will ascend in union with the Holy Spirit above all creatures to worship God with gratitude and praise. Praising Him in her life more than her words, she will become magnanimous, robust, and unconquerable. The more sharply provocation or temptation assails her, the more vigorous she will grow, combating with the conscious and invincible power of God. In contemplating the greatness and majesty of God the mind will become simple, free from all narrow views and feelings, and in her growing insight of His goodness she will not know how to praise Him enough. Through this praise of God the soul will feel her own insufficiency, and the very consciousness of what she herself is in the presence of His unspeakable excellency will fill her spirit with joy, salvation, and the beginning of beatitude. She may therefore say with the Blessed Virgin: "My soul doth magnify the Lord; and my spirit hath rejoiced in God my Saviour"[40].

The gift of fortitude inspires courage to undertake great things. What are those great things? If we limit them to what rises above the ordinary events of life, the gift would be rarely needed. What are the great things for which it is habitually given? To understand this it will suffice to consider that man is a fallen king who has lost his royal state. Deny this who may, it is revealed to every man in every hour of his life. He finds it within him in the strife between good and evil. He finds it in those sublime instincts of his heart that perpetually rebuke his degrading propensities. We are called upon to reconquer the kingdom from which we have fallen. This truth is the foundation of all religion, and of all wise legislation; it rests on the distinction between good and evil. What brings us to God is good; what takes us from God is evil. Our great work is to recover the lost kingdom of Heaven.

The means of recovering this kingdom are of the same supernatural character with our final end. God is the supreme object of the soul, and those great means must come from God. To employ them with courage and perseverance is therefore the great thing to be accomplished, and for this the gift of fortitude is essential. The great means to be used are the theological and moral virtues, summed up in the creed and the commandments. Endowed with these virtues, and living in them, the man is restored to God, becomes a king, possesses and rules himself, and inherits the kingdom of Heaven.

This is the greatest and most difficult of all enterprises. Three frightful powers are leagued against its success, and strive to cause its failure: these are the world, the flesh, and the devil. We need not speak here of the craft, cruelty, and hatred of the devil and his legions. The flesh is the body that belongs to us, a heated furnace that burns day and night with the fuel of unlawful affections; with covetousness, with disorderly appetites, with insubordination and vanity; with aversion, anger, hatred, audacity and sadness; with the love of lawless delights, with fear, with despondency. Like another Eve, the flesh offers us the forbidden fruit, and invites the soul to take delight in evil. Like the wife of Putiphar, it solicits Joseph to dishonour. Like Delilah, it shears away the strength of Sampson with his locks, and delivers the man up to the devil as she gave up Sampson to the Philistines. Not only does the body ensnare the soul to evil, but turns her away from good. There is no kind of war which the body will not wage against the soul, and no kind of sacrifice that the soul may not be called upon to make to ensure her safety from the attacks of the body, and that not merely in the interest of one virtue, but of all the virtues.

What is the world but a motley and immense crowd of renegades from God, or from the virtues? Yet this same world is not always seen even by its own members for what it is; notwithstanding its foul errors, false philosophies, loose maxims, pretentious manners, covert vices, and seductive charms. And yet, like the three children in the Babylonian furnace, we must live in the midst of this unruly conflagration, without being scorched by its flames. To conquer the world, the flesh, and the devil is the most arduous of all undertakings, and far exceeds our strength without the presence, light, and power of the Holy Ghost. This is the first part of our task. The second is to suffer.

To suffer well requires much greater fortitude than to act well To act against evil, and to face the danger of evil, comes first in point of time. But to suffer and endure is more essential to accumulating internal strength. This last is also more difficult more noble, and more perfect. St. Antoninus, following St. Thomas, puts the argument in this shape. It is more difficult to combat with the strong than with the weak. But the attack takes the position of the strong, and the defence the position of the weak. He who attacks another sees nothing but a mere possible and distant danger to himself. But he who receives the attack must endure an evil that is actually present, and which must be endured at the present time. An attack is made in an instant; but those who have to bear the attack must suffer for an indefinite and uncertain length of time. It therefore requires much greater fortitude and constancy of will to be firm and patient under the danger, the attack, the pain and suffering of present evil, than to enter actively upon a difficult work. Hence it is well known that the most valiant soldiers are not those who are alert in attack, but those who are patient and strong to endure assaults.

What has man to suffer? It should rather be asked: What things has he not to suffer? Pains and distress of body; pains and griefs of soul; pains and sorrows of conscience; and the dread which they inspire. "Conflicts without, fears within." Maladies to which every part of his mortal frame is exposed; poverty, contradiction, injury, injustice; the attacks of the world, the flesh, and the devil. These are our attendants from the cradle to the grave. Often is the devout Christian predestined to exceptional sufferings, especially of the interior kind, that the spirit may be made strong for eternity. Then, again, his virtues irritate the devil and the world; and at their hands he receives providential sufferings for his purification and perfection in virtue.

But what is man? Who is he that he should undertake to scale Heaven, and to do this mighty feat in the face of all these enemies? His nature, his very name is weakness. Measure the grandeur of his undertaking by the weakness of his nature, and the difference between them represents the divine force of which he stands in constant need. This feeble man, this feebler woman, must become a strong living force through the Holy Spirit dwelling within them.

Thanks to the divine gift of fortitude, the world for nearly nineteen hundred years has witnessed wonders almost incredible.

It has seen millions of souls, poor and rich, ignorant and learned, young and aged, men, women, and even children, in all climes, of all races, courageous and constant to one grand and holy purpose; strong and vigorous in conquering temptations; brave and magnanimous in enduring pain, adversity, and sorrow, for the sake of the kingdom of Heaven. The world has seen the peaceful patience and heroic constancy of the Christian Martyrs. The world has seen the gentle fortitude, so gentle in its strength, of the confessors of Christ, and their joy amidst countless sufferings. The world has witnessed the patient toils and privations of the missioners of truth, and of the daughters of charity. But quickly does the world forget what its children should most take to heart.

Yet all this the world has seen. And what has it heard? It heard St. Paul throwing defiance to the enemies of the soul in the name of all the children of the cross. "I fear not"—"I can do all things in Him that strengtheneth me."—"Who shall separate us from the love of Christ?" The world has heard St. Francis taking poverty for his spouse, and greeting patience as her sister. It has heard St. Teresa taking for the heroic maxim of her life: "To suffer or to die". It has heard the yet more heroic maxim of St. Mary Magdalen de Pazzi: "To suffer, not to die". It has heard St. John of the Cross uniting these two maxims into one: "To suffer, and be despised for God's sake". How many like notes breathed from the gift of fortitude, and praising the blessed good of sufferings, have resounded from the hearts and lives of the Saints since the day when the Holy Ghost came in fire upon the heads of the Apostles[41].

The first branch on the right hand of the golden candlestick is the gift of knowledge. In this gift the Holy Spirit moves the mind and the will to form just and sure judgments in what belongs to faith, and to distinguish what is from what is not of faith, independently of all reasoning from secondary or created causes. By this gift we also know what to do, and what to leave undone, according to the law of justice. This is the science of the Saints, of which the Book of Wisdom says: "The Lord hath led the just man through right ways, and showed him the kingdom of God, and hath given him the knowledge of holy things"[42]. St. Thomas thus explains the gift: "The divine knowledge is not from reasoning, it is absolute and simple; and the gift of knowledge from the Holy Ghost is like to this, it is a certain partaken resemblance of the divine knowledge. Distinct from the virtue of faith, it perfects that virtue with greater light and knowledge."[43]

In the first place, the gift of knowledge gives us light to distinguish what is true from what is false, what is of God from what is of the creature, what is solid from what is vain and imaginary, and what is truly great from what only appears to be great, although not so in reality. For example, it enables us to see the perfect harmony that exists between humiliation, poverty, and suffering, and the real wants of the fallen man; and thus we learn to accept them as the sick man takes his medicines, to save him from death and restore him to health. It is a holy commerce, in which we exchange what is temporary and trivial for a wealth that is imperishable. St. Paul understood this commerce well. "The things," he says, "that were gain to me, I have accounted loss for Christ. Furthermore, I count all things to be loss for the excellent knowledge of Jesus Christ my Lord: for whom I have suffered the loss of all things, and count them all but filth that I may gain Jesus Christ."[44]

Secondly, the divine gift of knowledge acts upon the will, and brings judgment and action into harmony with the truth in the mind. Thirdly, this knowledge radiates the light of truth upon the sciences, shows their true place, and gives them their due order, whilst it confirms, ennobles, and fertilizes them.

The gift of counsel is the second luminous lamp on the right of the golden candlestick. We can never run well or wisely unless we know at what object and end we are aiming, and by what course the prize may best be obtained. St. Antoninus defines the gift of counsel to be that gift of the Holy Ghost which directs us in all things that are ordained to bring us to our final end in God, whether needful to our salvation or not. But in the searchings of counsel man needs to be directed by God, to whom all things are known. This is the gift of counsel.

[45]And St. Thomas observes that the gift of counsel responds to the virtue of prudence, which it keeps and perfects.[46] Prudence results from the good use of counsel in what regards the conduct of life and the management of affairs. But human prudence often fails, whilst divine prudence never fails those souls who act by its inspiration. At first there may be doubts and hesitations, but this is only the sifting and cleaning off of what is human, fanciful, or erroneous in our deliberations, of which the light of counsel makes us conscious; whilst, with the help of patience and humility, the counsel of the Holy Spirit will shine out clear in the end, and that in a way that cannot be mistaken, because it puts the mind at peace. There is also

given a grace to the will to carry out in action what has been resolved upon by counsel.

But we should much mistake the gift of counsel in supposing that its light is always given to the individual whom it concerns directly. The Holy Spirit provides for the fundamental and essential virtue of humility, without which the plenitude of the gift cannot be received. He therefore often conceals from one what He makes known to another, and guides the one to seek light from the other, that the humility of the act may open the mind to receive the light of counsel. Again, it is written, that "where there is much counsel there is safety"[47]. Counsel collects into one what the Divine Wisdom distributes to several, giving light to one and the desire of light to another, who obtains it by consultation. Hence holy Tobias admonishes his son: "Seek counsel always of a wise man".[48] And we are taught by the Holy Spirit: "Be at peace with all men, but let one in a thousand be thy counsellor",[49] St. Bernard points to a double leprosy that eats into the soundness of counsel, self-will and self-interest, both of which listen more to the perversity of nature than to the guidance of God.

The third lamp on the right is the gift of understanding. This gift is a supernatural light that descends through the mind into our spiritual nature, and lifts up our spiritual sense to penetrate that truth which is given to the receptive mind or memory, enabling us to comprehend it, and make it our own; and so to bring it into use and application in the practical intelligence. It is of little avail to have truth in the mind unless it be received into the understanding. But by bringing the understanding through the act of the will into commerce with the light of truth in the mind, that is, by attention, by consideration, by reflection, and by meditation, we bring the truth presented to the mind into our spiritual nature, and thus make it our own. But the knowledge that God offers to us can never really become our own, until, by the searching which the Holy Spirit moves us to make, that truth descends into our spiritual sense, and takes possession of the powers of the will, that what we see with our understanding we may feel in our inmost life, giving our active consent to the light in us that accords with the light in God. Then, as St. Augustine observes: "Understanding of truth cleans the heart of carnal affection, that pure intention may direct us towards our final end".[50]

By the gift of understanding the Holy Spirit purifies the eye of the soul, and leads us into ourselves, where we begin to understand what we are and what God is. And whilst we subject our understanding to God, His truth makes us children of the light. Moving upwards through that light, we rise above our senses, above our imagination, above the instincts of our nature, and enter with intelligence into the presence of God. There we receive the gift more abundantly in proportion as we die to ourselves; and from the gift there grows a singular virtue, having its origin in God and its life in the will, a virtue that makes us watchful of good, and conservative of the light of life. This vivid and luminous appetite for good looks to God with great contentment, thanks Him, and feels after Him through His manifold gifts. In this sense of God the mortification of nature is constantly renewed, the spirit grows in the grace of the Holy Ghost, and the divine light is preserved in the soul. The soul delights in God, and the interior man is renewed day by day.

The seventh lamp upon the golden stem crowns the other six with the sovereign gift of wisdom. Who can declare the splendour of this gift? Implanted in the human heart, it illuminates divine and eternal things, and gives us the sense of eternal good. Human wisdom consists in the knowledge of things in their causes, and especially in their supreme cause. But the gift of divine wisdom is a certain created participation of the Holy Spirit as He is the Eternal Wisdom. That Eternal Wisdom is the infinite light of the infinite love of the Father and the Son in the person of the Holy Ghost. In the words of St. Bonaventure: "The wisdom that descends to us from above is the splendour of truth in the delightful sense of good. Having God for its chief object, as He is the true good that attracts our will to Him, it draws us to love God, and to delight in Him. Wherefore," concludes the great Doctor and Saint, "the gift of wisdom is a supernatural habit infused into the soul by the Holy Spirit, enabling us to know, to love, and to delight in God."[51]

This gift is given in its abundance to the pure of heart, and is chiefly cultivated in contemplation. For contemplation brings the soul nigh to God, where she receives the impress of His likeness in much simplicity, and where, ascending above the creature, the soul absorbs the sense of God. But the sense of God is wisdom. "We begin with the gift of fear," says St. Augustine, "and passing step by step through the intermediate gifts, we reach their consummation at last in the gift of wisdom. This is the final gift, because it tranquillizes the soul, and makes her peaceful, fruitful, and joyful."[52] "The Holy Spirit," observes St. Anselm, "accumulates this gift upon His other gifts, when He breathes wisdom into the soul, enabling what is correctly known by the gift of understanding to be sweetly relished in the gift of wisdom, in virtue of which we pursue what is excellent from pure love. Dwelling in this house of the soul with His gifts, the Holy Spirit rules the whole family of the soul's interior senses, and so disposes them in His service that they ascend to God, and, without departing from God, they descend to the service of our neighbour. That soul is therefore able to say with the Psalmist: 'The Lord ruleth me, and I shall want for nothing. He hath set me in a place of pasture.'"[53]

This wisdom is the "unction from the Holy One" that teacheth all things: the light that illuminates all darkness: the lambent fire that played on the heads of the Apostles. The Wise Man had experience of this light, this unction, this ardent fire when he wrote this praise of wisdom. "I wished, and understanding was given to me: and I called upon God, and the Spirit of wisdom came to me, and I preferred her to kingdoms and thrones, and esteemed riches as nothing in comparison of her.... I loved her above health and beauty, and chose to have her instead of light. For her light cannot be put out. She is an infinite treasure to men, which they that use become the friends of God, being commended for the gift of discipline. For in her is the spirit of understanding: holy, one manifold, subtle, eloquent, active, undefiled, sure, sweet, loving that which is good, quick, which nothing hindereth, beneficent, gentle, kind, steadfast, assured, secure, having all power, overseeing all things, and reacheth everywhere by reason of her purity. Her have I loved, and have sought her from my youth, and have desired to take her for my spouse, and I became a lover of her beauty. Give me wisdom, that sitteth by Thy throne, and cast me not off from among Thy children. Send her out of Thy holy Heaven, and from the throne of Thy Majesty, that she may be with me, and may labour with me, that I may know what is acceptable to Thee.[54]

# 10

## ON PRAYER

"All things, whatsoever you ask when you pray, believe that you shall receive, and they shall come to you."—S. MARK xi 24.

Before entering upon the important subject of patience in prayer, it will be expedient to give some instruction on the true spirit of prayer. The path of prayer is the King's highway from earth to Heaven. Whilst the body remains on its kindred earth, the spirit ascends on the wings of grace into that divine region of light and good for which she was created. This royal path leads the soul into the Eternal Presence, there to plead her cause with her Creator and Sovereign Lord; there to converse in the humble spirit of child-like affection with her Heavenly Father; there to receive His good and perfect gifts. This royal highway to God was opened for us by our Lord Jesus Christ; was consecrated by His prayers and sufferings; and was illuminated by His ascension to Heaven through the path which He opened. By His Incarnation He bridged the whole distance between the creature and the Creator. He is Himself the way, the light of the way, and its security. Through Him we have access to the Father, who answers us with mercy and benignity. "I go to the Father:

and whatsoever you ask the Father in My name, that will I do: that the Father may be glorified in the Son."[1]

This holy path of prayer was figured in the vision of Jacob. Reposing in solitude with his head upon a stone, he saw a ladder ascending from earth to Heaven, and the Lord leaned upon the ladder, and the Angels of the Lord ascended and descended. They ascended with the prayers of mortals, and descended with the gifts of God. Prayer is the golden key that unlocks the celestial treasury to our spiritual wants, and opens the door of God's providence to our temporal necessities. In bountiful reply to the cry of our hearts, comes that holy light which enlightens our minds, that grace of life which removes our offences, that fire of charity that kindles our soul with love, that fortitude which strengthens us with the gifts of the Holy Ghost. In a word, prayer is the commerce of the soul with God through Jesus Christ in the supreme affair of our salvation and perfection. "I am the way, and the truth, and the life. No one cometh to the Father but by Me."[2]

Prayer is, therefore, the noblest and most exalted action of which man is capable through the grace of God. It is the sublimest act of the human intelligence, and the greatest act of the human will. If we put its whole grandeur into a sentence, it is the action of God's created image seeking union with her Divine Original, and seeking it so that this image may be healed from offence, and perfected into likeness by the reception of life from the Eternal Life, and be prepared for beatitude through the gifts that descend from God's infinite perfection. So wonderful is the power of true prayer as to make it evident to reason as well as to faith that its efficacy can never depend upon such weak and sinful creatures as we are. Again, there are obstacles in our own nature, in those many and strong attractions to ourselves, against the exercise of true and pure prayer, which not only require a Divine Mediator of prayer, but a Divine Mover of prayer. This Mover is the Holy Spirit of God. St. Paul has taught us this: "We hope for that which we see not: we wait for it in patience. Likewise the Spirit helpeth our infirmity. For, we know not what we should pray for as we ought: but the Spirit Himself asketh for us with unspeakable groanings, and He that searcheth the hearts, knoweth what the Spirit desireth: because He asketh for the saints according to God."[3]

The Holy Spirit is the prime mover of all the true prayer that created spirits offer in supplication or adoration to the Holy Trinity. He is also the helper and supporter of our supplications. But these prayers obtain their effective power from the sacrifice and the pleadings of our Lord Jesus Christ. Such is the sublime dignity of prayer. What, then, is our part in this holy exercise? To follow the inspirations, to obey the movements and attractions of the Holy Spirit. The Divine Comforter of souls, whom Jesus Christ promised us to be our Paraclete, our other Advocate with the Father, moves us to repentance, dwells in our heart by charity, and helps our infirmity with the light of His wisdom and the power of His gifts. Our prayers are then attached to the prayers of Jesus Christ, our sufferings to His sufferings, and our patience to His patience. The Holy Spirit, the most sublime lover of our souls, moves our will by His grace, and sustains our humble petitions; and we, when we pray in spirit and in truth, respond to His movements, and, whilst groaning under our mortal burden, sigh in desire beyond what words can express to be delivered from all that is weak, sinful, and miserable in ourselves, and to be brought to the perfect charity and peace of God.

Such is the sublimity of Christian prayer. Moved and helped by the Holy Spirit, resting for its efficacy on the merits of Christ, and formed in the soul by humble obedience to those divine inspirations, the prayer of the Christian transcends the whole order of creation, and for the love of His Incarnate and Crucified Son, and of the loving action of His Holy Spirit, the Father beholds that prayer with clemency, and repays it with mercy and bounty. The soul herself is drawn to follow her prayer, and, in following, approaches near to God. The spirit is humbled in the consciousness of her wants; the heart is opened, and filled with reverence; the virtues rise into our prayer, and receive greater perfection from this holy exercise. Truth is enlightened to us, hope is elevated, love is enkindled, repentance deepened. For the divine virtues rest the soul on God, and adhere to Him as their one true object. Such is the spirit of true prayer. If trial comes to darken the understanding and dry the affections, so long as right intention remains, the efficacy of prayer is not lessened; but it is rendered more effectual through the greater faith and patience with which it is continued. For the object of prayer is not to please ourselves, but to honour God, and to open to Him the desires of our heart; and the more our prayer costs us, the more precious it is in the sight of God. We then fully realize the words of St. Paul: "We hope for that which we see not: we wait for it in patience".

Prayer, then, is not an affair of words, but an action of the internal spirit. Words are but an imperfect instrument for the manifestation of the deeper movements of the soul. There is a great deal in the action of true prayer which words are incapable of expressing. The truest word of prayer is the interior and spiritual word, that word of the spirit which consists in the silent movement of the soul's desires towards God. The posture of the body, again, should be a kind of silent word expressive of the interior posture of the soul. Of the prayer of words without the prayer of the heart the Almighty speaks with indignation. "This people draw near Me with their mouth, and with their lips glorify Me, but their heart is far from Me, and they have feared Me with the doctrines and commandments of men."[4]

"The hour cometh," saith our Lord, "and now is, when the true adorers shall adore the Father in spirit and in truth. For the Father seeketh such to adore Him. God is a spirit, and they that adore Him must adore Him in spirit and in truth."[5] When therefore our Lord gave us a form of prayer, made His sacrifice the centre of worship, and ordained His sacraments, He required that we should put our spirit into His prayer, and our heart into His sacrifice and sacraments. St. Paul has indicated the vast difference between the spiritual prayer of the New Law and the ceremonial prayer of the Old, where he says: "I will pray with the spirit, I will pray also with the understanding: I will sing with the spirit, I will sing also with the understanding"[6] We adore the Father in truth when we pray in the faith of Christ Jesus, the Eternal Truth; we adore Him in spirit when we pray in the grace of His Holy Spirit. For "grace and truth came by Jesus Christ".[7] When therefore we assist at the Holy Sacrifice in which Jesus Christ the very truth pleads for us, or join in the solemn offices of the Church, or, "having shut the door, pray to the Father in secret," our prayer must be in spirit and in truth, and the words we use must express the inward movements and desires of the heart. "For the Father seeketh such to adore Him."

Hence vocal prayer should be mental as well as vocal, and spiritual as well as mental. Whenever we say the Lord's prayer, or the devout prayers which the Church provides, or recite the inspired psalms, we must remember that the words are given us to waken up in our souls the profound sense of what they signify, and to move us by spiritual action to put that sense into the words we utter, that the mind may accord with the voice. "True prayer," observes St. Gregory the Great, "is not to be found in the words of the voice, but in the thoughts of the heart. The voices that reach the ears of God are not words but desires. If we seek the eternal life with our lips, without desiring that life with our heart, our outcry is nothing but silence. But when we desire that life from our heart, though our mouth be silent, in that silence we cry to God."[8] Hence holy Job exclaims: "Who will grant me a hearer, that the Almighty may hear my desire?"[9] And the Psalmist says: "The Lord hath heard the desire of the poor: Thy ear hath heard the preparation of their heart."[10] All true prayer, even that which is called vocal, resolves itself into mental and spiritual prayer. It includes the internal motives that enlighten and elevate the mind, and the internal aspirations of desire that move the soul towards God; and the words are but the outward expression of those internal motives and movements. True vocal prayer, therefore, is the outward language of internal adoration and supplication in spirit and in truth.

Pure mental prayer uses no external words, but only internal words. The more the soul is habituated to this interior prayer, the more perfectly will she make her vocal prayer. This needs no proof: for it is obvious that when the soul is accustomed to interior recollection, she will carry that recollection with ease into her vocal prayer; and as the truly recollected soul sees God everywhere, she will especially find Him in the language of prayer, which, to the recollected heart, is the most congenial of all languages.

The hand has five pliant and docile fingers which lay hold of their objects and do their work, but the three first have the chief power. The soul has also five faculties, which are employed in mental prayer, and by means of which we take hold of the objects of the soul and work with them. But of these faculties three are principal and purely spiritual: the memory, in which our light and knowledge are stored; the understanding, by which we draw light and knowledge from the stores of memory; and the will, by which we consent to or refuse what is before us, by which we love or hate, by which we desire or refuse to desire, by which we assent or dissent, and by which we make resolutions to determine and guide our actions.

But besides these three superior faculties there are two others which, when they work in their right and proper order, are subordinate to them. These are the imagination, which gives to the mind the images of external and visible things; and the interior sense, which on its inferior side is in communication with the corporal senses, and on its superior side is in communication with the spiritual gifts of God, whereby we feel the things of God that move our spiritual affections. St. Paul says: "They that are according to the spirit mind the things that are of the spirit."[11] And again: "Strong meat is for the perfect: for them who have their senses exercised in the discerning of good and evil".[12]

Through the help of the imagination we represent to ourselves the life of Christ, the truths of the gospel, and the mysteries of faith, but in ways that are more or less figurative. These pictures of the mind are illuminated by the light given us, and are perfected from the stores of truth in our memory. The next step is to penetrate with the understanding through these sensible images, or words, into their interior and spiritual sense, and thus rise from the visible representation to the pure truth as it is in God, feeling that truth, feeding upon it, and absorbing it into the soul, as the bee extracts honey from the flowers. Thus meditation is a gradual ascent of the mind by the act of the will from the sensible representation of sacred things formed in the imagination with the help of memory to their interior and spiritual sense and signification; and from their interior sense and signification the mind ascends to the pure truth as it is in God; so that what begins in meditation ends in contemplation.

"In my meditation," says holy David, "a fire shall flame out."[13] As truth enters the soul her desires open, the Holy Spirit of truth moves the affections, the spiritual sense is touched with the flame of love, and the soul is moved to love, to adore, and to resolve upon her conduct. Meditation leads to contemplation as the soul ascends in greater simplicity from the figures and images of truth to the very truth as it is in God, divested by degrees of that sensible and multiplied imagery with which it is clothed to our senses and imagination. The soul looks into that truth, and feels that truth with a simple eye and a simple heart, and so receives it by dwelling upon it, that it greatly increases the knowledge of God and of ourselves. For when by the divine attraction the soul rises from the labour of meditation to the simple tranquillity of contemplation, God makes a partial revelation of Himself to the contemplating soul, and "in His light we see light".[14]

Thus the will uses the imagination to represent those visible things that help to bring the mind to God, and especially, with the help of memory, brings the mind into contact with the person, life, words, actions, sufferings, death, and glorious mysteries of our God and Saviour Jesus Christ. The understanding, enlightened by faith, penetrates into the interior spirit and sense of what the imagination externally represents to us. But it is the will that moves the understanding to "dispose ascensions in the heart,' rising from truth to truth until our soul rests upon the One Supreme Truth and Infinite Good, who is the final end of all desire, and therefore of all prayer. Our spiritual sense, most intimately connected with the will, and the receptive cause of our spiritual affections, when it is touched by the Spirit of God, is that which gives us the feeling of refreshment and consolation in prayer. Touched by the light and sense of God, the will bends down our whole being to His divine influence; and illuminated by His truth, lays open her infirmities and her wants to His mercy and goodness, and performs all the offices of prayer and praise.

The great obstacles to prayer are self-love, the inconstancy of the will, and the sadness that results from self-love and inconstancy. Self-love draws our sense, thought, and will to ourselves, instead of surrendering them to God and to the guidance of His Holy Spirit. This causes the will to vibrate like a pendulum, but in a very unsteady way, between God and one's self, making the soul restless, impatient, inattentive, and wandering. Yet we cannot look to God and to ourselves at the same time: we cannot feel after God and after ourselves at the same moment. This is not pure prayer, but prayer mixed with distraction, self-love, and confusion. This generates sadness, which injures or destroys the zest for prayer. Yet this gives us no knowledge of ourselves, because we learn to know ourselves as we are reflected in the light of God.

Prayer is either public or private. Public prayer is essentially vocal, that all who are assembled for its performance may unite and pray in common. To all who are thus united, with one heart and soul, especially in the Church, or in the family, our Lord has promised that He will be in the midst of them. But if the Father seeks the true adorers to adore Him in spirit and in truth, why do we use vocal prayer? First, because Christ has taught us to use vocal prayer, and has given us a perfect form of it by way of example. Secondly, because as members of the Church we owe to God and to each other the public communion of prayer, as well as mutual edification. Thirdly, because vocal prayer is designed for the outward expression of internal prayer, the prayer in spirit and truth. Fourthly, because the words and signs of prayer, especially those provided by the Church, awaken the inward mind and heart to apprehend the light and sense of prayer, and move the affections to lift up the soul in prayer. As St. Augustine says: "By words and signs we are more keenly wakened up to holy desires"[15]. Fifthly, as our body has been the instrument of sin, it should be made the submissive instrument of the service of God.

Sixthly, the united supplication of heart and voice especially becomes those who pray for the remission of their sins. The Prophet Osee says to sinful Israel: "Take with you words, and return to the Lord, and say to Him: Take away all iniquity, and receive good: and we will render the calves of the lips"[16]. The calves of the lips is a figurative expression for the sacrificial offerings of the voice. The tongue is a great offender; it should therefore be a great expiator. Seventhly, it may be added that a humble posture of body, responsive to the humility of soul, especially becomes us in penitential and supplicatory prayer, that the whole man may be vocal as well as the voice. Hence the custom from the beginning of the Church of not only kneeling, striking the breast, and prostrating, but also of extending the arms in supplication towards heaven, that the body may not only not oppose or contradict the movements of the soul, but may express and help her pious movements.

St. Augustine has pointed out another excellence of vocal prayer, namely, that whilst the words help to take us from distraction and raise our mind to God, they remind us of what we are, of what we want, and of what we ought to desire from God. When, for example, we cast our eyes on the words of the Lord's prayer, they become as a luminous mirror in which the Divine Master of prayer shows us the excellence and fruitfulness of prayer, the chief wants of the soul, and the virtues to be put forth in prayer.

The fundamental condition of prayer, essential for obtaining its end, is attention. But this attention depends for its constancy and perseverance on the virtue of patience, as we shall explain in the next lecture. We shall here give the doctrine of attention from St. Thomas, the prince of theologians, because anxious and timid souls stand in need of a great authority to quiet their apprehensions, and to put them at peace with respect to distractions in prayer.

Even holy persons are subject at times to wanderings in prayer, and the holy Psalmist says of himself: "My heart is troubled, my strength hath left me, and the light of my eyes is not with me". Yet he had said just before: "Lord, all my desire is before Thee".[17] Vocal prayer requires two kinds of attention: attention to the words, and attention towards God. But the first and most necessary attention is to the end of prayer, which is an elevation of our attention to God. This is necessary to prayer. The second is the attention necessary for obtaining the effects or fruits of prayer. The fruits of prayer are of three kinds; these are the merit of prayer, the obtaining of what we ask for in prayer, and the refreshment given to the soul in prayer.

The first effect or fruit of prayer, as of all good works done in a state of grace and charity, is its merit, always, be it understood, through the merits of our Lord Jesus Christ. To obtain this fruit it is not necessary that actual intention should continue through the whole prayer; because the force of the first intention with which the prayer is begun continues virtually throughout, and renders the whole prayer meritorious.

The second effect, and that which is proper to prayer, is to obtain the divine answer to our prayer. To obtain this result the first intention will also suffice, because God looks principally to that intention. But if there is no first intention begun, prayer cannot be meritorious, nor will it obtain the good we came to ask for. For, as St. Gregory says, God hears not the prayer of him who gives no attention to his prayer. But it should be noted, that attention to God whilst we pray is attention to prayer.

The third effect or fruit of prayer is its immediate influence on the soul, in giving that soul a certain refreshment and consolation. This of necessity requires a continual attention to prayer. Hence St. Paul says: "If I pray in a tongue, my spirit prayeth, but my understanding is without fruit".[18] The Apostle speaks of a tongue that is unknown to him who prays, and which he therefore cannot understand.

We must next understand that there are three kinds of attention, any of which may be given to the words of vocal prayer. We may attend to the words alone, so as to make no mistake in repeating them; or to the sense of the words as well; or to the object and end of prayer, that is to God, and to the good that we seek of God. This last is the necessary and essential attention, an attention which even the simplest and most unlettered minds can give. Sometimes, as Hugo of St. Victor observes, in holy souls devoted to prayer, this attention to God is so abundant, that for the time all things else are forgotten. And we ourselves have known certain holy souls with such a gift of prayer, and from time to time so absorbed in God, that on first returning to themselves they knew not where they were, nor what was around them.

From these principles and their explanation, we are now in a position to draw the following conclusions. First, we pray in spirit and in truth when we approach to prayer from the movement of the Holy Spirit, even though in the course of prayer the mind should wander owing to infirmity. Secondly, we must understand that the human mind, on account of its infirmity, cannot remain in an elevated state of recollected prayer for long, because the weight of infirmity brings the soul down to inferior things. It thus happens that when the mind has ascended to God in contemplation, after a time it will suddenly go astray, and that from no other cause than the infirmity of nature. Thirdly, if any one of set intention wanders away in mind from attention to prayer, this is sinful, and it hinders the fruit of prayer. But those distractions of mind that are not intentional do not take away the fruit of prayer. St. Basil says: "If, through being enfeebled by sin, you cannot pray with fixed attention, hold your attention together as much as you can, and God will pardon your defects; because it is not from negligence but from frailty that you cannot keep yourself in God's presence as you ought"[19].

Fourthly, it will give a most valuable light to prayer, if we further consider with St. Thomas how great the distinction is between the present consolation received in prayer and the future benefits to be derived from it. Consolation is not always felt in prayer; and when it is absent, the soul is sometimes tempted to imagine that the essential rewards of prayer have not been obtained, because they have not been made sensible to us in the time of prayer. But this notwithstanding, they are in the hands of God for our future good. To express the truth briefly, and in the words of the famous Doctor Alexander Hales: In our present state, in which our fallen nature is undergoing reparation, we advance to God more through adversity than through prosperity, and this is true even in prayer. Our faith, trust, love, humility, and patience are perfected by adhering to God without present consolation, whenever God so wills it, and without our having the present knowledge of the good things which God has in store for us.

Like every other good act, prayer obtains its merit from the root of charity which the Holy Spirit gives us; but the proper object of charity is the Eternal Good, which it prepares us to enjoy. The prayer that proceeds from charity, and obtains the good things of Heaven, is also accompanied in a special manner by those other virtues that belong to the good of prayer, by faith, by humility, by patience, and devotion. Faith believes that we shall obtain what we seek; humility knows how much we stand in need of what we seek; patience gives steadfastness to our attention; and devotion prefers God to all things.

The granting of our petitions is from the grace of God by whom we are attracted to pray. But, as St. Augustine observes, God would not move us to pray if He did not wish to give. And St. Chrysostom remarks that God never denies His benefits to those whom His paternal piety instigates in such a manner that they do not fail in praying to Him. Our Divine Lord Himself assures us that "Whatsoever you shall ask the Father in My name, that will I do, that the Father may be glorified in the Son"[20] These are divine words, words of truth addressed to our belief, and deserving to be diligently taken to heart. In the same divine discourse our Lord says again: "Amen, amen I say to you, if you ask the Father anything in My name, He will give it you"[21]. How He will give it we shall see presently.

But the prayer that proceeds not from sanctifying grace has no divine element in it, and has no more merit than any other good action that is not done in charity. Yet even the prayer that implores the grace of conversion and the gift of sanctifying grace proceeds from an awakening grace, for prayer is always the gift of God.

We shall better understand the merit of prayer, if we keep this principle in mind, that prayer is chiefly and before all things ordained with respect to our final beatitude. When, therefore, we ask for other things, if they stand in the way of our beatitude, they will not be granted, because this would not contribute to our greater good. If then we ask anything of God for ourselves which He sees would not be useful towards our beatitude, it would be of no merit to obtain what we ask for. But when our intention is good, God in His goodness will give us, not what we think it would be best to receive, but what He sees it will be best to give, and what will contribute to our eternal life. Hence St. Augustine says: "When we ask of God in good faith for the necessities of this life, He is as merciful when He does not hear as when He does hear us; for the physician knows better what is good for the sick man than the sick man knows himself"[22]. When St Paul prayed to be freed from the thorn in his flesh his prayer was not granted because it was not expedient for him, but grace was given him to bear it.

It remains to consider the words of St. Luke: "And He spoke to them a parable, that we ought always to pray, and not to faint"[23]. And the words of St. Paul: "Pray without ceasing. In all things give thanks: for this is the will of God in Jesus Christ concerning you all."[24] And those words to Timothy: "I will therefore that men pray in every place, lifting up pure hands without anger or contention".[25] To understand this doctrine of perpetual prayer we must draw a distinction between the spirit of prayer and the formal exercise of prayer; or, as St. Thomas puts it, between the cause of prayer and actual prayer. The spirit or cause of prayer is in the desires of charity, from which all prayer ought to proceed. These desires of charity ought to be continual, if not in act, at least in habit and virtually; for this virtual desire abides in all that we do from the love of God. It is in this sense that our prayer should be continual and never ceasing. So St. Augustine instructs Proba: "As long as our desires continue in faith, hope, and charity, we are always praying."

But the actual exercise of prayer cannot be continual, because we have other works to do and other duties to engage our minds. But, as St. Augustine teaches in the same instruction: "We have certain hours and intervals of time in which to pray to God in words, that helped by those signs we may admonish ourselves, and know how far we have advanced in holy desires, and may more keenly awaken up ourselves to increase them"[26]. In God's sight holy desires are prayers.

As food is proportioned to corporal health, prayer should be proportioned to spiritual health. Whilst we perform our due share of public prayer and our regulated duty of private prayer, what is left to free choice should not be continued further than will do us the good of keeping up the fervour of interior desire. Beyond this measure it will become tedious and distracting, and will cause a distaste for prayer. But this measure is very different for different persons. There are highly privileged souls, though rare, whose interior habit of prayer is almost continual, though not in words yet in recollection. Yet so far from interfering with external duties and conversation, this interior recollection is of great profit to them.

This brings us to that method of prayer which is called aspirative or ejaculatory. This prayer consists of brief aspirations, or short and fervid sentences, sped like arrows from the heart. It is a prayer of inestimable value, that can be used at all times and in all places, and interiorly amidst all occupations. It keeps up the flame of desire, fosters the interior life, and when it becomes habitual is an unspeakable consolation. Owing to its brevity, purity, and simplicity, it neither wearies the soul nor is subject to distraction. These qualities, and especially its efficacy in nourishing the flame of spiritual desire, made it the favourite devotion of the hermits and conventuals of the desert; and it is still the favourite method of all truly devout persons. It is suited to every mind and disposition, even to those who find it difficult to fix their attention in other kinds of prayer. It is an invaluable resource to those who have difficulties in meditation. It also forms the more active part of contemplation.

To quote again the celebrated letter on prayer addressed by St. Augustine to Proba: "The body may be sound, but the soul can never be sound and healthy that prefers temporal to eternal things. But where the love of eternal things exists, this kind of prayer is not only easy but delightful. We are told that the brethren in Egypt use frequent prayers that are brief and swiftly ejaculated. This they prefer to slower methods, that the vigilant and elevated attention so necessary in prayer may not be dulled or dissipated. In this they show that when attention cannot be sustained it ought not to be deadened, but that when it is sustained it should not be readily interrupted."[27]

Let us hear what those brethren in Egypt say themselves of this aspirative prayer. They call it "brief and pure prayer," and St. Benedict does the same in his Rule. They chose it for their private prayer both in their cells and at their work. They said of it that it was not subject to distractions or to temptations. Abbot Isaac in the Conferences calls these short and frequent aspirations the secret and familiar prayer within the cell of the heart, which is open to none but God, the searcher of hearts; so that the adverse powers do not see this kind of petition, and cannot interfere with it. "This brief and frequent prayer," he says, "allows the deceiver of souls no time to put anything into the heart. It is true sacrifice, for a sacrifice to God is a contrite heart. It is the sacrifice of justice, and the sacrifice of praise. These are rich victims, holocausts with the marrow when offered by humble and contrite hearts. When we make these offerings with spiritual discipline and pure intention, we may sing with faithful virtue: 'Let my prayer be directed as incense in Thy sight: the lifting of my hands as the evening sacrifice'."[28]

All the prayers of the Church are reducible to aspirations. The Lord's Prayer consists of seven aspirations in form of petition, and they can be used separately as well as unitedly. The Collects of the Church consist each of a briefly expressed motive to inspire confidence, and an aspiration in form of petition. The Psalms are full of brief forms of aspiration alternating with motives. The Saints have left us many examples of their favourite aspirations, which are fervent, luminous, and beautiful. But they are always best when they come fresh and simple from the abundance of the heart. Nor is repetition, and even frequent repetition, undesirable when the soul is so inclined. On the contrary, for love delights to dwell on the same sense, and to prolong the same sweet melody of prayer and praise, returning to it again and again, sustaining and deepening the same devout affection.

When our Blessed Lord rebuked the use of much speaking in prayer, and called it a heathenish custom, He admonished us to look to the spirit, object, and intent of prayer rather than to the uttering of many words. God looks not to words but to desires. On this subject St. Augustine has said everything in his instruction to Proba: "It is one thing," he says, "to speak much in prayer; it is another thing to pray much, and to extend the time of prayer. It is written of our Lord that He passed whole nights in prayer, and that 'He prayed the longer'; but this was for an example to us. Let there be much prayer when the intention is fervent, but without much speaking; for to speak much encumbers the action of the spirit with superfluous words. To pray much is to ascend towards God with the continual elevation of a devout heart." There is nothing more injurious to the spirit of prayer than the artificial composition of fine speeches: this is the work of vanity and self-love, destructive of simplicity and sincerity of heart.[29]

Mental prayer is purely interior, although interior words are not absent, and especially the mental use of aspirative sentences.

According to the method pursued, mental prayer is divided into meditation and contemplation. Meditation begins with visible things presented to the imagination, and ascends by degrees to the invisible things of God. Contemplation has already found the invisible things of God, and dwells upon them with wonder, awe, and delight, whilst the soul is profoundly humbled into her nothingness before the infinite majesty of God. Meditation searches and feels after that truth and goodness which contemplation has found, so that what begins in meditation may end in contemplation.

When, placed in a narrow valley, our prospect is closed in on every side, the view of the heavens above us is limited as well, and we can only conjecture what there is beyond. But if we toilsomely ascend the mountain side, on reaching the top the prospect opens in all its magnificence, and the expansion of the heavens above exalts the mind, and reveals to us what the earth contains below. This laborious ascent resembles meditation; but contemplation is already on the mountain, and has neither to imagine nor to reason, but only to look with admiration into the prospect of truth which God from His heavens reveals to us. Yet conscious of the limitations of our mind, and of the obscurity of the created medium through which we see, we feel how little and feeble is the creature before the Creator. Meditation is fruitful with labour; contemplation is more fruitful without labour. Hence contemplation is a special gift of the Holy Ghost, and perseverance in its exercise is founded upon the gift of fundamental patience or fortitude. Yet almost all souls have to make their first beginnings of mental prayer with meditation.

St. Thomas observes that in our free and private prayer we use words and signs, the crucifix for example, so long as they help to dispose us to mental or interior prayer. But when they become a distraction and a hindrance to interior recollection, the use of them should yield to pure mental prayer.[30] When meditation itself becomes a distraction, because the mind and heart tend to pure recollection, and this habitually, it is the sign of a call to contemplation. This prayer the Psalmist describes in the following words: "My heart hath said to Thee: my face hath sought Thee: Thy face, O Lord, will I still seek"

[31]. But the Saints have a maxim that the meditation or contemplation of our Lord's Passion should never be abandoned.

There are so many valuable manuals on the method of meditation that it will be unnecessary here to say more on the subject. Those who are still novices in interior prayer; who have not yet mortified the restlessness of their interior faculties into tranquillity; who are still much engaged with the senses and with sensual things; who have not yet gained much control over the imagination of sensible things; these will often require the help of a book to steady their attention; and when their meditative faculties are dull and refuse to act, they should have recourse to aspirations, an exercise of prayer that is always easy. One thing should be especially avoided, that is, the converting of meditation into a study, as though it were a literary exercise. This snare should be shunned most carefully; it not only destroys the child-like simplicity of prayer, but takes the mind from God, the true object and end of prayer, and occupies us with the vanities of self-love.

But "where the spirit of the Lord is, there is liberty".[32] The Holy Spirit is the mover of prayer; and though every one should learn a good method of meditation, yet to tie the soul always to that method in all its rules, would not only injure freedom, but cause the soul to lose the touch and attraction of the Holy Spirit. No one thinks of putting all the rules of grammar into every letter that he writes; no one thinks of putting all the rules of rhetoric into every discourse that he delivers. His production would be a chained-up folly. Rules are of value when required, not when out of place. Those who look more to rules than to the spirit of prayer are the pedants of prayer. They will never make much progress in this holy exercise.

When one point in the meditation fills the soul with light, and brings us to the divine end of prayer, why leave the end of prayer already gained to go in search of another point? This is to go backwards instead of forwards, and will only bring distraction. When the soul is ardently moved to aspirations in the sight of God, she has reached the essence of prayer; why return from this pure prayer to the things of imagination? This is to come down from spiritual to visible things, and from the fervour of prayer to its first beginnings. When meditation raises the soul to contemplation, to abandon that contemplation for the sake of obeying the rules of meditation is like descending the steps of Jacob's ladder for no other object than to endeavour to reascend. It is to come down from the mountain of light into the valley of shadows. A little of that pure and serene light will do more to teach us the knowledge of God and of self than all that can be seen through the shadows of the imagination. The Holy Spirit is the true teacher of prayer, and the liberty of prayer consists in freely following the divine attraction, which always leads to greater simplicity, humility, love, patience, and union with God. "Commit thy way to the Lord, and trust in Him. . . . Be subject to the Lord and pray to Him."[33]

"The work of justice shall be peace, and the service of justice quietness and security for ever."[34] It is very important for the peace of the soul in prayer to remember that present consolation is not the essential answer to prayer, and that its greatest effects are obtainable without sensible consolation. The answer to prayer is not always felt at the time, or even given at the time; and its greatest fruits are laid up in eternity.

Contemplation rises above the senses, above the imagination, above all processes of the reasoning powers. Collected within herself, the soul rises above herself, and with a simple view beholds, though "darkly as through a glass," some manifestation of the beauty, goodness, and greatness of God, which deepens her sense of God, and affects her with wonder, admiration, and love, giving her some foretaste of blessedness. Sometimes, however, this contemplation is very obscure, and the presence and goodness of God are felt as it were, through thick darkness rather than seen in open light. It gives to the humble and adoring soul either great light and refreshment, or a secret sense of God, according as it is luminous or obscure; but in the latter case it gives us a more humiliating knowledge of ourselves. The holy Psalmist describes the divine source of contemplation in these words: "With Thee is the fountain of life; and in Thy light we shall see light"[35]. And he aspirates his gratitude for the gift in these words: "The light of Thy countenance, O Lord, is sealed upon us: Thou hast given gladness to my heart".[36]

The acts of contemplation are four: to seek after God, to find Him, to feel His sacred touch in the soul, and to be united with Him and enjoy Him. St. Paul has expressed all this in a certain way in his discourse to the Athenians. "That they should seek God, if haply they may feel after Him, or find Him: although He be not far from every one of us: for in Him we live and move, and have our being."[37] We seek after Him with our mind, feel after Him with our spirit, find Him when the light of His countenance shines upon us and the sense of His goodness penetrates our heart, and have our life and movement in Him when we love Him with our whole heart, soul, and strength. We know that we have our being in Him when He gives us the light to see that He is all things to us, and that we are nothing in ourselves. Wherefore the Psalmist says: "Seek ye the Lord, and be strengthened; seek His face ever more".[38] He must be sought ever more, says St. Gregory, because He must be loved ever more.[39]

To contemplate is to be on the mountain of revelations with Moses, or on the mountain of Transfiguration with the three chosen Apostles, or at the feet of Jesus with Mary Magdalen. It demands an abstraction, for the time at least, from mortal cares and solicitudes. It not only calls for a mortified body but for a mortified spirit, that the interior powers may be collected, may become serene and peaceful, and the soul arise above all that is not God. Hence the active life and the combat with nature precede the gift of contemplation. "Contemplation," says St. Gregory, "is a sepulchre in which all depraved works and things of this world are buried together with the contumelies of the body and the petulance of the imagination, whilst the spirit ascends by a holy operation to behold the things of God. For you are dead; that is to yourself; and your life is hidden with Christ in God."

The same great Pontiff and Doctor in another place draws this distinction between the two kinds of life which God allots to those who serve Him. Almighty God in His Holy Word instructs His servants in two kinds of life, the active and the contemplative. The active life feeds the hungry, instructs the ignorant, and corrects the erring; brings back the proud into the way of humility, has care of the infirm, and provides subsistence for those who are dependent on us. The contemplative life maintains the love of God and of our neighbour with the whole mind and heart, but rests in peace from extreme activity, and adheres to the one desire of God alone. Casting away all other cares, the soul burns with the desire of seeing the face of her Creator. Knowing with grief that she bears the load of her corruptible body, she thinks with ardent desires how she may be present among the angelic choirs, and with the heavenly citizens, there to enjoy the vision of her incorruptible Creator for evermore. Yet she can only obtain the sight of God's beauty in a certain measure, but a hand's breadth as it were. For with whatever love she may be enkindled, with whatever strength she may tend towards God, she is so far from perfectly seeing what she loves, that in this life she only begins to see. As the strenuous Apostle says: "We see now through a glass in a dark manner; but then face to face. Now I know in part: but then I shall know even as I am known."[40]

To continue the celebrated instruction of St. Gregory: In contemplation the mind strives to rise above the man, and stretches forward unto spiritual things, endeavouring to transcend what is visible to the senses, and to reach what is celestial. Thus the spirit is drawn upwards that it may expand upon things divine. At times the spirit conquers, and soars above the contentious darkness with which at other times it is blinded, and the soul is secretly and slightly touched by something from the incomprehensible light of God. But by reason of her infirmity she soon returns from that wonderful light, and falls back upon her darkness anew, there to sigh in her obscuration. It should however be plainly understood, that no one can advance so far in contemplation as to penetrate even to one single ray of God's incomprehensible light. The Almighty cannot be seen in His brightness. What is seen is something beneath God; but it greatly refreshes the soul, whilst the glorious vision of God is reserved for the world to come.

St. Gregory himself is one of the greatest examples of the union of the contemplative with the active life. Whilst governing the Universal Church with vigorous energy, he never abandoned that gift of contemplation which gave light and force to all his active works. It is the privilege of saints and holy persons, when called to the duties of the active life, to keep always within them a cell of quiet recollection, into which God alone is allowed to enter; and being faithful to detachment as well as to recollection, they are able to put aside external things in the tranquil hour devoted to contemplation, the spirit of which continues with them amidst the most energetic employments. This St. Gregory himself observes in the same discourse: "Be it known that as the good order of life tends from action to contemplation; it is also often useful to transform contemplation into action, that what contemplation enkindles in the soul may come forth in the active duties of life to make them more perfect"[41].

To understand the conduct of the soul in contemplation, it must be clearly comprehended how much depends on the conduct of the will. For although the mind is the medium, and as it were the mirror in which we see, it is the will, as St. Thomas remarks, that moves and elevates the mind, and holds it firm and steadfast to the object of contemplation. Hence the great authorities on this kind of prayer insist that the fortitude of the will is the moral foundation of contemplation. The spiritual appetite is the spring that moves the desire of contemplating the divine beauty of truth; but what awakens the appetite is the love and desire of beholding and feeling the beautiful things of God. As our Divine Lord teaches us: "Where thy treasure is, there is thy heart also"[42].

Hence contemplation begins with love and ends in greater love.[43]

All pious souls are not called to contemplation, but it is open nevertheless to every state of life, to the poor as much as to the well provided, to the simple as well as to the learned. Nay, the simple are often better disposed for this holy exercise than the learned, because of their singleness of mind and simplicity of heart. Most of the great writers on the subject have observed that the lovers of learning are often too curious, too much devoted to reasoning, and too fond of wandering through the regions of human knowledge, to be well disposed for interior recollection, and for the simple, childlike contemplation of Eternal Truth, however profoundly it would enlighten them. Yet not only among the servants of the altar, and among those devoted to religion, observes St. Gregory, but even in the married life some are found who receive this precious gift. But those who are by nature restless and unquiet, or who have not subdued their spirit by interior mortification, or who have not brought themselves into habits of recollection, are unfit for this kind of prayer. Again, as holy Job tells us, wisdom is not to be found by him who "knoweth not the price thereof, neither is it to be found in the land of them who live in delights"[44].

The man who receives the light of contemplation has his heart within him. He is not immoderately taken up with external things. That light cannot be infused into the things of the senses, nor can it enter into those corporal images that fill the imagination; it is the spiritual light of spiritual things known only to spirits. Whoever desires this light should have great care to keep the soul in a state of humility, and should never suffer the soul to be elated over the grace received. That light enters obliquely as it were through the window of the mind, but the thief should not be allowed to enter after it. For true contemplation keeps down the sense of self and the spirit of selfishness as well. The divine truth enters through the window of the mind, but the boastings of elation should be kept out. The window of contemplation admits light, but excludes the storm; it opens to the entrance of grace, but is closed against the admission of pride[45].

We say nothing here respecting those rare and extraordinary gifts of contemplation to which no one should have the presumption to aspire; they come of some wonderful and unexpected visit of God, and can never be obtained by human industry. But the effects that follow the ordinary exercise of contemplation are these three. The first is wonder, admiration, and awe at beholding some manifestation, however remote, of the beauty, power, and sublimity of God in His Divine Attributes, or in His divine goodness to His creatures; in the presence of which the soul is humbled down in veneration and adoration. The second effect is the infusion of heavenly sweetness, that fills the soul with love and gratitude. For the soul converses with that Eternal Wisdom of whom the Scripture says: "Her conversation hath no bitterness, nor her company any tediousness, but gladness and joy"[46]. The third effect is the revelation to the creature of her littleness and nothingness apart from God. Searched as with lamps, the soul sees her defects and failings laid open to her eyes. The light of the Sun of Justice penetrates the soul, and the beauty of goodness enters the heart, withering up the desires of earthly and carnal things, and drawing those desires into aspirations towards the God of all beauty and goodness.

The soul that has been once illuminated with the light of contemplation, though but for a short time, can never forget it, nor can ever be the same as before. A higher and purer standard of good is implanted in the mind and in the conscience. To turn to evil would be much more fearful and loathsome than before; the rending of the conscience would be more terrible. To abandon God after the light of His countenance had shone with sweetness and power on the soul, would be a spiritual apostasy to which the words of St. Paul are but too applicable. "It is impossible [that is to say, very difficult] for those who were once illuminated, have tasted also the heavenly gift, and were made partakers of the Holy Ghost, have moreover tasted the good word of God, and the powers of the world to come, and are fallen away, to be renewed again to penance."[47]

Such falls after true contemplation must be rare indeed. The causes are more numerous where a pretension to the gift is false, a mere delusion of the imagination rather than a union of mind and heart with the divine light, generating conceit in place of humility. But true contemplation brings with it such a knowledge of God and of self, generates so much charity and humility, and inspires such a horror of sin, that the soul is drawn ever closer to God and further from selfishness.

From this exposition of the several kinds of prayer three paramount instructions may be gathered. First, in every kind of prayer, whether vocal, meditative, aspiratory, or contemplative, whilst the manner is different the spirit is the same. All prayer has one final end, that of our beatitude in God; and all should be exercised in spirit and in truth. Secondly, every kind of prayer leads to interior recollection according to each one's gift and disposition; and when this recollection ascends to contemplation the summit of prayer is reached; there is nothing between the soul and God but His own gifts; it is a certain foreshadowing within the brevity of time of the eternal contemplation of God. Thirdly, the greatest fruits of prayer are not visible in the time of prayer; but only a certain light, refreshment, and consolation. Even this is often withheld for the correction, or the probation, or the discipline of the soul; but the memory of that refreshment is a great encouragement in the time of trial. The great reward of prayer is reserved for eternity; and the generous soul will say: Give me now the thorns, and keep the crown for eternity.

## 11

## ON PATIENCE IN PRAYER

"Because thou hast kept the word of my patience, I will keep thee from the hour of temptation."—APOCALYPSE iii, 10.

When we reflect on the inconstancy of the mind and the instability of the will, we have most painful proofs of the weakness of human nature. Restless as the weathercock on the steeple, the mind shifts from point to point, incapable when left to its own nature of dwelling long on any subject without many deviations and distractions. The cause of this infirmity is not so much the mind itself as the restlessness of the senses, the petulance of the imagination, the waywardness of curiosity, and impatience of the conditions of each present moment. The will is shaken from its constancy and stability by the same causes, and by the continual changes which our feelings undergo. Every movement around us, every voice that speaks to us, produces some change in us. The eye of the soul is now here, now there; her affections are now up, now down; she is too weak to hold on her course without being in a greater or less degree affected and turned about by every varying attraction that brings its influence to bear upon her tremulous mobility.

Such is human nature left to its native infirmity, and without the discipline of the virtues. This restless inconstancy gives melancholy evidence that we are not firmly united with the object for which we were created. For whatever has obtained its end is at peace through being united with that end, and is at rest from perturbations, and from wanderings without reasonable purpose. It is clear that what the soul most needs is some steadying power that will not only give stability to the mind and will, but a preservation of the balance of stability by resistance to whatever would disturb it. But as the object of such a power is to heal the weakness which causes this instability, it is evident that it cannot be looked for within our nature, but must come from One who is by nature strong, constant, and unchangeable. This power is the grace and virtue of Christian patience, which strengthens and steadies the will, and through the will the mind and all the powers. Hence all things weak within us look to patience for their remedy. This virtuous power strengthens and unites in us what weakness disunites and dissipates.

But as that which is weak is strengthened by resting on what is strong, the soul is made strong by resting with her interior centre upon the strengthening power of God. "Be thou, O my soul, subject to God; for from Him is my patience."[1] As God is above us, and we beneath, to be subject to God is to rest on Him, that is to be united with Him. What is restless by nature can only be made calm and peaceful by union with what is calm and peaceful. We obtain peace from our troubles by union with the God of peace. "It is good for me to adhere to God, to set my hope on the Lord God."[2] As we can only obtain stability of mind and heart by union with what is unchangeable, our soul obtains stability by union with the unchangeable God. The principle of that union is charity, and God has placed the power of patience in the gift of charity, that we may be able to adhere with our spirit to Him in a firm, stable, and patient love. "Charity is patient."

Whatever is created is made for an object and an end which is different from itself, from which it receives its fulness, peace, and perfection. God has created us for Himself, and only by union with God can we receive our fulness, peace, and perfection. This union we seek in prayer, and obtain through prayer, and by prayer we prepare ourselves for our eternal union with God. For the final end of prayer, as of all good works, is our eternal union with God in His beatifying vision.

It is therefore of great importance to understand what we ought to put into our prayer; for the value and merit of our good works depend less on their show than on the spirit and virtue put into them. It has been acutely observed in human actions, that God looks less to the verbs than to the adverbs, that is, to the spirit and manner in which we do our actions, to the virtues we put into them. And Cassian says with great truth, that "we come to the perfection of prayer with the construction of all the virtues; for unless they are collected and compacted in the elevation of prayer, they can in nowise be firm or enduring in their stability".[3] This is a great light. It shows that not only must the virtues enter into prayer, be united in prayer, and blended together in prayer; but that it is in prayer they receive their stability for the performance of other good works.

The first condition of prayer is attention. The second is humility, whereby the soul is opened and made subject to God. The third is faith in God, and trust that He will hear our prayer, and grant us according to His promises. The fourth is the love of God, which makes our prayer generous and acceptable. The fifth is obedience to the interior movements of the Holy Spirit. The sixth is patience. And as attention wholly depends on patience, this virtue should be present throughout every good prayer, not only to keep our mind firm and steady to the presence of God, but also that the soul may adhere to Him in faith, hope, and love. Hence that most enlightened and experienced guide of souls, Father Louis of Granada, tells us that "patience is not only necessary, but is marvellously necessary for obtaining and preserving the fruits of prayer".[4]

Let us consider what attention is, and what it is in prayer. Taken literally, the word attention signifies a stretching forth. We stretch forth the ear to listen, the eye to see, and the mind to understand. As an interior act attention is the act of directing and applying the mind to some special object presented to our thoughts. Attention in prayer is the stretching forth and applying the mind to God and to divine things. It is evident that this action of the mind depends upon the energy of the will, which both directs and applies the mind to its object. It is equally obvious that our attention will be generous in proportion to our detachment from sensual self-love. The mind tends to God by command of the will, and takes heed of what we see, think, feel, and say to Him. Perfect attention in prayer excludes attention to whatever belongs not to that duty. This attention ought to be humble, loving, trusting, free, peaceful, patient, and persevering.

The hindrances to fixed, steadfast, and patient attention are well known to be numerous. But they are by no means the same to all persons; for the power of attention is gained as the fruit of habitual recollection. Those souls that have disciplined themselves into habits of recollection obtain the patient possession of themselves, and the custody of their mind and heart frees their attention from many impediments. Some, again, are by nature of a firmer and less irritable texture than others, and respond more readily to that grace of patience which sustains and protects attention. Let us enumerate the chief hindrances that interfere with recollection and attention in prayer, not in detail—that would be impracticable—but in their kinds, and we shall find that they are all conquered by patience.

The first hindrance to attention is the restlessness of the body, with its nerves in constant play and its senses in unpeaceful movement. Unless the will has obtained patience to disregard the restless emotions of the body, and to keep the attention abstracted from them, they will make the mind restless and the attention unsteady. The patient mind attends to God and to her prayer, and refuses to be disturbed by the animal feelings, which cease to trouble when the soul is not with them. Restlessness of body arises from various causes; one of which is the very quietude of posture in prayer, and the greater consciousness of any movement in that quietude. Another is due to the habit of giving too much attention of mind to the sensual feelings at all times, which greatly fosters their power over the mind. Another may arise from intemperance of diet, which is apt to cause local irritability as well as weakness in the mental powers. Another cause is want of habitual control of temper, which disposes the soul to fret at small things, and disturbs the tranquility of the senses.

Sometimes when the body is in a state of restlessness, a change of position will give considerable relief. Some, who are by nature restless, are best able to think and reflect when in motion. But holy souls who are truly patient will not even allow great sufferings of body to interfere with their recollection, except to bring them closer to God. But if the soul is distracted from attention by only moderate irritation in the earthly frame, there can be no true patience in the will. For true patience adheres to the object of prayer regardless for the time of all inferior things.

The second hindrance to attention is from the imagination. This volatile and many coloured intruder is excellent in its place as the servant of truth, and is the first help to meditation, and when rightly used gives much instruction and delight. But it is also the chief cause of our distractions, wanderings from attention, and delusions. There is nothing that the uncontrolled imagination will not at times protrude upon the recollection of devout attention, from mere flitting distractions to gross images of vice. As the imagination is closely connected with the senses, from which its action originates, it is apt to cause disturbance in the senses as well as the mind, and even to awaken passions, such as resentment or sadness. When, again, the subtle movements of self-love gain entrance into the imagination, not only is the attention diverted from God to self, but the imagination becomes imbued with the vanities of self-love, and will bring that self with its petty interests before the mind in a way to eclipse the light of prayer. But when these disturbing shadows are first perceived, it is the duty of patience to increase the energy of attention, and to adhere with greater application to the object of prayer, leaving these distractions to fall away for want of notice.

The third hindrance to attention is the intrusion of things from the memory that have no proper connection with prayer. These ordinarily come, though not always, through the medium of the imagination. They are caused by association of ideas, and frequently by association of contraries, which are sometimes painful as well as troublesome. When these memories are connected with ourselves, or with our external pursuits, or with any one towards whom we have strong feelings of any kind, unless the mind holds on with patience, they have much power to distract attention. Distractions from the memory or the imagination become very troublesome if the least importance is attached to them, if the soul yields to any anxiety about them. They may at times take shadowy forms that seem to touch faith, or to sound like blasphemy, or even touch on purity. Yet this in pious souls will be nothing perhaps but the mechanical association of what is directly contrary to the desires of the soul. To attend to such suggestions, to be anxious about them, to attach any importance to them, is to give them a power of troubling and tormenting which they have not in themselves. The effective way of treating such intrusions on attention is to adhere with patience to God, to help that adhesion with active aspirations, and utterly to disregard them. When the mind perseveres in attention to the Divine Object of prayer, despite of accidental perturbations, the soul cannot become engaged with herself, and those intrusive images dissolve and vanish for want of attention to nourish them. To be anxious about them is to give them entertainment; this enables them to trouble both recollection and peace, and so the end of the tempter is gained.

It is of great importance to understand that where evil spirits tempt us, they have no power allowed them except on the corporal senses and the imagination. They cannot act in the substance of the soul without the soul's consent. It is equally important to understand that, though the imagination acts on the mind, it has its origin from the corporal senses. When this was explained to Saint Teresa it became an epoch of light in her spiritual life. She then understood how to manage her imagination, and what degree of importance was to be attached to that which St. Paul calls "the spirit of the flesh".

There are celebrated pictures by great artists which profess to represent the temptations of St. Antony the Hermit whilst in prayer, and some of them are widely known by engravings. Properly understood, these pictures give a valuable instruction. They represent in visible shapes the solicitations and temptations with which the imagination besets the mind in prayer. Some of these figures are grave, others refined and seductive, others grotesque and ridiculous. But whilst these creatures of the imagination seek to attract the attention of the Saint, to allure him from recollection, or to dissipate his prayer by their charms, illusions, antics, or seductions, the Saint himself kneels with his whole soul concentrated on God; his features exhibit the strain upon his fortitude, and there is a consciousness of the siege with which his soul is beset; but his patience does not waver, his will holds his attention with steadfastness towards God, and refuses to be diverted even for an instant from the object of his prayer. He has mastered these solicitations, he has mastered the ridiculous, he has mastered the anxieties of temptation and distraction, and that simply and solely by adhering to God with patience.

The fourth hindrance to attention is a very subtle one, and the more mischievous because it springs directly from self-love. So long as the soul abides in the humble sense of her nothingness before God, and looks to Him with patient confidence as the giver of all she stands in need of, temptation will slide off and leave her prayer uninjured. But if the soul begins to lose sight of what she is before God, and departing from her humility takes delight in what she fancies the success of her prayer, her attention will secretly glide off from God to herself, a shadow of that imaginary self will come between her real self and God, and though it may not efface the divine presence from her mind, it will nevertheless obscure that holy presence, whilst it will raise the spirit of self-conceit. Self-love and vanity will come into action, and show themselves in petty fancies and weak sentimentalities; there may be industrious compositions of sentences, and other dressings of vanity, making a silly display before God for one's own entertainment; just as vain people do in their conversation with their neighbours.

This loquacious prayer of self-love is very offensive; it is an example of that much speaking which our Lord rebuked in the prayer of the heathens, who thought much of themselves and little of God. The prayer in spirit and in truth moves not from self-love, but from the grace of the Holy Spirit, and moves towards God with love and veneration. It consists not in fine words or pleasant poetry, but is penetrated with the power and goodness of God, and with the sense of our own lowliness, poverty, and want. When the heart is truly touched with light and grace, and subdued into earnest desire, the soul will express herself in the simplest words, springing without art or effort from the spirit that moves within. This is the prayer of humble fervour, which is not easily distracted because of its patience and simplicity; but the prayer which is corrupted by the vanity of self-love invites distraction. Can such a prayer be pleasing to God? Not when we are in labour with our vanity. He hath said: "To whom shall I have respect, but to him that is poor and little, and of a contrite spirit, and that trembleth at my words?"[5] And the Proverb says: "His will is in them that walk in simplicity"[6]

The moment this vain spirit is detected, everything should give way to profound humiliation before God, and to a deep sense of shame at having thus behaved in the divine presence. Whoever is subject to this infirmity will find in it the proof of an unmortified will, and such a one should not only begin prayer with an act of profound humility and subjection to God, but should repeat that act from time to time in the course of prayer. This should be accompanied with the consideration of one's nothingness before God, who sees through all our weaknesses, and who demands of the fallen creature humility before all things, and the 'simplicity of a helpless child in the presence of his Creator. At the end of prayer he should consider how he has yielded to presumption, or has borne himself with single-hearted simplicity, that he may ask pardon where he has erred from vanity or conceit.

The fifth hindrance to attention arises from confusion of mind. There are some persons who at certain times know not where to begin or how to pursue their prayer. They flounder in confusion of mind from beginning to end. In such cases recourse should be had to a book, and that book should be used freely, not only as a guide but as a support to reflection. There are few persons who cannot meditate on the Passion of Christ, and they can have nothing better. This state of mind requires a great deal of patience. When the mind can do nothing else, the will can always wait on God, which with patience is an excellent prayer. But when the mind cannot meditate the heart can always use simple aspirations, which are the very essence of prayer.

But the greatest cause of mental confusion is scrupulosity, which greatly impedes the freedom of the mind. Scrupulosity is a real malady. It has its seat in the imagination, and it gravely affects the action of the will as well as of the judgment. It is a kind of mania, ruled by the fixed image of sin, which oversways the balance of the judgment, so that the just distinction between right and wrong is no longer discerned in our acts or thoughts. As a person suffering from jaundice has his eyes so filled with yellow bile that everything he looks upon seems tinted with that colour; so the scrupulous person has his mental sight so filled with the image and fear of sin, that it hangs like a phantom before his eyes, and seems to give its colour to all his acts. Hence he attaches the notion of sin to his most innocent thoughts and actions, and lives in constant dread that what he does is sinful, and this more especially in his acts of piety. In some persons this malady is constitutional, and may be detected by a person of spiritual discernment by external signs. In others the trial is only temporary.

It is obvious from the nature of this malady that those who suffer from it cannot be judges in their own cause. For the disease affects the judgment itself, which is unable to decide except on the judgment of another. Where there is pride, and that is seldom absent, there is great obstinacy of will, and this makes the malady much more difficult to cure. There is but one remedy for this suffering state of soul, and that is absolute and implicit obedience to the Spiritual Physician. When the physician pronounces that the patient is suffering from scrupulosity, the first and indispensable duty of the sufferer is to believe that such is the case, although the scrupulous person may neither see nor understand how that can be. For unless the patient trusts the physician the cure cannot be effected. The second duty of the scrupulous is to faithfully follow the few and simple rules given by the director for its cure, however unreasonable they may appear to the disordered judgment of the sufferer. That judgment may be perfectly sound in every other respect, excepting where there is question of sin, or of the imagination and dread of sin. When this malady gives rise to disquiet and anxiety disturbing to the peace of prayer, the sufferer should seek special direction as to the kind of prayer most suited to the case, and as to the conduct to be pursued in prayer. It will greatly encourage the obedience of the scrupulous if they will only assure themselves that they are only responsible to God for their obedience, and that the director is responsible for all that is enjoined them.

The sixth hindrance to attention in souls not already purified by trials is dryness of heart. When the affections lose their pleasant sensibilities and find that their enjoyment is gone, the soul is liable to become anxious and uneasy, and to imagine that something serious, she knows not what, is wrong within her, and that God is not with her. This anxiety is much increased if there be obscurity or darkness in the mind as well as dryness in the heart. Accustomed to the light, refreshment, and consolation of prayer, when deprived of them, the soul is inclined to lose courage, to become occupied with herself and with her changed feelings, and not unfrequently yields herself to sadness, which greatly relaxes attention to God, and brings an uneasy apprehension about her state. She has yet to learn the stronger and less selfish virtues of prayer, and, however well instructed in theory, to discover in practice that there are far greater rewards of prayer than its actual and present enjoyment.

What is the faith that swims in light compared with that strong and energetic faith which adheres to God and His truth when the soul is surrounded with dark clouds and obscurations? It is a noble courage to believe that God is still present, hearing our prayers and providing their reward, notwithstanding the darkness that hides His presence from us. "Blessed are they who have not seen, and have believed."[7] What is the hope that enjoys the foretaste of the promises, compared with that unbounded confidence that cleaves to God with undiminished trust when everything wears the appearance of discouragement? This was the patient trust of holy Job. Tortured in body, overwhelmed with darkness and dryness of spirit, assaulted with fears and perplexities, he exclaimed amidst his sorrows and privations: "Even though He should kill me, I will trust in Him: but yet I will reprove my ways in His sight."[8] The Psalms of David are the voice of a soul that frequently alternates between light and obscuration, between consolation and desolation, between delight in God and fear of self; and they are written for our instruction. When trial comes, what is the conduct of the Prophet of souls? He adheres to God with hope; he abides with him in patience. He is subject to God and prays to Him; he awaits with fortitude the coming of God.

St. Paul knew how to abound and how to suffer loss. He has humbly recorded the alternations of his soul, even to the humiliation that he suffered, lest he should be lifted up with the greatness of his revelations. "For which thing," he says, "thrice I besought the Lord, that it might depart from me; and He said to me: My grace is sufficient for thee: for power is perfected in infirmity." What then did the Apostle? Knowing the will of God, he troubled himself no more, but patiently bore the trial. "Gladly therefore will I glory in my infirmities, that the power of Christ may dwell in me. For which cause I please myself in my infirmities."[9] We read the lives of the Saints of all ages, and find that they had their times of refreshment and their times of interior trial and desolation, and were deeply conscious of their infirmites. But what truly distinguished them was the simple faith, the confident trust, and the untiring patience with which they adhered to God in every trial and every state of feeling, indifferent to all but the will of God and His sanctifying influences.

What is the charity that loves God with the sweet sense of love compared with that greater charity in which, though without the sense of enjoyment, our desires of God are sent forth to Him with greater earnestness? God measures our love by our desires, and not by the refreshment with which He sometimes rewards them. Consolation is not prayer, but an encouragement given to the weakness of souls. Prayer is the strongest, fullest of virtue, and obtains the greatest reward in eternity, when our desires ascend to God, and our adoration is given to Him without regard to greater consolation than it pleases God to give us. What is the patience of a soul in which all goes pleasantly on the path of prayer, and when she has only to exclude what interferes with recollection, compared with that firm and constant patience that adheres to God amidst obscurity and desolation?

This strong meat is not given to the babes of spiritual life, but to those who are chosen for great rewards in eternity. This severe diet purifies the affections from what is sensual, feeble, irritable, or selfish in them, and strengthens the virtues with a view to their perfection. The rewards of prayer are given to its humility, its patience, its charity and purity. Let no one mistake present consolation for the great reward. The first is a grace given to the soul to encourage her to labour for the eternal reward. When prayer is pure it looks more to God and less to present enjoyment. When prayer is patient it abides more steadfastly with God, waits upon His will, and is less attentive to one's inward perturbations. This dry prayer is generous, and most peaceful when most patient. The great final reward, to which all prayer should be directed, is God Himself.

If it please God that the soul should have her winter as well as her summer season, this is a divine policy and a spiritual providence. For just as the providence of God sends the bracing cold, the rainy clouds, and cleansing winds to prepare the earth, that its fruits may gush forth in the summer; so are these trials ordained to brace the soul, to purify the heart, and eradicate the weeds of self-love; to make the spirit strong in fortitude and patience, and to change our soft habits into a more vigorous constitution of life. Hence in the language of theology these trials are called purgations; either purgations of sense, or purgations of the intellect, or purga-tions of the will.

Purgation of the sense is effected by that drying-up of the affections, by which we learn that spiritual consolation comes not from one's self, but is the gift and encouragement of the Holy Spirit, who both gives and takes it away. This trial also purifies the spiritual affections from whatever is sensual or savouring of self-love that has got mixed with them. They thus become more purely spiritual, and when consolation returns it is felt more in God and less in one's self. The purgation of the intellect is effected by that withdrawing of divine light which leaves the soul in obscurity, except in what regards the light of conscience, and the soul more clearly sees that this light is in the hand of God to give or take away. We put many images of vanity into that light, and many reflections of self-love. and make the holy light a mirror in which to admire our own mental efforts, forgetful that it is by God's gift of light that we believe, and think, and obtain knowledge and understanding. But when darkness comes upon the mind, we find ourselves out; we see that our light comes from God, and that by no labour of our own can we produce a single ray of its illumination. We are left to faith, and to the light of justice, needful to guide us on our way; and we learn how insig-nificant our mental efforts are without the light of God. The pride of intellect is mortified and humbled, the intellect itself is purified of its vanities and conceits, and from the reflected images of self-love; and when the cheering light returns, it comes more serene into a purer mind, so that we make our prayer and conduct our mental operations with truer dependence on the divine illumination. Thus the intellect is purged from pride and vanity that we may see the truths of God and the laws of wisdom with purer eyes, and respond to them with greater fidelity.

The purgation of the will is effected by the crucifixion of our inordinate loves and desires. This is accomplished by the sufferings, privations, and disappointments which the will has to endure in things that tend to God. When the dispositions of the will have been thus purified from seeking their own way in the things of God, and when the desires of nature have been cleansed away from impeding the will of God in that soul, the soul accepts all privations and sufferings here below with indifference. The gift of charity is purified from the interests of nature and self-seeking, and, divested of its accidental encumbrances, the flame of divine love obtains an increase of purity and force, of fortitude and patience, that gives it wonderful capacity both for unity with God and for every good work.

It will become evident from these explanations that the chief virtues to be exercised in times of dryness, darkness, and interior suffering are patient faith, patient hope, and patient charity, raised to the degree of fortitude. We must endure for the love of God, believe in His loving care of us, wait in patience for the light of His countenance, and persevere in our prayer. But remember that it is with ourselves that we have to be patient. The Italians have a proverb, that time and patience change the mulberry leaf into fine satin. It is wonderful what time does for a soul when helped by patience. Patience with time matures everything. God is the governor of your soul: have patience with His mysterious ways, and let Him govern you. A hundred have perseverance for one who has patience; but without patience that perseverance is of a restless, broken, and unpeaceful kind. Devout surrender to the ways of God is the summit of patience.

The seventh hindrance to steadfast attention and recollection arises from the timidities, fears, and discouragements to which the soul gives way amidst the trials and desolations of prayer. This repining fear is very different from the filial fear of God; it is a sinking of hope and courage, and a failure of the confidence that God is present and hears the desires of our heart. These timid misgivings do not proceed from grace but from the weakness of nature deprived of consolation. People who will go through a great deal of patient labour, and will endure privations with cheerfulness to obtain success in other things, will often shrink from labour and endurance, and lose their patience, when what they ask of God is deferred; they lose both heart and much of what they have already gained. They will not reflect that God delays His graces to try their faith in Him, and their patience, or for other beneficial reasons that He alone knows. Hence their attention is disturbed, becomes divided between God and their own discomforts, and is sometimes overwhelmed with the gloom and sadness of their discontented nature. Sometimes this goes further; they imagine their own displeasure to be God's displeasure with them, that He has abandoned them, and that their prayer is displeasing to God, and useless. Thus patience breaks down into melancholy, and the soul becomes wholly occupied with self.

Yet all this is but a mischievous delusion, of which presumption is the origin and self-love the feeder. This will show itself in various ways. The imagination will wander away to other scenes in search of relief. The soul will fancy that she could do better in some other place and under other conditions. For one of the effects of this kind of discontent is to imagine that one is not in one's right vocation, and might do better in some other; forgetting that we carry ourselves with us wherever we go. Yet all this weakness comes from want of patience with ourselves. But the question arises: Are we to do God's will or our own? What will our own will profit us? We are abundantly taught by Holy Scripture and the Saints, that the trials which God sends us are among His greatest benefits, and we are quite ready to teach this truth to others under their trials. But when it comes to our own case, our self-love will not let us understand. Yet to remove self-love is that trial given us. If we practically knew God's ways in the soul, we should believe in them, trust in them, love them, and patiently wait through the winter of trial for the returning spring. But self-love is blind, voracious for present enjoyment, and sad and sorrowful when it is not granted. The true question for the soul is this: Do we deserve it? Is it good for us? And the answer is: God knows.

In the 87th Psalm King David puts before us the fear, anxiety, and desolation with which his soul is beset in his prayer. He begins his prayer with earnest supplication: "O Lord, the God of my salvation: I have cried in the day, and in the night before Thee". He then compares his interior privations to those of a man who is buried in a sepulchre: "in the dark places, and in the shadow of death". Yet with patient fortitude he perseveres in his prayer: "My eyes languished through poverty, all the day I cried to Thee, O Lord; I stretched out my hands to Thee". And again he continues his prayer: "Shall any one in the sepulchre declare Thy mercy; and Thy truth in destruction? Shall Thy wonders be known in the dark; and Thy justice in the land of forgetfulness? But I, O Lord, have cried to Thee: and in the morning my prayers shall prevent Thee." This is the inspired prayer of one whose attention to God is not destroyed by his fears and discouragements.

The Prophet Habacuc begins his prophesying with a prayer of

great desolation: "How long, O Lord, shall I cry; and Thou wilt not hear? Shall I cry out to Thee suffering violence, and Thou wilt not save?"[10] But at the end of his dolorous prophecies his patient grief is rewarded, and his words are joyful: "But I will rejoice in the Lord: and will joy in God my Jesus. The Lord God is my strength: and He will make my feet like the feet of harts; and He the conqueror will lead me on my high places singing psalms."[11]

The true remedy for all these fears and discouragements is to adhere to God in the darkness, and wait with patience the hour of deliverance. Then will God infuse a secret strength into the soul that will carry her through her trial. "Wait on God with patience; join thyself to God, and endure, that thy life may be increased in the latter end. Take all that shall be brought upon thee; and in thy sorrow endure, and in thy humiliation keep patience: for gold is tried in the fire, but acceptable man in the furnace of humiliation. Believe in God, and He will recover thee; and direct thy way, and trust in Him."[12] You will also find out the truth of the words of Solomon: "Better is the end of prayer than the beginning. Better is the patient man than the presumptuous one."[13]

We must not forget that the will as well as the mind is liable to become fatigued, not as they are spiritual powers, but in the corporal organs which they use. Hence in this our mortal state attention cannot be very long sustained on one subject without varying the method of attention. The power of attention is very different in different persons, and that for various reasons: the difference of natural constitution, the difference of the habits in which the soul has been trained, and the greater or less degree in which the soul has been disciplined to patience. The mind and its faculties should not be strained, or weariness and dulness will be the consequence. Meditation, which the Fathers call investigation, is more fatiguing than the aspirative prayer of the affections. Contemplation is less laborious because the movements of the mind are more simple. But what really fatigues the mind is not tranquil prayer, but any anxiety or sadness mixed with it. When aspirative and affective prayer is mixed with meditation it is not only less fatiguing but more fruitful. This will be particularly found in long retreats.

Let any one who would feel the value of patient prayer take the Our Father, or the Creed, or a Hymn of the Holy Ghost, and repeat it slowly and attentively, with the heart on God and the mind on the sense of the prayer, and he will find, perhaps with some surprise, how much more light will come to his mind, how much more sweetness to his heart, how much nearer he will feel himself to God, than when these customary prayers are little better than gabbled without their full and solemn sense. One Our Father thus meditatively recited with mind, heart, and patient attention, will do more for the soul than several repetitions that are little better than verbal. Sometimes the mind will enter with affection into the sublime truths expressed; sometimes the heart will use them as pious aspirations; sometimes the soul will repose more fully on the divine presence; sometimes she will examine herself by their light; sometimes she will more definitely receive their influence in determining her conduct. These solemn petitions will constantly bring new lights and new refreshments; the spirit of God is in them, and "where is the spirit of the Lord there is liberty".

In his Moral Exposition of the Book of Job, St. Gregory the Great has given us such a solid explanation of the value of interior trials, that we gladly give his reflections at length. The text on which the great Pontiff builds his comment is the words of the messenger to Job. "While thy sons and daughters were eating and drinking wine in the house of their elder brother, a violent wind came on a sudden from the side of the desert, and shook the four corners of the house, and it fell upon thy children, and they are dead, and I alone have escaped to tell thee."[14] Upon this St. Gregory observes that the interior house of the soul is built up in the four cardinal virtues, and within are the other virtues, children of the heart, that mutually feed each other. Justice, fortitude, prudence, and temperance frame a house for the Spirit of God. Then the Spirit of God prepares the house of the soul against her several trials by tempering her with seven virtues; with wisdom against folly, with understanding against stupidity, with counsel against precipitation, with fortitude against fear, with knowledge against ignorance, with piety against hard-heartedness, and with the fear of the Lord against pride.

Yet sometimes whilst the soul is upheld in the plenteous abundance of the divine gift, were that gift left constantly with us, giving us always sweet enjoyment, we should forget from whom the gift comes, and think it our own. It is therefore useful that sometimes this grace should be withdrawn to check our presumption, and to show us how weak we are. When we lose it for a time we learn to know whence our good comes; and that we have not the power to keep it. Sometimes, to teach us humility, temptation rushes upon us, and that with a violence that strikes our wisdom into folly. Not knowing how to deal with the temptation, we become troubled as to how we can meet the pressure of evil. But by this very folly the heart is taught prudence; our momentary folly makes us more humble, and therefore more truly wise; and the wisdom lost in a manner for the time is henceforth held in greater security.

Sometimes, after the understanding has ascended to sublime things, there comes a dull obtuseness that sinks the mind down to things low and vile, and even inferior truths leave the mind that recently soared aloft on rapid wings. Yet this very stupidity, that comes upon the temporary loss of the mental powers, saves the understanding; for the heart is humbled, and is therefore more justly strengthened to understand what is truly sublime. Sometimes, whilst rejoicing in the steady counsel that rules our actions, there comes a crisis that hurries us into thoughtless precipitation, so that whilst we imagined that all was well regulated within us, our interior becomes devastated with confusion. Yet this very confusion teaches us to beware of ascribing our counsel to our own virtue, and after we have returned to the gift of counsel that seemed lost, we hold to that counsel with greater firmness.

Sometimes, whilst bravely despising adversities, some new trouble beyond what we looked for comes upon us, and the soul is struck with unusual fear; yet after suffering this confusion the soul learns to whom she should ascribe the strength that sustains her under tribulations; and in proportion to the danger she has incurred of losing her fortitude, she will adhere more firmly to her Divine Strengthener. Sometimes, whilst rejoicing in the knowledge of divine things, the mind becomes torpid, and struck as it were with blindness; yet though the eye of the mind is closed in ignorance for a time, it afterwards opens to true knowledge; for this visitation of blindness instructs us in the right kind of knowledge, and teaches us from whom true knowledge comes.

Sometimes, when all things seem to be disposed religiously within us, and we congratulate ourselves on being filled with pious feelings, a sudden hardness comes upon us; yet whilst made sensible of the natural hardness of our heart, we learn from whom we receive the gift of piety; and after its partial extinction that piety returns more perfect, and we love it the more for having lost it for a time. Sometimes, when the soul is rejoicing in the holy fear of God, she becomes suddenly stiffened with temptations to pride; yet roused by the dread of losing the fear of God, she bends down anew to humility, and in proportion to her dread of losing a virtue so momentous, she receives it back with greater solidity.

When the house of Job was overwhelmed the seven sons died. When the strong wind of temptation troubles the conscience, for the gaining of self-knowledge the virtues born of the heart are overwhelmed. Yet those sons of the heart still live through the spirit within them, although externally dead to the sensibilities. For though the hour of trial troubles the virtues in a moment, through the perseverance of right intention they live secure in the root of the soul. With the sons of Job their three sisters were overwhelmed. When heavy trials come it will sometimes befall us that charity is troubled in the heart, hope is shaken with alarm, and faith is assaulted with questionings. For at times our love of our Creator will languish under the thought that we are made to suffer beyond our strength; and yielding more to fear than we ought, the confidence of our hope becomes enfeebled. At times also the mind stretches to immense questions, and faith suffers fatigue as though it were failing. Yet these daughters of grace are alive, though they seem overwhelmed; for when conscience seems to say that faith, hope, and charity have almost failed, they are kept alive in the sight of God by the perseverance of right intention.

The servant who brought these tidings to Job alone escaped. Amidst our greatest trials one thing remains safe and secure, and that is the light and discretion by which we distinguish what is just from what is unjust. In the wonderful dispensation under which we live the soul is stricken at times with the sense of guiltiness. Were a man never to feel his weakness he would imagine himself the lord of his powers. But when shaken by the inrush of temptations he becomes fatigued beyond what suffices him, there is shown him the fortress of humility, where he will find an ample protection against his enemies; and from the very fear that his weakness may bring him to a fall, he receives a strength that enables him to stand with firmness. He not only learns from his trials from whom he receives his power, but knows with what watchfulness that power must be preserved. Often when temptation might be easily defeated in the combat, the conceit of self-security brings him to a fall. For when the soul is dissolved in idleness she becomes an easy prey to the corrupter. But when the Divine Piety disposes in such a manner that temptation shall not rush with vehemence upon us, but is only permitted to approach with moderated steps for our instruction, this is granted that we may arm ourselves with caution against the coming foe.[15]

And Job said: "The Lord hath given, the Lord hath taken away. Blessed be the name of the Lord." See how the trials of Job instruct him. In what he has received he confesses the bounty of God: in what is taken from him, to the perturbation of his fortitude, he confesses the power of God. Yet fortitude itself is not taken from him; it is only fatigued with perturbation. From moment to moment his soul is shaken with the fear of losing it; but growing ever more humble through that fear, his humility saves him from losing his fortitude.[16]

No one has treated the subject of patience in prayer, and in the conduct of life, with greater breadth, clearness, and fulness, than St. Catherine of Siena; and it must be remembered that in the decree of her canonization her doctrine was pronounced to have been not acquired but infused. With a summary of what this profoundly enlightened Saint dictated on the subject, we will close this instruction. She listens to the Eternal Truth, and then speaks to souls.

In the Old Testament, when sacrifice was offered to God, there came a fire that drew the victim to Him, and made it acceptable. So the Sweet Truth sends the fire of the Holy Spirit to draw to Him the sacrifice of desire whereby the soul makes the oblation of herself to God. And He says to the soul: 'Knowest thou not that all the pains thou endurest, or canst endure in this life, are insufficient to punish the least of thy sins? An offence against God, the Infinite Good, requires an infinite satisfaction. But all the pains sent thee in this life are not sent for punishment; some are sent for the correction of the offending child. This however is true, that the soul can satisfy by her desires, when they are accompanied with true contrition and displeasure of sin. True contrition satisfies both for sin and punishment, not because of the limited sufferings endured, but because of the infinite desire of God which accompanies them. For He who is infinite would have infinite love and infinite sorrow. He would have infinite sorrow for the offence of God, and also of our neighbour. But souls have infinite desires when they are made infinite through their union with God in love, and in grief, for having offended Him. Whatever sufferings they endure, whether spiritual or corporal, receive an infinite merit through being moved by the Holy Spirit of love, although the acts themselves are limited in time and intensity. The virtue of endurance prevails because it is accompanied by this infinite desire, together with contrition and detestation of sin. This truth is demonstrated by St. Paul. "If I speak with the tongues of men and of angels, and have not charity, I am become as sounding brass or a tinkling cymbal. And if I should have prophecy, and should know all mysteries, and have not charity, I am nothing. And if I should distribute all my goods to feed the poor, and if I should deliver my body to be burned, and have not charity, it profiteth me nothing."[17] The glorious Apostle thus demonstrates that no limited acts or sufferings can satisfy unless seasoned with the unlimited desires of charity.

Every virtue has life and avails through Jesus Christ the Only-begotten Son of God, Crucified, and avails as far as the soul draws love from Him with which to follow His steps in the virtues. In this way they avail, and in no other; in this way sufferings satisfy for sin, that is, from the sweet and unitive love obtained from the sweet knowledge of the Divine Goodness; and through bitter contrition of heart, derived from the knowledge of thyself and thy sins. This knowledge produces hatred of self, of sin, and of sensuality, the effect of which is to account one's self deserving of suffering, and undeserving of consolation. Thou seest, then, how by contrition of heart, by love of patience, and by true humility, thy sufferings should be borne with patience through humility; whilst thou accountest thyself worthy of suffering, and unworthy of consolation. Thou wilt then ask to suffer as a satisfaction for thy offences against thy Creator, and wilt desire to know the Sovereign Truth, that thou mayest love Him.

But the way to gain perfect knowledge, and to taste the Eternal Truth is this, that thou never depart from the knowledge of thyself, but abide in the valley of humility, where thou shalt know God within thee, and shalt draw from that knowledge what is needful for thee. No virtue can have life without charity, nor without humility, which is the nurse of charity. Thou shalt humble thyself in the knowledge of thyself, and shalt see that thy being is not from thyself, but from God, who loved thee before thou wast; and, through unspeakable love, re-created thee in grace; and washed thee; and re-created thee in the Blood of His Only-begotten Son, shed with great fire of love. This love makes the Truth known to every one who but lifts the cloud of self-love from off him through self-knowledge. Then will the soul ascend to the knowledge of God with unspeakable love; yet this love will keep the soul in continual suffering, because it is a love that sorrows in the knowledge of the truth, and suffers exceedingly because of one's sin and ingratitude, and because of the blindness of those who love not God. Yet this is not an afflicting sorrow, not a sorrow that withers the soul, but an enriching sorrow. The soul thus satisfies for her sins, and for the sins of the other servants of God; and her sufferings may suffice because she receives the fruits of life through the virtue of charity.[18]

Patience is the Queen of the soul. She is seated on the rock of fortitude. She conquers, and is never conquered. This virtue is the marrow of charity. By its presence we know whether the garment of charity with which we are clothed is the true nuptial garment or not. If this garment have rents in it, it is an imperfect garment, and impatience will escape through the rents. The other virtues may be for a time concealed, or may seem to be perfect when in reality they are imperfect. But thou, O Patience, canst not be hidden! Let this sweet patience, this marrow of charity be in the soul, and it will demonstrate that all the other virtues are there, and living in perfection. But if patience be absent, that absence will show that all the other virtues are imperfect, and not yet united to the most holy Cross. Patience is conceived of self-knowledge through the knowledge of God's infinite goodness, is born of self-hatred, and is anointed with true humility.

Nothing is refused to the virtue of patience; neither the honour of God nor the salvation of souls; it enjoys them continually. Look at the glorious Martyrs. How many souls were given to their patience. Death brought them life: they raised the dead: they drove mortal sin away from souls. The world exhibited its grandeur, the lords of the world put forth their power; yet they could not prevail against the Martyrs, so strong were they in the sweet power of patience. This virtue is a light placed on a candlestick. It is the glorious fruit of tears united with the love of God and of our neighbour; it partakes of the Immaculate Lamb with anxious and crucified desires. The pain suffered by this virtue is not afflicting, even though suffered for the offences committed against our Divine Creator; because loving patience destroys all fear and self-love. It is consoling, because founded in charity: it brings joy, because it is the demonstrative proof that God dwells by grace in the soul.[19]

Impatience springs from one of two causes: from spiritual death when the soul is in mortal sin; from imperfection of life when the root of self-love is not mortified. Those imperfect souls live by grace, but they are tender about themselves, sensitive from sensuality, and have a soft compassion for their own weakness. They expect other people to compassionate them, and suffer when they are not compassionated. This leads them to murmuring, and to judging the wills of other persons. All this comes from self-love, and impatience is the proof of it. They love their own way, and what tongue can tell the troubles of self-will? In these self-willed persons the eye of the understanding is obscured; their faith, the very pupil of the eye, is clouded with self-love, and they are unfaithful to their light. The impatience that follows makes them disobedient; this weakens their judgment; and this, again, leads them to murmuring. Although they live in grace their souls are imperfect; their self-love obscures their sight, and their virtues are imperfect.

For they accept not the discipline of God with patience, nor even with becoming reverence, nor with the love which God has given them. They do not properly understand that what God sends them, or permits, is for their sanctification, and is consequently to be accepted with gratitude. But this disobedience to God's will results from pride, which chooses to serve God in their own way, and not in His way. For if we believed in very truth that everything except sin proceeds from God, and that He wills nothing but what is for our good, a truth we taste in the Blood of Christ crucified; did we believe this in very truth, and were not warped from it by this tenderness for ourselves, we should be reverentially obedient, and accept whatever God sends us, and should judge that what He sends us is sent in love, and for our good. But because we are unfaithful to this belief, we suffer pains and troubles, and become impatient under the pains that we suffer.

Impatience is the habitual outcome of infidelity to what God ordains for us. We can see this in others, and can be disedified with it; such persons can be quite content that superiors should direct things in their own way as a rule, but they are pained and troubled if their own private ways are contradicted. Whence comes all this pain? If they had no conflict between their nature and their living grace, they would not suffer. But they are weak, and their infirmity is owing to their not having patience in their charity. Instead of humbling themselves beneath the mighty hand of God, and receiving, as they can do, what comes from Him, they will have their pains and fatigues at a time, in a place, and in a way that they choose for themselves. If they cannot pay their debt of duty like other people, they should at least pay their debt of patience. God requires nothing of us beyond what we are able to do, but He always requires charity, and always requires patience to endure the pains and toils that He sends us.[20]

O Patience, how delightful thou art to those who have thee! What hope thou bringest to those who possess thee! Thou art the sovereign of the soul. Thou art the corrector of sensuality. Let but anger or impatience appear, and with the two-edged sword of hatred and love anger is cut down, pride is severed away by the roots, and impatience is made to vanish. Clothed in thy garment of self-knowledge as with sunlight, and casting keen rays of ardent charity on those who would injure thee, thou heapest coals of fire on their heads. In the might of self-knowledge thou art begirt with the virtues as with the stars of heaven; and after the night of self-knowledge comes the day of great light, and the sun's high fervour, clothing thee in beautiful robes. Who then will not love this beautiful patience that endures all things for Christ Crucified.[21]

Where shall we find this valiant virtue of patience? We shall find it, says St. Catherine, where we find charity, and find it in the same way. We shall find it in the Blood of Christ Crucified, where amidst the torments of the Cross no murmur is heard but that of prayer and pardon. There shall we find the patience that bears all our iniquities and infirmities, and that gives the grace of patience to all who live in that Blood. We shall find it in the Blood that is embraced and possessed by the Eternal Divinity, to whom adhering the soul is filled with the holy fire of charity, and with the patience by which that Blood was shed. We shall find that patience in the unspeakable love with which God has loved us, and with which He has endured us.[22]

## 12

## ON THE CHEERFULNESS OF PATIENCE

"That you may walk worthy of God, in all things pleasing.... Strengthened with all might according to the power of His glory, in all patience and long-suffering with joy."—COLOSSIANS i. 10, 11.

There can be no better proof of a healthy soul than habitual cheerfulness. Christian cheerfulness is that modest, hopeful, and peaceful joy which springs from charity and is protected by patience. It is as far removed from the bacchic outbursts of sensual mirth and the egotistical thrills of self-applauding laughter, as from melancholy gloom or self-absorbing sadness; of all which disorderly excesses true cheerfulness is the gentle but most decided adversary. It is the well regulated vigour of spiritual life that throws off all morbid humours and depressing influences, refusing them a lodgment in the soul devoted to God. Cheerfulness gives freedom to our thoughts, and a generous spirit to our actions. It makes our services to God acceptable, and our services to our neighbour grateful. It is revealed in Holy Scripture that "God loveth the cheerful giver"[1]. And, as Ecclesiasticus says: "He that adoreth God with joy shall be acceptable"[2]. As this spirit of cheerfulness is born of charity and patience, it is charity that expands the soul with grateful affection, and infuses sweetness;

and patience that keeps the soul in peace, and protects the spring of cheerfulness from being troubled or diminished.

It is observed by St. Thomas that "although spiritual joy is not of itself a virtue, it is the fruit produced by the virtues, and is chiefly the fruit of charity, flowing from the love of God"[3]. But whilst the great theologian assigns the chief cause of spiritual joy to charity, he gives the due share of that joy to patience. "We must distinguish," he says, "between the virtue and the fruit of patience. As a habit of the soul patience is a virtue; but the pleasure which flows from the exercise of patience is its fruit, and especially in this respect, that it preserves the soul from sadness."[4] Hence St. Paul places patience among the fruits of the Holy Ghost.

This cheerfulness of soul springs from the divine good which God has placed within us, which acts within us, of which we are partakers, and with which our affections are united. Hence purity of conscience is a great promoter of cheerfulness, for when the conscience is clean the affections are pure. But the moving cause of cheerfulness is in the exercise of the virtues, especially as they are the ready servants of the joy of loving God. Yet even the joy of charity is very imperfect, and is often troubled, unless that charity be patient. For it is by the more difficult virtue of patience that we conquer within us what is adverse to cheerfulness, suppress our selfish passions, and obtain freedom for charity to expand untroubled, that it may enlarge and fill our souls. No one can have perfect cheerfulness without perfect charity, or perfect charity without perfect patience.

Who has ever made an effort of will to be patient under trial or temptation, who did not find peace and joy in the conquest? Who has ever upheld his will with patient resolution above the under current of invading sadness, who has not found cheerfulness as the reward of his resolute action? Let the ignorant speak as their sensuality prompts them; we know that those who are the most mortified and patient for the love of God are always the most cheerful and happy. Their spirit is free, their inward sense is drawn to spiritual good, they are not encumbered with moodiness, their souls delight in God.

If we had no greater joys than the world can give the body, or the body give the soul, we should be poor creatures indeed. We should be nothing but animals, oppressed with the gross shadows of sensual enjoyment, which like our bodies are predestined to sufferings and death. "Let us eat and drink to-day for to-morrow we die." This is the philosophy of the sensualist, most abhorrent to the soul. If we had no greater joys than society can give us, with its vain rivalries and fictitious sentimentalities, we should still be poor creatures. Our minds and hearts would not have much more to feed on than the uncertain vanities of this uncertain life. This is the philosophy of the sentimentalist, whose conversation and literature is but too often imbued with subtle poison. The great joys of the soul are secret, known to heaven, unknown to the world. What is ambition but a scrambling to rise one over another, to the humiliation of our neighbours, the confusion of order, and the destruction of peace and content? This is the philosophy of pride.

If we had no greater enjoyment than the material scientists can give us, we should be unhappy creatures. Poring into matter until they lose sight of their immortal souls, they materialize their souls, and wish to materialize us. Losing the power of ascending from the creature to the Creator, by an immense abuse of their intelligence they drown their souls in their senses, cast a shadow of gloom and sadness over the world, and do their best to make it a dreary habitation for immortal souls. They leave the spiritual nature of man without object, without purpose, without development, without meaning, without anything immortal with which to satisfy her immortal yearnings. But God is infinitely patient. Religion is the first, the grandest, the most ennobling of all sciences, for it brings us to the Fountain of intelligence and wisdom. As all other sciences deal with the works of God, in their right place they are the servants of religion. Without His light who made and governs them, how can we understand the works of God? But with His light they minister to our cheerfulness, because they speak of Him and lead to Him.

The Christian soul lives in communion with God, and to that soul a prospect is opened into infinite and unchangeable truth. Within that soul a sense is opened that tastes the infinite and eternal good.

What opens this eye in the soul? The light of faith descending from God. What awakes this sense in the soul? The grace of charity from the Holy Spirit of God. Can anything be so cheering to the soul as her growth in truth except her growth in good? As truth and good come to our soul from God, can anything secure their increase like prayer and communion with God? By this holy converse hope is ever growing of greater things to come. Unlike our converse with the world, it is inexhaustible in expectation of eternal good.

Add patience to these divine gifts, and the restless soul, brought to order and tranquillity, is enabled to profit by these divine visitations to the full of her capacity. If nature becomes fatigued by its exaltation above its powers, patience steps in to sustain the weary spirit, and keep her tranquil and resigned in hope. We may be left in a certain obscuration at times; but we know that the light is near us. We may suffer interior hunger and privation for our trial; but we know that God is secretly with us. We may feel the weight of trial as a burden; but patience will make that burden light, and the love that bears it will cheer the soul; because it is the joy of sacrifice filled with the hope of eternal good to come.

The children of the world, who live for themselves, know nothing of the enjoyments of the children of grace, who live for God. Bent upon the things beneath them, their enjoyments come from nothing that is equal to their spiritual nature, and certainly from nothing that is superior to that nature; and what they do enjoy contains the seeds of sadness and decay. Loving but mortal things with an immortal soul, they pervert the order of their nature until their desires contradict their wants. The flowers of their gladness fade and die, and the fruits of sadness come in their place.

They thus detach themselves from the order of the universe, separate themselves from the Eternal Fountain of light, life, and joy, and are reduced to isolation from the God who gives peace and happiness, and from the society of the blessed who are happy in God. How can they understand those joys of the spirit that spring up to eternal life? They are estranged from them by their state of isolation. But the spirit of charity carries cheerfulness into every part of life; its innocent pleasures and relaxations have the same basis of the love of God as its graver duties; so that whilst what is transient in them quickly passes, what is divine in the motive lasts for ever.

The joys of the spirit are like the spirit; they have no visible shape by which they can be seen, no sensible form by which they can be touched; they are joys of the spirit that flow from God's gifts and the soul's virtues; they are guarded by patience, possessed in God, and give a sweet and attractive sense of God. Spiritual cheerfulness can only belong habitually to the superior soul of those who by loving patience have made the conquest of their inferior nature, that its inordinate movements may not mix with the acts of the superior soul to sadden or disturb them. What is beneath the superior soul, be it the body, the senses, the animal life, or that inferior region of the soul which is in contact with the body, all this may be exposed to pains, to afflictions, or to any kind of suffering; but so long as the superior soul is united with God, and responds to the ruling of His grace with patient love, those sufferings in the region beneath are kept in their place. They are looked down upon by the superior soul for what they are, and for no more than what they are; they are not allowed to invade the superior soul, to disturb her peace, to make her anxious, fretful, or distracted, or to lessen the cheerfulness of her self-possession and resignation.

No one without experience can have an idea how much of this detachment of our superior from our inferior nature can be effected by the patient love of God, or what power this gives the spirit to command the imagination and the senses, enabling the spirit to rise superior to suffering and sadness. Then that patient love brings those sufferings with a cheerful spirit to Christ Jesus on the Cross, where, blended with His sufferings, they open to her the mysteries of eternal life, there seen with wonderful clearness, and grace and comfort flow to the sufferer from that life-giving fountain. Hence St. Paul has taught us in many places that hope springs from suffering with Christ, and brings joy and consolation to the soul. "Rejoicing in hope, patient in tribulation, instant in prayer."[5] This interior habit of tranquillity alike in prosperity and adversity shines from the interior into the countenance of the man of patient charity with a bland irradiation. A beautiful expression sits like a seal of the Holy Ghost upon the features of the Saints, and has often been recorded by those who knew them. To give but one example out of thousands, St. Athanasius, who was intimately acquainted with St. Antony the hermit, and knew his austere life and the great patience of his combats with his spiritual enemies, tells us in his Life of the Saint, that "if any stranger came to see Antony, although personally unknown to him, if he saw him first from a distance, and among a crowd of the brethren, he recognised the Saint the moment he cast eyes on him, and would hasten past the others to reach him. For his purity of soul shone through his features, and the grace of his holy mind was reflected on his earthly frame; whilst the cheerfulness of his countenance never failed to show that he was inwardly engaged upon divine things."

Ruffinus also informs us, that whenever St. Antony had to try the spiritual condition of other souls, he invariably applied the test of patience. Hearing that the brethren were extolling one man to the skies for his wonderful virtues, St. Antony sent for him and put his patience to the trial, and finding him fail in that virtue he made but small account of the rest, and said to him: "Brother, you are like a fine house with a very ornamental front door, whilst you leave the back door open to thieves". If he saw signs of sadness in any one he asked the reason of it, and would say: "No one ought ever to be sad in whom is the salvation of God, and the hope of the kingdom of Heaven. Pagans may be sad, they have reason to be so, and so have unrepenting sinners; but let the just rejoice in God." This also was one of his sayings: "There is but one way of conquering the enemy, and that is by keeping the spirit cheerful and the mind fixed on God".

When our hearts are free from envy, that deadly bane of charity that shows itself in disparaging speech, we find joy in the good which others possess, and this makes us partakers of their good. But we delight in the good which is united with ourselves. Delight, therefore, in its spiritual sense, is the pleasure we receive from good obtained; but joy is the pleasure we receive from the good we perceive in others, or that we expect to receive ourselves. For the communion of charity has a breadth without limits, in which we rejoice or are delighted with all the good we see in God, and in all that He gives to ourselves or to our fellow-creatures, conscious that by love we are in communion with all that good. This joy also moves us to desire that this good may be more and more increased and diffused to the honour of God and the blessing of His creatures. But the spiritual gifts that bind us to God are more in God than they are in us, and God is the cause of all spiritual joy; wherefore St. Paul exhorts us: "Rejoice in the Lord always; again, I say, rejoice"[6].

But delight is the enjoyment of good in our actual possession, which tranquillizes and satisfies our appetite for good, and makes it peaceful, pleasant, and contented. It enlarges the soul into a greater life. Remembering that meekness is the fruit of patience, we shall better understand the words of the Psalmist: "The meek shall inherit the land, and shall delight in abundance of peace"[7]. And he says again: "My soul shall rejoice in the Lord, and shall be delighted in His salvation"[8]. And he shows the reward of this delighting in God: "Delight in the Lord, and He will give thee the requests of thy heart"[9]. Our Heavenly Father loves to see His children free in His love without servile fears. He loves to see them trusting in Him and rejoicing in Him. He loves to see them living in the consciousness of His goodness. To delight in God is to honour, praise, and glorify Him. To delight in God is the effectual way of opening the soul to His divine influences. This delight is a bright shadow of the good things to come.

But to have this calm and cheering sense the heart must habitually look to God, live in the sense of God, and often converse with Him. I say converse with God, because the sense of the soul receives the answers to our prayers. There are two states of the soul that desires God which are immeasurably different. There is a state in which the inward sense of the soul is set on God, with humble, reverent, and devout attention, and in which the soul lives more in God than in herself. And there is a state in which the soul lives more in herself than in God, conscious of God but much more conscious of herself; in which state self-love plays a great part. The soul finds herself in a net of the earthly senses, filled with self-consciousness, shadowed with gloom, or restless with levity. Thus imprisoned, the soul will imagine that she cannot rise above her nature to seek the cheering light of God. Nay, this self-love in the inferior soul will play shameful tricks with the superior soul, will suggest the shame of her faults, or the plea of her unworthiness, and thus dishearten her from making efforts to rise out of her entanglements. Or the busy sense and consciousness of self, infected with levity or imbued with sadness, according to the tone and temper of the time, will grasp the heart as with ligaments of fear or with bonds of dulness, and make the will reluctant to snap the strings of self-love, that the mind may rise to God. Then prayers are muttered distractedly or murmured painfully within the soul. There is no clear outlook above one's self, no lifting of the mind, no going forth of the heart to God, no resting of the affections on God. Hence cheerlessness, impatience, and a tendency to sadness.

But to lend the will to those tricks of self-love that incline the soul to unreasonable fears and sadness, is unworthy of a child of God, who ought to cherish unbounded confidence in a Father of such unbounded goodness, and ought to foster that unbounded confidence which inspires generosity. For what has self-love ever done for us that is not to our shame and discouragement? And what has the confiding love of God ever done for us that is not to our joy and content? True faith knows the unbounded goodness and mercy of God, and how ready He is at all times to accept our good will. True humility knows what infirm creatures we are, and how our Heavenly Father is disposed to help us in our infirmities, whatever they may be, provided we have recourse to Him. True patience withstands all the fears and misgivings of self-love that interfere with hope, and adheres with unbounded trust to the Divine Helper of our infirmities. The true love of God, however humbled, is never ashamed to bring every weakness and failing before our Heavenly Father; gladly knowing that He expects this of us, and that to open the soul to Him is to secure pardon, light, and peace. "Wait on God with patience: join thyself to God and endure, that thy life may be increased."

Only those souls that are disciplined in the patience of charity can be truly cheerful under grave trials. For this depends upon the magnanimity with which the spirit upholds herself above the pressure and pain of her inferior nature, and this can only be done by the brave and patient love of the spirit which looks to God, and by virtue of the trust which that love inspires, that if we are resigned to the trial, God will show us a way out of it, and will deliver us from it in His own good time. Cheerfulness implies hope, courage, confidence in God, the turning a deaf ear to the complaints of self-love, and a certain modest joy in the consciousness that in the hands of God, "in whom we live, and move, and have our being," we are safe. But when we are beset by serious trials, a certain effort of patience is required to keep the spirit uppermost, and to keep the door closed through which sadness would invade the soul. Yet it is surprising to any one who tries with what a small amount of effort on the part of the will this cheerfulness, when lost, may be recovered, and how much evil and discomfort this cheerful spirit will prevent.

No one should allow his peace to be disturbed by what is not a rebuke of conscience. There are a number of pious people who greatly injure their freedom as well as their cheerfulness by attaching unquiet feelings to their conscience without cause, and make themselves miseries out of their own fancies. Brooding over their dull or unpleasant sensations, or over little things said about them, they indulge in the art of self-torment, and make such a set of discomforts for themselves, that nothing works at ease in them, and they can neither rejoice in God nor be cheerful in themselves. Yet these discomforts may be nothing more than humours in the body, or little irritations in the nerves that are not worth attention, or depression caused by change in the atmosphere, or some obstruction or other in the corporal system, or something of sadness allowed to be engendered from annoyance of no moment. Yet these good people will mistake these petty disturbances or depressions of their sensibilities for something wrong in the conscience, they know not what, which engages them with themselves, alarms them with apprehensions, and fills them with uneasiness. But these and similar things have no relation whatever in their origin with the will or the conscience, and only become a mischief by being made the subject of a great deal of self-consciousness and self-love, wearing and wasting the spirits in discomfort, sadness and discouragement. This is not the way of patience but of impatience, not the way of peace but of trouble, not the way of the cheerful giver but of the selfish self-disturber. The generous soul sets her heart on God, not on herself; thinks of God, and not of her own mechanical discomforts.

If any one should take this brooding over himself for self-knowledge, he would be very much mistaken. He is simply making discouragements for himself by looking for them, and so conjuring them up. Self-knowledge is not to be found in our own darkness but in God's light. There is an immense deal of selfishness in this dull and dreary self-introspection, excepting when we examine ourselves before God, and in His light.

Peace of conscience should not be disturbed by venial weaknesses; they cause no surprise in humble souls that have a sincere disposition to reform them. Nor should venial faults of the will be allowed to disturb its patience, and so open the door to sadness, causing irritating frets instead of peaceful regrets. For, as St. Bonaventure observes, if we keep our patience it will remove our sins of weakness; and the Council of Trent teaches that there is no obligation of confessing these venial sins, because every good act is removing them. It is commended, but not required. A good act of the love of God or for the love of God will do more to remove them than the fretting and disconsolation and shame at failure which have less of contrition than self-love in them, and are therefore more offensive than the mere faults of surprise, weakness, or inadvertence from which this interior disturbance has been allowed to rise. Beware of that shame, humiliation, and self-disturbance which is neither humility, patience, nor contrition. It is good to have sincere contrition for even the least of our faults, and to submit them to the tribunal of penance; but they ought not to injure our cheerfulness, because that is to injure our childlike confidence in God. Without failures of which we are conscious, and that help to keep us humble, we should have deeper sins of pride of which we should be less conscious.

Trials of darkness and dryness are not to be assumed for proofs of the presence of sin, but as demands on patience and resignation. If on examination the conscience is silent, they have no other object than to strengthen us in the more solid virtues, such as faith, trust, patience, humility, detachment, and resignation. The peace of a good conscience inspires cheerfulness under all trials, because God in His goodness has enabled us to keep the great points of His law. In the words of St. Paul: "We glory in this, the testimony of our conscience, that in simplicity of heart and sincerity of God, and not in carnal wisdom, but in the grace of God, we have conversed in this world"[10].

There is another error of judgment, seldom noticed, but a not unfrequent cause of interior discouragement. A soul that has had a long and trying conflict with interior darkness, temptation, or trial will suffer fatigue and weariness, and may even mistake the consequent depression for a wound in the conscience. The will may have been firm and patient, but the fatigue will be all the greater from the strain. Let not that soul mistake the depression of fatigue either for sadness or reproach of conscience. A little tranquil recollection, raising the spirit above the exhausted sense, will restore her cheerfulness.

Nothing contributes more to cheerfulness than the habit of looking at the good side of things. The good side is God's side of them. But even on their human side, what makes them appear worse than they are is conferred on them by the envy, jealousy, and malice of our hearts, falsely imagining that what depresses others exalts ourselves. This is one of the most false and miserable of human weaknesses. The evil it produces is incalculable; for what begins in the jealousy of the heart ends in the scandal of the tongue. Inordinate self-love is never without the inclination to exalt one's dear self at the expense of others, and to take a secret enjoyment out of their humiliation. Hence comes the disposition to look to the weak rather than the good side of persons and things; and hence the habit of rash judgment, making things appear much worse than they are. Let patience keep down envy and repress the fancy of our own superiority, and we shall see a great deal more for which to praise God, that will make us more cheerful and thankful. For all good is from God, and is to His honour and praise. Wherever we find a single-hearted Catholic people full of faith, their constant praising of God for all the good they see or receive forms the most beautiful element of their language. But the pleasure of seeing and imagining what is wrong or imprudent in our neighbours indicates a jealous disposition of soul that is fruitful in uncharity and evil.

Why should we not rejoice in the good things of God? We can rejoice in the good things of the senses, why not in the good things of the soul? If the day is pure and serene we enjoy its gladness. Why should we not rejoice in the serene light of truth that shines from Heaven upon our mind? If the sun warms us with His beneficent rays our whole frame is cheerful. Why should we not be cheerful under the radiation of God's divine charity. If we look at beautiful flowers or hear delightful music, our heart expands with pleasure. Why should not our soul expand with delight when God puts beautiful flowers of grace into our souls, or gives us a sense of the eternal harmonies? We find a joy in the presence and cheerful greeting of our friends. Why should we not look up to Heaven, whence so many pure and most loving faces look upon us with divine affection, and with most tender desires to cheer and help us? We feel honoured and cheered by the arrival of beautiful gifts, chiefly because they are embalmed with the kind affections of our friends. Why should we not delight in the beautiful gifts of God, so many, so frequent, so various, bringing to our soul the celestial balsam of His eternal love? Having an Almighty and most loving Father, in whom we live, and move, and have our being, let us rejoice in Him. Having a most loving Saviour, very God of God, who has made Himself our brother, and feeds us with His life, we ought surely to rejoice in Him. Having the Holy Spirit of God with us, dwelling in us with wonderful condescension, making us His temples, and pouring His love into our hearts, we ought certainly to answer His love, and rejoice in His overflowing goodness. "Rejoice in the Lord always; again I say, rejoice."

Sensual joy is from a mortal cause, and we soon find out its mortality. Spiritual joy is from a spiritual and eternal cause, and nothing but sin or sadness can bring it to an end in us. For true spiritual delight springs from the divine truth in the intelligence and the divine love in the will, and is pure, simple, innocent, peaceful, contenting to the spirit, and filled with the promise of eternal good things. Why should we ever set a gloomy face against a guest so beautiful and generous? That heavenly guest will never disturb us, will never derange the good order of our being as sensual pleasures do; but will give the soul in which it dwells a sweet growth, a tranquil energy, and a loving cheerfulness proportioned to the welcome that we give to a guest so divine. And, as St. Thomas truly observes: "This spiritual cheerfulness perfects the work of the will by giving pleasure to its operations"[11].

As every spiritual good that we receive comes from the Eternal Fountain of happiness, when gratefully received and rightly used it ought to promote that cheerfulness which is the beginning of all happiness. For what the Book of Wisdom tells us of the manna with which God fed the Israelites in the wilderness is applicable to every divine gift. "Thou didst feed Thy people with the food of angels, and gavest them bread from heaven prepared without labour; having in it all that is delightful, and the sweetness of every taste. For Thy sustenance showed Thy sweetness, and serving every man's will, it was turned to what every man liked."[12] But whether we shall taste the varied and abundant sweetness of those heavenly gifts or not, depends upon what patient control we exercise over our earthly desires and sensual appetites, which hinder us from relishing divine and eternal things. When the Israelites lost this control and longed for the fleshpots of Egypt, their souls nauseated the food that God had provided for them, and they fell into a sadness and a murmuring with which God was greatly offended. Of what profit are the divinest gifts unless we give our heart and will to them? How can they make us cheerful if we prefer the sadness that sensual self-love engenders?

Then, as we have said from St. Bonaventure, the patience of charity purifies the soul from sin, which is the chief obstacle to cheerfulness; and here we will give the whole teaching of the Seraphic Doctor on this important subject, and that nearly in his own words.

First, patience purifies the soul from past sins, and by keeping the will apart from those temptations that move us to sin, it preserves us from future sins. Patience effects this by holding back the will from entering into temptation.

Secondly, by keeping the soul in just order, regularity, and peace, patience disposes us for the receiving of greater graces and diviner gifts, and prepares us for the exercise of stronger virtues.

Thirdly, patience tests and proves all the virtues. For as St. Gregory says: "The trials of a man prove what is in him". Gold is purified from dross in the fire. The grain of iron is tested by the file. Wheat is separated from straw by the flail. What is false or defective in the soul is cast out by patience.

Fourthly, the patient soul perfects her charity to a high degree, and obtains greater glory in Heaven. She therefore welcomes the sufferings that give occasion for exercising this virtue; that she may be able to say with the Psalmist: "According to the multitude of my sorrows in my heart, Thy comforts have given joy to my soul"[13].

Fifthly, when patience works by charity the soul is prudent in the ruling of herself, strenuous in combating for her own protection, and reigns like a peaceful sovereign in her own domain, of which she holds free and firm possession; whilst by her calm vigour she becomes the mistress of her adversaries.

Sixthly, patience is a singular retributor of the Passion of Christ. It repays Him in kind for what we receive from Him who bore our sorrows. This is the special joy of the Saints. Whatever comes to them in likeness to the sufferings of Christ, that they welcome, that they suffer with patience, and rejoice in their sufferings. They rejoice because they have opportunities of repaying the Lord as far as they are able for the exceeding love with which He gave His life for them. Not that He is in need of our goods, who have none of our own to give Him; but when He enters into judgment with us, and we come before Him with the marks of His sufferings upon us, then will they have great confusion who have had no will to suffer for His sake, and they will have great glory who have endured much with patience for the love of Him. It would seem, then, that our Lord shows special love to those to whom He sends many things to be endured; He honours them with a part of His burden, as He honoured Simon of Cyrene with a part of His Cross.

A number of persons, each with his own burden, are travelling the same road in company. If one of them gets exhausted with fatigue, he will naturally look to some one on whose affection he can rely to help him for a time with his burden. He will trust to love, and not to the grudging help of those to whom he is indifferent. So our divine Lord, walking with us all the days of our lives, looks out for those who are ready for His love to carry a part of the burden that He still must bear in His mystical body the Church. He distributes that Passion, which as our Head He endured for us, among His faithful and compassionate members, who, being of the body of which He is the Head, love to suffer with Him, that with Him they may be glorified. For as the sufferings of Christ abound in us, so also shall His glory abound. Partaking of His death we partake also of His resurrection; and the more we suffer with Him, the more gloriously shall we reign with Him.[14]

When the Royal Psalmist is in affliction, and his life is "wasted with grief," he exclaims to God: "O how great is the multitude of thy sweetness, O Lord, which Thou hast hidden for them that fear Thee! Which Thou hast wrought for them that hope in Thee, in the sight of the sons of men. Thou shalt hide them in the secret of Thy face from the disturbance of men. Thou shalt protect them in Thy tabernacle from the contradiction of tongues.[15]

Among the treasures of His goodness God has provided an unspeakable sweetness for those who fear Him with a loving fear, and a singular protection for those who, in patient hope, refer the trials and contradictions they endure to their Divine Protector. The Psalmist has before him two states of soul: the state of one who seeks God in solitude and silence, and the state of one who is exposed to the combats and vexations of the active life, and the contradiction of tongues. The souls that seek God in silence He hides in His face, and gives them a divine intimacy with Him. A great sweetness is hidden for those souls, which is sometimes given to them and sometimes concealed from them. When this luminous sweetness is communicated, it fills them with delight; when it is concealed from them, it is not lost, but is hidden in the secret of God's face for them, that their faith may be exercised, their patience put to the proof, and their desire of God increased. The law of justice is in their heart, but there is a cloud before them; yet they know that the Sun of Justice is in the cloud. Then sensible delight is changed into a secret sustaining strength; and they wait in the outer court. In the root of the soul there is hope, desire, and a chaste fear that is not afraid of God. But where is the source of cheerfulness? In the faith that God is in the cloud, and very near the soul. In the confidence that the sweetness is not lost, but only hidden in the face of God for them. In the trust that their trial is purifying them for greater good. In the courage that still adheres to God with patience, and waits His will with magnanimity. Meanwhile it is ordained that the soul prove her love by the constancy of her patience, and wait in peace until consolation returns.

Two things try the patience of the souls set in open combat: persecution in their persons or goods; and provoking, offensive, or calumnious speeches. But when they silently commit their cause to God, and patiently leave themselves to His care, He protects their souls from injury, and hides them in His tabernacle, or sanctuary, words that signify their secret union with Him, in which He shows them special favours and proofs of tenderness.

To those who are in the charity of God St. Paul addresses these magnificent words: "Know you not that your members are the temple of the Holy Ghost, who is in you, whom you have from God: and you are not your own. For you were bought with a great price."[16] And in another place the Apostle tells us: "Whosoever are led by the Spirit of God, they are the sons of God. For you have not received the spirit of bondage again in fear: but you have received the adoption of sons, whereby we cry: Abba (Father). For the Spirit giveth testimony to our spirit, that we are the sons of God. And if sons, heirs also; heirs indeed of God, and joint-heirs with Christ: yet so if we suffer with Him, that we may be also glorified with Him."[17]

Here is a list of most noble prerogatives and privileges that belong to the lovers of God. They are delivered from servile fear, and are free with that freedom with which God makes them free. They have the joy of being God's children, a joy that should remove all sadness from their hearts. They are the living temples of God's Holy Spirit, who bears them witness that they are the sons of God. They are joint-heirs with Christ of the good things of God. But one condition is attached to these exalted privileges. "Yet so if we suffer with Him, that we may also be glorified with Him." This condition is required for proof and for earnest that we do love God with sincere affection and gratitude, and are ready to suffer with cheerfulness for His sake, who bought us this love with His sufferings. And as our present sufferings prepare us for the future glory, they ought already to have in them the seeds of that glory in the cheerfulness and joy that comes of the patient love with which we suffer.

Why should the children of God raise the question in fear and sadness, that they know not whether they love God or not? You know whether you prefer God to all things else. You know whether you desire God above all things. You know whether you would consent to die rather than offend Him mortally. You know whether, trusting in His grace, you are ready to suffer with Christ. It is these dispositions of the will, and not the emotions of sensibility, that decide the question whether you love God or not. Why, then, should you deprive yourself of the cheering joy of loving God? Why should you check and restrain the expansion of that love with saddening thoughts and servile fears? The Apostles and Saints give us the maxim that the proof of the presence of charity is in its patience. When we are ready, and cheerfully ready to suffer and to endure for the love of God, we have the full proof of the presence of that love in our soul.

Why should the Sacred Scriptures exhort us so continually to rejoice in God, to delight in God, and to rejoice in suffering for His sake, if we are to turn a deaf ear to them, as though they were not the revealed will of God to our faith, as though they were not His own divine invitations that we should love and serve Him cheerfully. To rejoice in God is to put His enemies to flight. The cheerful love and service of God disperse gloom, scatter morbidity to the winds, and leave no room for self-love to indulge in sadness. Nor need this cheerfulness be lowered by the advent of tribulation, if patience be there to sustain the spirit in its right position. "We may always rejoice," observes St. Chrysostom, "if we will only keep our heads a little raised above the flood of human things."

Cheerfulness is the beauty of patience, the play of freedom, the radiation of charity, the glow of spiritual health. It is an emanation from the gifts and the fruits of the Holy Ghost, and a certain sign of the happy order of the virtues, braced into the love of God by peace-giving patience. This cheerful spirit, this joy of devotedness, completes and perfects our acts in the service of God and of our neighbours. It crowns our good deeds, and without it they are without their best ornament. When our good acts are accompanied with reluctance or constraint, they lose their freedom, power, and influence, because they are mingled with pain and sadness.

It is said in the Ethics, which give us the voice of nature, that "the generous man, who expends his gifts joyfully, does a noble action: whereas he who gives reluctantly and with regret does an unworthy deed". Holy Scripture proclaims that to serve God with joy and gladness makes our service acceptable. It was said to the Israelites: "Because thou didst not serve the Lord thy God with joy and gladness of heart, for the abundance of all things: thou shalt serve thy enemy, whom the Lord will send upon thee, in hunger, and thirst, and nakedness, and in the want of all things."[18] This was their punishment for not serving God gratefully but grudgingly. The sacred psalmist exhorts us: "Serve ye the Lord with gladness"[19]. And he gives it as the blessing of the hopeful: "Let all them be glad who hope in Thee: they shall rejoice for ever, and Thou shalt dwell in them"[20].

If the Old Testament abounds in exhortations to serve God with cheerfulness and with joy, the New Testament is even yet more instant in exhorting us to be cheerful and thankful under sufferings and trials. Who ever suffered more than St. Paul? Yet he tells the

Corinthians: "I exceedingly abound in joy in all our tribulations"[21]. In which of his epistles does he not proclaim his joy amidst his sufferings, profoundly conscious that they bound him to the cross of Christ and the love of God? St. Peter gives a sublime reason for this joy in suffering: "If you partake of the sufferings of Christ, rejoice, that when His glory shall be revealed you also may be glad with exceeding joy"[22]. But the most touching instruction is that of our Blessed Lord after His Last Supper. He tells His disciples that He is going to leave them; He describes all the sufferings that will come upon them after His departure. He then says to them: "Peace I leave with you, My peace I give unto you; not as the world giveth do I give unto you. Let not your heart be troubled, nor let it be afraid." And after exhorting them to abide in Him, and in His love, He says to them: "These things I have spoken to you, that my joy may be in you, and your joy may be filled"[23].

How joy meets suffering on the ground of patience St. Augustine will explain. Expounding the text of the psalm: "My bone is not hidden from Thee, which Thou hast made in secret," he asks: "What is this bone that is known to God, but hidden from man? It is a certain interior firmness and fortitude that is not easily broken down. Whatever troubles, whatever trials or adversities come upon us, God has made a firmness within us that neither yields nor breaks under them. This firmness is a certain patience that God forms within us, and of which the Psalmist says: 'Shall not my soul be subject to God? For from Him is my patience.' The Apostle had this firmness, 'Sorrowful as it were yet always rejoicing'. The persecutors strove their best to make the martyrs miserable, and judging them by their own weakness they thought them miserable. To the eyes of men they seemed in a miserable plight; but within themselves they rejoiced in God, to whom the bone was not hidden that He had made for them."[24]

The man born blind has no sense of colours. The man born deaf has no knowledge of the sound of the human voice. The fishes that live in the waters have no experience of fire. The body has eyes, but they cannot see the soul. Man without the grace and virtue of patient charity can form no true conception how peace and joy can coexist with great pain and suffering. It is not sensually but spiritually examined; but in the case supposed this union of joy with suffering is not in the soul to be examined, nor is the spiritual power there by which it can be examined. The gifts of the Holy Ghost give the joy and the power to feel the joy. Where God acts, and the soul acts with God, human weakness is not the point for consideration, but divine strength; and the grace of patient charity is stronger than all suffering. Hence a St. Felicitas could cheerfully encourage her seven sons to look up to heaven where Jesus Christ expected them; to be faithful in their love and suffer bravely for their souls. With joy she saw them expire in torments one after another, and then followed them on their ensanguined path to heaven. A St. Agnes, so young and tender, surveyed the cruel fire and the instruments of torture with a cheerful countenance, expressed her joy at the spectacle, and still more at the sight of her barbarous executioner; and "went more cheerfully to her sufferings than other maidens to their bridals". A St. Lawrence could playfully jest with his executioners in the midst of his cruel torments. A Sir Thomas More could calmly use his gentle wit at the moment of laying his head upon the block. When St. Tiburtius was sentenced to bitter tortures before the death stroke, he said to the judge: "To the Christian whose conscience is pure all your torments are but trifles". The Acts of the Holy Martyrs and Confessors abound in evidence of the consolations that carried them through their sufferings. In return for their patient love God gave them the hidden bone of fortitude, and the refreshment of His Holy Spirit; and they experienced the truth of the eternal promise: "He shall cry to me, and I will hear him: I am with him in tribulation, I will deliver him, and glorify him"[25].

But after all our greatest trials are interior. Those that come from without are open, palpable, and definable in their causes; but those within are often obscure and mysterious. They go to the very core of our affections, and to the inexperienced they cause anxiety and solicitude, owing to the privation of light and of sensible joy. Yet are they the most important part of the discipline of the soul. They correct negligence, punish conceit and pride, and are very often trials of fidelity. They are at all times great instructions in self-knowledge, humility, and patience. Under this kind of trial the wants of the soul are keenly felt; our nothingness before God is keenly impressed upon us; our dependence on God is struck deeply into the conscience; and the craving of the heart for God is so much awakened, that, where patience is truly present, self-love, which is the greatest enemy to spiritual cheerfulness and joy, is in great measure purified from the soul.

What shall we say to those who are in the first experiences of this kind of trial? Let them first understand that such trials are not exceptional, but common to souls called to greater perfection of life. First comes the season of flowering, then the season of the hard and unripe fruit, and afterwards the mellowing of the fruit into sweetness. We first enjoy the beauty and perfume of the blossoms; but they must decay before the fruit can come. The time of flowering is the novitiate of the soul. Then comes the hard, acid, and unripe fruit. This is the time of patience and hope, of strengthening and maturing. But during all this time of patient endurance the hard, dry, and acid fruit is being strengthened in its virtues, increased and ripened by the sun into sweetness and perfection, and then we enjoy its matured beauty and nourishing sweetness with delight.

It is unreasonable to expect the ripe fruit in the time of flowering, or in the time of maturing. Yet we may be cheered with their beauty and their promise, and with the hope of greater enjoyment in the future. There is no present good of the spiritual kind without the promise of greater good, and even of eternal good. The trial is the pruning of the tree of its harmful superfluities, giving it strength and vigour to be fruitful. Know that you must pass from the flower to the green fruit of piety, and that the fruit must be hardened before it is ripened. Do not frighten your imagination as if yours were an exceptional and singular case. Your books of instruction will tell you differently. Look not to your sensibilities as if true piety consisted in them, but look well to your will and desires. In the winter season of your soul fret not for the summer's sunshine; you are soft, and must be hardened. It is the season of patience, of resignation, of waiting, of enduring. Why should not your winter be cheerfully undergone? There is nothing to prevent it, if by patient love you keep sadness away.

The great enemy of the soul is not trial but sadness, which is the bleeding wound of self-love. It takes many shapes, and many shades of colour, all of the darker hues, and is often subtle and unperceived in its depressing influence. It is fertile of evils, chokes a great deal of good, resists the operations of divine grace, and is the great adversary of cheerfulness. It contracts the heart, darkens the mind, and insinuates the morbid elements of self-love like a virulent poison into the soul. Shall we call it blood-poisoning or soul-poisoning? It is both. It is noxious to the whole spirit of life, natural, as well as supernatural. There are but two remedies for this malignant evil. The preventive remedy is in that patience of will that resists its entrance into the soul from the outset, and by adhering to God keeps the spirit from descending into the entanglements of self-love. But when sadness has arisen, has got some hold of the will, and already caused some moodiness and trouble, the remedy will be in an effort to break through the slimy net in which the spirit has become entangled.

As the effect of sadness is to close us up within ourselves, the short way of deliverance is to break away from one's self, and this by some act of kindness and attention to others. This will be a reluctant effort at first, but with a little effort to overcome reluctance, self-conquest and freedom will be quickly gained; and it will be discovered with surprise that there was nothing in this contemptible moodiness but pride. For self-love was entertaining a resolve to be unhappy, and will feel the humiliation of giving up the dark conceit, which was nothing but the dregs of self, nothing but the bitter consciousness of nature warped to sullenness; whilst the effort to be cheerful and kind is in fact the separation of the will from self-love, to which it clings like a limpet to a rock, not because it is happiness, but because it is self. Yet no humiliation imposed by another could be more severely felt than this tearing away the will from one's morbid self. It is like giving up a fortress.

It looks like something too strong to conquer, yet nothing can be weaker. All that is required to break the fascinating spell is some little effort of the will, and it is amazing how small is the effort required. A few kind words, a kind act, even a kind look, though reluctant at first, will set the will free, and dissolve the gloomy phantoms that have held the soul in bondage. Then will patient charity recover her ascendency, and will open first the green bud and then the bright flower of cheerfulness, giving graciousness and beauty to the virtues.

Let us conclude these instructions. The heart is the centre of our corporal life, from which every member of the body receives its renovation. The calm, regular, and musical time of its pulsations gives us the best assurance we can have that our material frame is in a healthy condition. In virtue of those steadfast and constant pulsations every part of the body receives fresh elements of life, and rejects what is noxious or destructive of life. The will, in like manner, is the centre of our spiritual nature, the spring and fountain of its action. Hence the Scriptures place the heart for the will, which is truly the vital principle of the soul,—the principle of action, love, and endurance. But there is this essential difference between the spring of our material and the spring of our spiritual life, that the material heart acts by a fixed law that is independent of the will; but the spiritual heart, or font of action is the will, which is free in its action, and formed to work with the supernatural grace of God.

But among the divine gifts of grace there are two chief principles of power, and when the will works faithfully with them they give the soul that perfection of life which prepares her for her final union with God. The one is the fervid and generous action of charity, the other is the regulating and controlling action of patience. This last power is essential for the protection and defence of the first, so long as we are in this mortal state of trial and probation. Not charity alone, nor patience alone, but the charity which is patient prepares the soul for God. As the twofold movement of the heart gives the action that renews life, and the action which expels what is injurious to life; the movement of charity brings life, and the movement of patience repels what is injurious to life. The charity of the will makes the whole man charitable and holy; the patience of the will makes the whole man strong and peaceful.

The custody of the heart is the custody of the man, and this custody of the heart is the work of patience. When the will is patient the mind is patient, the heart is patient, the tongue is patient, the hand is patient. When the will is patient charity is patient, and all the virtues are patient. But this implies the exercise of a tranquil violence over our restless and wayward nature; of which our Lord tells us: "The kingdom of heaven suffereth violence, and the violent bear it away".[26] What is weak and restless in our nature looks to patience for strength and consistency, and we must reign over ourselves before we can enter our Saviour's Kingdom.

To the angels the heavens are natural because they are pure spirits; but before the heavens can be natural to us a great change must be effected in us. Yet, as St. Jerome observes: "He who is created man desires to be an angel, the earthly man seeks a heavenly habitation".[27] Heavenly grace must work the change, and be woven by the will into our nature through the virtues. But this cannot be effected without doing violence to the appetites, the passions, and irascibilities of our nature, which patience accomplishes through the instrumentality of the virtues, quelling the disorders that resist the light of God and the operations of His grace, and that oppose the free flowing of celestial charity, which prepares us for the atmosphere of heaven and the most delightful vision of God.

As a last word of encouragement to the cultivators of patience, it may be well to point out once more how the closing Book of the Sacred Scriptures ascribes the whole victory of the Saints to their patience. "Here," says St. John, "is the patience of the Saints, who keep the commandments of God, and the faith of Jesus."[28] From the Island of Patmos St. John salutes us, and calls himself our brother, and our "partner in tribulation, in the kingdom, and the patience of Christ"; and he makes known to us the visions he has seen and the voices he has heard, proclaiming the rewards of them who overcome themselves, the world, and the evil spirits by their patience. The beloved Evangelist beholds in a sublime vision the Son of God in His glory, arrayed as the Eternal Bishop and Pastor of His Church, and records His words to the churches on earth.

"He that hath an ear, let him hear what the Spirit saith to the churches. To him that overcometh, I will give to eat of the tree of life, which is in the paradise of my God."[29] "He that shall overcome shall not be hurt by the second death."[30] "He that overcometh, I will give him the hidden manna, and will give him a white counter, and in the counter a new name written, which no man knoweth but he that receiveth it."[31] This white counter, or hidden manna, is the Holy Eucharist of the glorified body and blood of the Lord. The white counter is an allusion to the ivory symbol bearing the name of the donor, which men of distinction gave to their friends as a claim to their hospitality. And it here signifies a claim to the hospitality of Christ in His Eternal Kingdom.

"That which you have hold fast till I come. And he that shall overcome and keep My words unto the end, I will give him power over the nations." "He that shall overcome shall thus be clothed in white garments, and I will not blot out his name out of the book of life, and I will confess his name before My Father, and before His angels."[32]

"Because thou hast kept the word of My patience, I also will keep thee from the hour of temptation, which shall come upon the whole world to try them that dwell upon the earth. Behold I come quickly: hold fast that which thou hast, that no man take away thy crown. He that shall overcome, I will make him a pillar in the temple of My God: and he shall go out no more: and I will write upon him the name of My God, and the name of the city of My God, the new Jerusalem, which cometh down out of the heaven of My God, and My new name."[33]

"I counsel thee to buy of Me gold fire-tried, that thou mayest be rich; and mayest be clothed in white garments, and that the shame of thy nakedness may not appear: and anoint thy eyes with eye-salve that thou mayest see. Such as I love, I rebuke and chastise. Be thou zealous therefore and do penance. Behold I stand at the gate, and knock. If any man shall hear My voice, and open to Me the door, I will come to him, and will sup with him, and he with Me. To him that shall overcome, I will give to sit with Me on my throne: as I also have overcome, and am set down with My Father in His throne."[34]

"And He showed me a river of water of life, clear as crystal, proceeding from the throne of God and the Lamb. In the midst of the street thereof, and on both sides of the river, was the tree of life, bearing twelve fruits, yielding its fruits every month, and the leaves of the tree were for the healing of the nations. And there shall be no curse anymore: but the throne of God and of the Lamb shall be in it; and His servants shall serve Him. And they shall see His face: and His name shall be on their foreheads. And night shall be no more: and they shall not need the light of the lamp, nor the light of the sun, because the Lord God shall enlighten them, and they shall reign for ever and ever. And He said to me: These words are most faithful and true."[35]

# NOTES

## 1. The Work Of Patience In The Soul

1. 2 S. Peter i. 4.
2. S. John xiv. 23.
3. Daniel vi. 9-10.
4. Apocalypse i. 14.
5. Psalm xiii, 1.
6. S. Matthew v. 44-45
7. Psalm xlv. 14.
8. James i. 4.
9. Hebrews x. 36.
10. Luke xxi. 19.
11. 1 Corinthians xiii. 4.
12. S. J. Climachus, Scala Cali, grad. 37, n. 31.
13. S. P. Damian. L. vi. Epist. 9.
14. Tertullian, De Palientio, c. 15.
15. Canticles ii. 4.
16. Apocalypse xiv. 12.
17. 2 Thessalonians iii. 5.
18. S. Zeno, De Patientia, c. 1.
19. Psalm lxi. 1-7.
20. Psalm lxx. 3-5.
21. Psalm lviii. 17.
22. Psalm lviii. 10.
23. S. Augustin. De Patientia, c. 2.
24. Tertullian, De Patientia, c.2.
25. Tertullian. De Patientia, c. 5.
26. St. Greg. Mag. Hom. 56, in Evangel.
27. S. Zeno, De Patientia.
28. Ephes. iii. 17.
29. S. Augustin. De Patientia, c. 2.
30. 1 Corinthians xiii. 4-7.
31. St. Cyprian. De Bono Patientiæ.
32. Prov. xix. 19.
33. Ib. II.
34. Gerson. De Distinctione Verarum Visionum a falsis.
35. S. Cyprian. De Bono Patientiæ, c. 14.
36. S. Zeno, De Patientia.

## 2. On The Nature And Object Of Christian Patience

1. Psalm lxi. 6.
2. St. Thomas, Sum. 2 a. q. 36. a. 1.
3. 2 Corinthians vii. 10.
4. Eccles. xxx. 25.
5. S. Greg. Mag. Moral. in Job, L. v. c. 30.
6. Silvio Pellico, Le mie Prigioni.
7. Hugo de S. Victore, De Septenariis, c. 11.
8. Galatians vi. 2.
9. Gerardus Blega, in cap. 58, S. Regula.
10. Galatians, v. 13-15 and 25-26.
11. Job i. 21-22.
12. Job xlii. 12.
13. Job iv. 3-6.
14. St. James i. 19-20.
15. Romans xii. 18-21.
16. St. Ambros. De Officiis, c. 21.
17. Psalm iv. 5.
18. St. Bernard, Epist. 69, ad Guidonem Abbatem.
19. St. Greg. Mag. in Job, L. v. c. 33.
20. Silvio Pellico, Le mie Prigioni, c. 17.
21. S. J. Chrysost. Hom. Quod nemo laeditur nisi a semetipso.
22. 2 Corinthians iv. 16—v. 1.
23. Cajetan. in Summam S. Thomæ, 2. a. q. 136.
24. 2 Corinthians vii. 10.
25. Psalm lxi. 6-7.
26. Ecclesiasticus ii. 1-13.
27. James v. 13.
28. S. Leo, Serm. Ult. De Passione Domini.
29. Hebrews xii, 1-4
30. Romans v, 3-5

## 3. On Patience As A Universal Virtue

1. S. Zeno, De Patientia, c. 3.
2. Daniel xii. 4.
3. Harphius, Theologia Mystica, L. i pt. 2. c. 72.
4. St. Cyprian. De Bono Patientia, c. 5.
5. St. Cyprian. De Bono Patientiæ, c. 20.
6. S. Dionysius, De Eccles. Hierarchia, c. 2.
7. Ripalda, De Fide, Spe et Charitate, disput. 39.
8. St. Maximus, Hom. De S. Michaele.
9. Albertus Magnus, De Virtutibus, c. De Discretion.

10. S. Caterina da Siena, Trat. De Discretion, c. 10.
11. S. Luke ix. 23.
12. Romans viii, 13.
13. Psalm xvii. 3.
14. St. Greg. Mag. Moral. in Job, L. ii. c. 16.
15. St. Matthew v. 3-12.
16. Dryden's Life of S. Francis Xavier, Book 5.

## 4. On Christian Fortitude

1. 3 Kings vii.
2. 1 Timothy iii 15. The word firmamentum in the Vulgate is imperfectly rendered in the Douai version by the word ground.
3. 2 Cor. v. 1.
4. Aristotle, Ethics, L. iii. c. 7.
5. Cicero, De Inventione, L. ii. c. 54.
6. Idem, Ad Herem, L. iii. c. I.
7. S. Augustin. Quæstiones, lxxxiii. q. 63.
8. Idem, De Moribus Eccles. Cathol. L. i. c. 54.
9. Idem, De Libero Arbitrio, L. i. c. 13.
10. Romans viii. 35-39.
11. S. Augustin. De Moribus Eccles. Cathol. L. i. c. 22.
12. Idem, in Psalm. xxiv.
13. S. Ambros. De Officiis, L. i. c. 35.
14. Hebrews xi 32-38.
15. Ephesians vi. 10-11.
16. S. Bernard. Epist. 129 ad Farnuses.
17. Isaias xvi. 6.
18. S. Cyprian. Epist. 8.
19. S. Greg. Mag. Hom. 3 in Evangel.
20. S. J. Chrysost. Serm. in S. Eustathium.
21. S. Greg. Mag. Hom. 177 in Evangel.
22. S. Greg. Mag. Hom. 27 in Evangel.
23. Romans viii. 13.
24. Gerson. Compend. Theolog. c. De Septem Donis.
25. 2 Corinthians xii. 9, 10.
26. Philippians iv. 11-13.
27. S. Ambros. De Officiis Ministrorum, L. i, c. 35-37.
28. Josue i. 7.
29. Apocalypse xiv. 12.

## 5. On The Patience Of The Son Of God

1. Wisdom xv. 1.
2. Tertullian, De Patientia, c. 3.
3. S. John iii. 16.
4. Ibid. xiv. 9.
5. Ibid. xvi. 15.
6. Ibid. xiv. 10.
7. Ibid. x. 30.
8. Ibid. xvi. 28.
9. St. John i. 14.
10. 2 St. Peter i. 16-18.
11. Luke ix. 55-56.
12. Tertullian. De Patientia.
13. S. Matthew xxiii. 37-38.
14. Hebrews xii. 29.
15. Canticles viii. 6.
16. S. Luke xii. 49-50.
17. S. John xv. 13.
18. S. Mark x. 32-34.
19. S. Leo, Serm. De Passione.
20. Psalm lxviii. 2-3.
21. Luke xxiv. 25.
22. Hebrews v. 7-10.
23. Philippians ii. 5-11.
24. Hebrews xii. 1-2.
25. 1 S. Peter ii. 20-21.
26. 2 Corinthians iv. 6-10.
27. Colossians i. 11.
28. Canticles viii. 8.
29. Isaias liii. 4-6.
30. See Harphius, Theologia Mystica, L. i. c. 28.
31. St. Matthew x. 38.

## 6. On Patience As The Discipline Of The Soul

1. Proverbs xix. 11.
2. Proverbs xvi. 32.
3. S. Greg. Mag. Hom. 35 in Evangel.
4. Psalm xvii. 3.
5. Psalm cxxi. 1-3.
6. Albertus Magnus, De Virtutibus, c. De Fortitudine.
7. Ibid. c. De Materiae.
8. Cassian, Collat. 18, c. 13.

9. S. Bernard, De Ordine Vitæ, c. 6.
10. S. Francis, Assis. Opusc. c. 6.
11. S. Bonaventura, De Præfectu Religios. L. ii. c. 36.
12. S. James i. 4.
13. Proverbs iv. 23.
14. St. James iii.
15. Proverbs xvi. 1.
16. St. Matthew xii. 34-36.
17. Canticles ii. 4.
18. 1. Corinthians xiv. 40.
19. S. August. De Natura Boni, c. 23.
20. Job x. 22.
21. S. Bonaventura, Speculum Disciplinae.
22. Romans xv. 1-3.
23. Psalm lxxvi. 5.
24. Psalm xxxviii. 2.
25. Romans xii. 21.
26. Proverbs xiv. 16.
27. Romans xii. 19.
28. Proverbs xv. 1.

## 7. On Patience As The Perfecter Of Our Daily Duties

1. S. Matthew v. 43-45.
2. See S. Francis of Sales, Introduction a la Vie Devote, Parte 3me, c. 10.
3. Psalm cvi 18; S. Thomas, De Malo, q. 11, a. 1.
4. 2 Corinthians vii. 9-10.
5. St. Matthew v. 5.
6. Plutarch, De Ira.
7. St. James v. 13.
8. Eccles. ii. 3.
9. Psalm, xxvi. 7-9 and 13-14.

## 8. Encouragements To Patience

1. 1 Timothy i. 16.
2. 2 Corinthians xii. 12.
3. Tertullian, Apologia, c. 50.
4. S. Maximus, Hom. De S. Michaele.
5. S. Matthew xx. 22.
6. Genesis viii. 21.
7. Psalm cii. 8-14.
8. Ecclesiasticus iv. 4.
9. Romans ii. 4.

10. Job xxiv. 23.
11. Romans ii. 7.
12. S. J. Chrysost. in locum.
13. Romans ix. 22-23.
14. Romans ii. 5.
15. Colossians i. 24.
16. Hebrews ii. 10.
17. S. Matthew xxv. 40.
18. Apocalypse xiv. 12.
19. 1 Corinthians xii. 26.
20. See the copious exposition of the text in Cornelius a Lapide.
21. Rusbrokius, De Præcipuis Virtutibus, L. v. c. 9.
22. S. Luke ii. 18-19. Ib. 34-35.
23. S. John xix. 25.
24. Job iv. 5-6.
25. Job xiii. 15.
26. See Blosius, Institutio Spiritualis, c. 8 sect.
27. Psalm xxxiii. 19.
28. Psalm xc. 15. See Blosius, Institutio Spiritualis, c. 8. sect. 3.
29. S. Caterina da Siena, Trat. l. c. 45; Trat. 2. c. 13.
30. S. Cyprian, De Bono Patientiæ, c 20.

## 9. On The Gifts Of The Holy Ghost

1. Ezechiel xxvi. 25-28
2. Ezechiel xxxvii. 1-14.
3. Luke iv. 18.
4. John xx. 22-23.
5. Acts ii. 4.
6. S. Thomas, Sum. 1. 2. q. 110. a. 4.
7. 2 S. Peter i. 2-4.
8. Romans v. 5.
9. 1 Corinthians iii. 16-17.
10. S. John xiv. 23.
11. S. Thomas, Sum. I. 2. q. 113. a. 9.
12. S. Thomas, Sum. 1. 2. q. 113. a. 9.
13. John xiv. 26.
14. 1 Corinthians ii. 12.
15. Colossians i. 9-12.
16. Romans viii. 25-27.
17. S. John xiv. 15-17.
18. Psalms cxlii. 10.
19. Romans viii. 14.
20. St. Thomas, Sum. I. 2 a. 68. q. 3.
21. 2 Corinthians iii. 17.

22. Ezechiel xl. 22.
23. Isaias lxvi. 2.
24. Psalm lxxxiii. 6, 7.
25. Psalm ciii. 10.
26. S. Greg. Mag. in Ezechiel. L. ii. Hom. 19.
27. Proverbs ix. 1.
28. S. Bernard. Serm. 23 in Cantic.
29. Wisdom viii. 14.
30. Philippians ii. 5.
31. S. Anselm. De Similitudinibus, c. 130.
32. Hugo de S. Victore, De Claustro Anima, L. iii. c. 5.
33. 1 Timothy iv. 8.
34. Hugo de S. Victore, De Claustro Anima, L. iii. c. 5.
35. 1 Corinthians vi. 17.
36. Psalm xvii. 30.
37. Job xvi. 3.
38. Philippians, iv. 13. S. Antoninus, In Sentent. p. 4 tit. 13. c. 1.
39. Gerson, Compend. Theolog. De Septem Donis.
40. See Rusbrockius In Tabernaculum Fœderis, c. 30.
41. See Gaume, Traité du Saint Esprit, Vol. ii. c. 30.
42. Wisdom x. 10.
43. S. Thomas, Sum. 2. 2. q. 9. a. 1.
44. Philippians iii. 7-8.
45. S. Antoninus, In Sentent. p. 4. tit. 12. c. 1.
46. St. Thomas, Sum. 2. 2. q. 52. a. 1.
47. Proverbs xi. 14
48. Tobias iv. 19.
49. Eccius. vi. 6.
50. S. August. Serm. De Timore.
51. S. Bonaventura, De Dono Sapientiæ, c. 1.
52. S. August. De Doctrina Christiana, c. 7.
53. Psalm xxii. 1-2. S. Anselm. De Similitudinibus, c. 31.
54. Wisdom vii.-ix.

## 10. On Prayer

1. S. John xiv. 13.
2. S. John xiv. 6.
3. Romans viii. 25-27.
4. Isaias xxix. 13.
5. S. John iv. 23-24.
6. 1 Corinthians xiv. 15.
7. S. John i. 17.
8. S. Greg. Mag. Moralia in Job, L. xxxi. c. 17.
9. Job xxxi. 35.

10. Psalm x. 17.
11. Rom. viii. 5.
12. Heb. v. 14
13. Psalm xxxviii, 4.
14. Psalm xxxv. 10
15. St. August. Epist. 130 ad Probam.
16. Osee xiv. 3.
17. Psalm xxxvii. 10-11.
18. 1 Corinthians xiv. 14.
19. S. Basil, De Constitutionibus Monasticis, c. i.
20. St. John xiv. 13.
21. St. John xvi. 23.
22. St. August. In Sententiis a S. Prospero collectis, Sent. 212.
23. St. Luke xviii. 1.
24. 1 Thessalonians v. 17-18.
25. 1 Timothy ii. 8.
26. S. Augustin. Epist. 130 ad Probam.
27. Augustin. Epist. 130 ad Probam.
28. Cassian. Collat. 9, c. 34-35.
29. See S. Thomas, Sum. 2. 2. q. 83. a. 12-15.
30. S. Thomas, Sum. 2. 2. q. 83. a. 12.
31. Psalm xxvi. 8.
32. 2 Corinthians iii. 17.
33. Psalm xxxvi. 5-7.
34. Isaias xxxii. 17.
35. Psalm xxxvi. 10.
36. Psalm iv. 7.
37. Acts xvii. 27-28.
38. Psalm civ. 4.
39. S. Greg. Mag. Moral. in Job, L. v. c 37.
40. 1 Corinthians xiii. 12.
41. S. Greg. Mag. Hom. 14 in Ezechiel.
42. S. Matthew vi. 21.
43. S. Thomas, Sum. 2. 2. q. 108. a. 5.
44. Job xxviii. 12-13.
45. St. Greg. Mag. Hom. 17 in Ezechiel.
46. Wisdom viii. 16.
47. Hebrews vi. 4-6.

## 11. On Patience In Prayer

1. Psalm lxi. 6.
2. Psalm lxii. 28.
3. Cassian, Collat. 9, c. 2.
4. Granada, Memoriale vita Christiana, Tract. 5, c. 2.

5. Isaias lxvi. 2.
6. Proverbs xi. 20.
7. John xx. 29.
8. Job xiii. 15.
9. Corinthians xii. 8-10.
10. Habacuc i. 2.
11. Id. iii. 18-19.
12. Ecclus. ii. 3-6.
13. Eccl. vii. 9.
14. Job i. 18-19.
15. S. Gregorius Magnus, Moralia in Job, L. ii. c. 49.
16. Id. Ibid. c. 54.
17. 1 Cor. xiii. 1-3.
18. S. Caterina de Siena, Trat. Della Divina Providenza, c. 3-4.
19. Eadem, Della Oration; c. 95.
20. Eadem, Lettere 55 Ed. Gigli.
21. Edem, Lettre 96.
22. Letter 218 and 342.

## 12. On The Cheerfulness Of Patience

1. 2 Corinthians ix. 7.
2. Eccius. xxxv. 20.
3. St. Thomas, Contra Gentiles, L. i. c. 90.
4. Id. Sum. 2. 2. q. 136. a. 1-3.
5. Romans xii. 12.
6. Philippians iv. 4.
7. Psalm xxxvi. 11.
8. Psalm xxxiv. 9.
9. Psalm xxxvi. 4.
10. 2 Corinthians I. 12.
11. S. Thomas, Contra Gentiles, L. i. c. 19.
12. Wisdom xvi. 20-21.
13. Psalm xciii. 19.
14. S. Bonaventura, De Profectu Religiosorum, L. ii. c. 36.
15. Psalm xx. 20-21.
16. 1 Corinthians vi. 19-20.
17. Romans viii. 14-17.
18. Deuteronomy xxviii. 47-48.
19. Psalm xcix. 2.
20. Psalm v. 12.
21. 2 Corinthians vii. 4
22. 1 Peter iv. 13.
23. St. John xv. 11.
24. S. Augustin. in Psalm cxxxviii. 15.

25. Psalm xc. 15.
26. St. Matthew xi. 12.
27. S. Hieron. Epist. ad Algiasim.
28. Apocalypse xiv. 12.
29. Apocalypse ii. 7.
30. Ibid. ii. 11.
31. Ibid. iii. 17.
32. Ibid. iii. 5.
33. Ibid. iii. 10-12.
34. Ibid. iii. 18-20.
35. Ibid. xxii. 1-6.